Skepticism and Belonging in Shakespeare's Comedy

This book recovers a sense of the high stakes of Shakespearean comedy, arguing that the comedies, no less than the tragedies, serve to dramatize responses to the condition of being human, responses that invite scholarly investigation and explanation. Taking its cue from Stanley Cavell's influential readings of *Othello* and *Lear*, the book argues that exposure or vulnerability to others is the source of both human happiness and human misery. Although the tragedies showcase attempts at evading such vulnerability through the self-defeating pursuit of epistemological certainty, the comedies present the drama and the difficulty involved in turning away from an epistemological register in order to productively respond to the fact of our humanity. Where Shakespeare's tragedies might be viewed in Cavellian terms as the drama of skepticism, Shakespeare's comedies can be seen as exemplifying the drama of acknowledgment. As both a parallel and a preamble, Gottlieb suggests that the field of literary studies is itself a site of such revealing responses: where competing research methods strive to foreclose upon (or, alternatively, rejoice in) epistemological uncertainty, such commitments bespeak an urge to avoid or circumvent the human in the practice of scholarship. Reading Shakespeare's comedies with a "defactoist" view of teaching and learning points in the direction of a new humanism, one that avoids both the relativism of old deconstruction and contemporary Presentism and the determinism of various kinds of structural accounts. This book offers something new in both a scholarly and popular understanding of Shakespeare's work, doing so with both philosophical rigor and literary attention to the difficult work of reading.

Derek Gottlieb is a research fellow at the University of Basel in Switzerland. He works in the domains of both Education and English Literature, and is the author of *Education Reform and the Concept of Good Teaching*.

Routledge Studies in Shakespeare

1 Shakespeare and Philosophy
  Stanley Stewart

2 Re-playing Shakespeare in Asia
  Edited by Poonam Trivedi and Minami Ryuta

3 Crossing Gender in Shakespeare
  Feminist Psychoanalysis and the Difference Within
  James W. Stone

4 Shakespeare, Trauma and Contemporary Performance
  Catherine Silverstone

5 Shakespeare, the Bible, and the Form of the Book
  Contested Scriptures
  Travis DeCook and Alan Galey

6 Radical Shakespeare
  Politics and Stagecraft in the Early Career
  Christopher Fitter

7 Retheorizing Shakespeare through Presentist Readings
  James O'Rourke

8 Memory in Shakespeare's Histories
  Stages of Forgetting in Early Modern England
  Jonathan Baldo

9 Reading Shakespeare through Philosophy
  Peter Kishore Saval

10 Embodied Cognition and Shakespeare's Theatre
  The Early Modern Body-Mind
  Edited by Laurie Johnson, John Sutton, and Evelyn Tribble

11 Mary Wroth and Shakespeare
  Edited by Paul Salzman and Marion Wynne-Davies

12 Disability, Health, and Happiness in the Shakespearean Body
  Edited by Sujata Iyengar

13 Skepticism and Belonging in Shakespeare's Comedy
  Derek Gottlieb

Skepticism and Belonging in Shakespeare's Comedy

Derek Gottlieb

LONDON AND NEW YORK

First published 2016
by Routledge

2 Park Square, Milton Park, Abingdon, Oxfordshire OX14 4RN
52 Vanderbilt Avenue, New York, NY 10017

Routledge is an imprint of the Taylor & Francis Group, an informa business

First issued in paperback 2019

Copyright © 2016 Taylor & Francis

The right of Derek Gottlieb to be identified as author of this work has been asserted by him in accordance with sections 77 and 78 of the Copyright, Designs and Patents Act 1988.

All rights reserved. No part of this book may be reprinted or reproduced or utilised in any form or by any electronic, mechanical, or other means, now known or hereafter invented, including photocopying and recording, or in any information storage or retrieval system, without permission in writing from the publishers.

Notice:
Product or corporate names may be trademarks or registered trademarks, and are used only for identification and explanation without intent to infringe.

Library of Congress Cataloging in Publication Data

Gottlieb, Derek.
Skepticism and Belonging in Shakespeare's Comedy / by Derek Gottlieb.
  pages cm. — (Routledge Studies in Shakespeare ; 13)
Includes bibliographical references and index.
  1. Shakespeare, William, 1564–1616—Comedies. 2. Skepticism in literature.
  3. Belonging (Social psychology) I. Title.
PR2981.G68 2015
822.3'3—dc23   2015008804

ISBN: 978-1-138-85955-5 (hbk)
ISBN: 978-0-367-87279-3 (pbk)

Typeset in Sabon
by codeMantra

For Chelsea, like everything else.

I wanted to put that picture before him, and his acceptance of the picture consists in his now being inclined to regard a given case differently: that is, to compare it with this sequence of pictures. I have changed his way of looking at things. (Indian mathematicians: "Look at this!")

—Ludwig Wittgenstein, PI §144

Cultures cherish artists because they are people who can say, Look at that!

—Marilynne Robinson

Contents

	Acknowledgments	ix
1	Introduction	1
	1.1 Not in Fact Mistaken but in Soul Muddled: The State of Literary Studies	4
	1.2 Situating Cavell's Readings of the Tragedies	13
2	A Defactoist Practice of Literary Scholarship	25
	2.1 The Place(s) of Skepticism and Doubt in our Lives with Words and Others	27
	2.2 On Teaching and Learning as Training or Initiation	32
	2.3 "Agreement Not in Opinions, but Rather in Form of Life"	37
	2.4 Skepticism, Agreement, and Inheritance	40
	2.5 "Essence Is Expressed in Grammar": Comedy, Belonging, and Education	43
3	Much Ado about Nothing	53
	3.1 Disquietudes and Problems	54
	3.2 A Miracle!	63
	3.3 Conclusion	81
4	A Midsummer Night's Dream	87
	4.1 Legal and Biological Determination in *Dream*	88
	4.2 A Handsome, Enchanted View of the World	100
	4.3 Mine Own and Not Mine Own	108
	4.4 Conclusion	119
5	As You Like It	125
	5.1 Teaching Differences and the Stakes of *As You Like It*	131
	5.2 The Madness in Love	144
	5.3 The Reason in Madness	154
	5.4 The Education(s) of Rosalind	162
	5.5 Conclusion	168
6	Coda	178
	Index	195

Acknowledgments

I would like to thank the numerous people and institutions that have made my research possible. The Englisches Seminar at the Universität Basel, for instance, lent financial and scholarly support to all of my work: it is difficult to imagine my research taking intelligible shape without the invaluable commentary of Prof. Drs. Ina Habermann and Philipp Schweighauser, in particular, nor without the friendship and stimulating, thoughtful conversations with Ridvan Askin and Michelle Witen.

I would also like to thank the University of Iowa for the T. Anne Cleary Graduate Research Fellowship, under whose auspices I conducted some of the research that ended up in this book, though it was originally undertaken with a different purpose in mind. This only goes to show a Cavellian sort of truism: you can never know in advance, with respect to scholarly research, what will turn out to be important, and where the connections might lead. You have to find out.

I owe a standing debt of gratitude for the mentorship of David Stern, as well, who, without ever occupying an official capacity as an advisor with respect to me, has nonetheless been an invaluable teacher in all matters pertaining to Wittgenstein's thought, including my introduction to the work of Stanley Cavell, and who has continued to provide advice and feedback long after I finished my graduate work at the University of Iowa.

The feedback I received from my anonymous reviewers on the prospectus was likewise of the utmost help to me, offering encouragement via their positive reactions and shining a light on areas where the manuscript might improve. Though their contributions were anonymous, it was not difficult to divine the identities of Richard Eldridge and Sarah Beckwith, and subsequent correspondence with these two thoughtful scholars on specific points of their critiques proved most helpful.

But most of all, I would like to thank my parents, whose insistence, during my teenage years, on making regular summertime visits to the American Players Theater in the idyllic countryside outside of Spring Green, Wisconsin, introduced me in the flesh as it were to Falstaff and Malvolio, Robin Goodfellow and Prospero, Troilus, Rosalind, Antony, Portia, Romeo, Macbeth, and the rest. Walking down the long hillside path from the theater to the car at the close of a play, under the great sweep of the Milky Way and accompanied by the local fireflies, those unforgettable and incantatory words would reverberate within me, and I would tingle with a special type of wonder and gratitude at being the creature that I am, born into language, with such spectacular possibilities arrayed before me, I do not know if there are thanks enough for that.

1 Introduction

In Act 5 of *Much Ado About Nothing*, immediately following the union of Hero and Claudio, Benedick whispers an aside to the Friar and calls for Beatrice. This pair of lovers, having already privately confessed their feelings for one another in Act 4, seem poised to follow the joyous nuptials of the younger pair. But things go awry. Each lover, too proud, and perhaps having too often publicly repudiated romantic love, rejects in turn the other's request to proclaim aloud the very love that they have earlier professed. Now standing before their community, before their friends and families, both aver that their investments in one another amount to "no more than reason." Face to face at the altar, and each for all the world prepared to marry the other, they find themselves contemplating each other across an unbridgeable abyss. Though so seemingly near to one another, an unreckonable distance separates them. Prior to this scene, nothing could be more obvious to other characters, or even to themselves, than the fact of their mutual love. But each, at this precise moment, feels (and acts upon) the temptation to deny the prima facie truth of the matter. "Do not you love me?" Benedick asks. "Why no; no more than reason," replies Beatrice, to the profound disappointment of all present, including, one imagines, herself.

This play, as everyone knows, ends happily. But such impasses, where they arise in Shakespeare, such temptations to deny or repudiate an obvious truth, also drive the great tragedies. *Much Ado*'s happy ending comes about, and the impasse is resolved, when Claudio and Hero produce sonnets that Benedick and Beatrice have written for each other, sonnets immediately taken to prove the truth of the love that Benedick and Beatrice share. Benedick's reaction to the appearance of this evidence will be prescient: "A miracle!" he proclaims.

But no such miracles intervene in *King Lear* or *Othello*. When love, devotion, and fidelity are held up to skeptical scrutiny in these tragedies and are made to depend upon theoretical sorts of proof or justification, nothing seems capable of answering the doubts that seem to demand settling. A great deal of Shakespearean action hinges upon characters' varying responses to running up against the boundaries of sense, or the limits of logic. When circumstances defy explanation and seeming facts resist formal proof, when characters turn a jaundiced and disengaged eye upon their own worlds, something momentous is in the offing. It is in this light that I will suggest that Benedick's connection of the miraculous with the presentation of the aforementioned sonnets is not misplaced.

The structure and the guiding impulse of this book originates in a way of exploring Shakespeare pioneered in the works of Stanley Cavell. In readings of *Othello* and *King Lear*, most famously, Cavell foregrounds the ways in which Shakespearean tragedy is, in a manner of speaking, the drama of skepticism.

Cavell reads the characters of Othello and Lear as two sides, as I take it, of the same skeptical coin. Each character seizes upon, or is impaled upon, a certain problem of privacy, the fact of the same unreckonable distance that divides Benedick and Beatrice from one another in *Much Ado*, the fact, that is, of human separateness. Once Iago throws Desdemona's love for the Moor into doubt and makes it a problem of knowledge and certainty, Othello finds that nothing can reestablish the unreflective nature of his previous attachment to his wife, that nothing can guarantee her fidelity to him. Othello's jealousy, on this view, manifests a frustration with the very fact that Desdemona is in a sense both his and yet also her own person, a frustration with the fact that any other person has a private and inaccessible sphere and is possessed in this sense of irremediable secrecy. He runs aground on the realization that he cannot relate even to someone as near to him as Desdemona in the way that he relates to himself. In this sense, Othello's jealousy speaks to the way in which the ground occupied by another is perpetually closed to us.

Lear's tragedy makes visible the other half of Cavell's reading of skepticism. Where Othello takes his relation to himself—the immediacy or felt certainty of his convictions—as a starting point or a model, subsequently raging at his absolute inability to silence doubts around Desdemona in the same way he finds or imagines his own feelings immune to doubt, Lear takes this inviolable separateness or alienation from the private worlds of others as something of an ideal state of affairs. What Lear cannot bear, on Cavell's reading, is Cordelia's obvious love for him, the way in which her love for him is *not* dependent upon any promises or payments from him, but instead expresses a certain claim upon him, or the threat, one might say, of her ability to reach across the abyss between them. His attempt to coerce her into accepting the commodification of her filial affection is, on this understanding, an attempt at protecting his own privacy, an attempt at asserting or defending his own unknowable inwardness, an attempt at denying others' knowledge of him. Othello's madness derives from the sense that others remain perpetually beyond our reach; in contrast, Lear's madness emerges from the sense that we are never fully beyond the reach of others. Othello gnashes at the inescapable privacy of the human condition; Lear gnashes at its inescapable publicness. Othello cannot adequately ground his convictions with respect to others; Lear cannot adequately shake others' convictions with respect to himself.

Although Cavell himself does not study Shakespeare's comedy in any depth, he suggests in passing that these temptations, as I have already hinted with the *Much Ado* example, pervade Shakespeare's comedies as well. Michael Fischer, in *Stanley Cavell and Literary Skepticism*, says that for Cavell, "the two genres overlap and even feed into one another" (Fischer 90). Cavell himself notes this overlap explicitly: "the tragedy is that comedy has its limits," he states, and he proceeds to point precisely to Othello's version of the problem: "Join hands here as we may, one of the hands is mine and the other is yours" (Cavell, *Disowning Knowledge in Seven Plays of Shakespeare* 110). While Cavell certainly explores in great detail the ways in which American "screwball comedies" of the 1930s and 1940s speak to similar skeptical impulses, and while these writings will be helpful in thinking of Shakespeare's comedies, the closest thing to a Shakespeare comedy that he takes up is a study of *The Winter's Tale*, which is famously difficult to classify.

The central argument of this book is that, if a failure to live with and within the twin poles of the unshirkable bonds to others and the inescapable fact of our separateness or isolation can account for the action of the great tragedies, then the ways in which the characters of certain among the high comedies in fact find ways of giving rest, however momentary, to these same anxieties will also bear investigation. Or, to put it another way: the comedy is that tragedy has its limits. Intrinsically separate though our hands may be, they can yet be joined together. The fact of our separateness no more dooms us to tragedy than the fact of our publicness fates us to comedy. The character of the responses to the arrival of these moments in the comedies, as in the tragedies, I will show, and the ways these impasses or abysses are addressed, possess what Sarah Beckwith has called a certain "therapeutic and diagnostic power" (Beckwith, *Shakespeare and the Grammar of Forgiveness* 9). Understanding the nature of this power—literature's ability, which is also the ability of others, to teach us about ourselves—will require revisiting some major tenets of literary scholarship as a whole.

If it is the case, as it is with Othello and with Lear, that the knowledge we require lies in plain view but that owning up to this knowledge remains a difficult achievement, then the methods and assumptions upon which literary scholarship proceeds will require some reformulation. What it means "to understand what we know, to take on our education" (Cavell, *Little Did I Know* 374) in overcoming or moving beyond skepticism with respect both to others and to literary art, as I will argue below, will differ from a model geared toward the discovery of new facts.

Although the particular sort of skepticism that besets the protagonists of the above tragedies and that threatens the comedies as well is best characterized as other-minds skepticism, no bright line separates this form of doubt from the external-world skepticism that drives modern epistemology from Descartes through the work of Hume and Kant into the present day. Stephen Mulhall even suggests that Cavell's mode of reading copes with both forms of skepticism at once, inseparable as they are: for Mulhall,

Cavell's "complex reflexivity of acknowledgment flows from the fact that words and their criteria have two faces—they not only link the individual speaker to the world, they also link him with other speakers" (Mulhall, *Stanley Cavell: Philosophy's Recounting of the Ordinary* 179). The internal links between these two kinds of skepticism bear upon this investigation to the extent that literary scholarship or literary criticism aspires to—and is often denigrated for its failures to achieve—the sort of objective knowledge about literary works that might overcome the possibilities of doubt originating in Cartesian epistemological procedures.

In this introductory chapter, I hope to make visible the ways in which various theoretical upheavals within the field of literary scholarship can be taken as responses to their predecessors' felt inadequacies in this regard. The nature of those inadequacies—the sense that what literary scholarship produces has failed to live up to, or to do, something that we take knowledge to straightforwardly entail—strikes me as internally related to the experienced inadequacies suggested in the Lear-Othello polarity.

In this way, the discussion in this book pertains simultaneously to Shakespeare's comedies in particular and to the aims of literary study as a whole. Cavell's suggestion that the tragedies of Lear and Othello reveal something about a human tendency to warp or distort the nature of our connections to others not only pertains to the comedies, as well, but also deserves commentary in terms of its ramifications for our scholarly relation to literary art. Various stripes of skeptical doubt come together in a peculiar way when we raise a question about the place of literature in our lives, and hence the ways in which literary works are open to productive inquiry. Such inquiry also includes what we seek to learn from and about literature, in addition to the types of responses we take literature to be capable of, and responsible for, providing to any first-person-plural public.

1.1 NOT IN FACT MISTAKEN BUT IN SOUL MUDDLED: THE STATE OF LITERARY STUDIES

I wish at this point merely to offer the outlines of a few particular moments in recent literary debates, and I wish to offer these outlines as a means of pivoting in a different direction, or of locating my study of Shakespeare as responsive to, and not blithely ignorant of, these various concerns, concerns that I take to be symptomatic of a certain way of reacting to a sense of crisis in the humanities. Taking up a few relevant discussions will help to reveal the warrant for what I will call, following Robert Fogelin, a *defactoist* stance on our relation to literary works in general and to Shakespeare in particular. It will also provide a mode of transitioning in that direction.[1]

The largest single critical or scholarly shift of the past century, one to which critical schools continue to respond, goes by the name of the "linguistic turn." While Cavell opens his famous reading of *Lear* by alluding to this transition from a Romantic or humanist focus on character to a post-Romantic attention to language, he is of course neither the only nor the most recent thinker to comment on this shift and its consequences. The attention to language that Cavell has in view—particularly in the 1960s, when his *Lear* essay appeared in print—is the type of structuralism typified in the pioneering work of Leavis and Richards, which dominated the American academy under the banner of New Criticism over the postwar decades.

Post-structuralist responses to the New Critics, of course, far from returning the field to a study of character, initially redoubled the emphasis on language, but under an altogether negative—some would say "nihilistic"—aspect. The post-structuralist upshot of the matter is that walling off "the text itself" from any outside world and then discerning meaning through an objective analysis of the text's formal properties is an impossible and misguided task. The method of demonstrating this impossibility to which deconstructionist critics, in particular, often resorted involved showing relentlessly that the boundary between "the text itself" and its putative outside was inevitably *drawn* rather than metaphysically *given*. That is to say, such critics often turned to etymological discussions in order to bring out the ways in which the meaning of a word—the meaning that was to undergird notions of structural "tension" and "paradox"—evolved over time, and the ways in which this evolution of a word's meaning pointed inexorably to shifts in the entire lexicon and the human practices surrounding a language. There was no such *object* as "the text itself" in the way the New Critics imagined it. But the insurgent method of showcasing the iterative nature of language favored by the deconstructionists—turning the words and evidence of New Critics against themselves—garnered complaints of parasitism from the New Critics, as is reflected in a famous exchange between Wayne Booth and J. Hillis Miller. It was a complaint to which Miller, for one, responded by etymologically establishing that "parasite" and "host" are not as neatly separable as Booth might think. Thus Miller made both his own point, and, to a degree, Booth's as well (Miller).

The spirit of this general charge against post-structuralist critics was (and remains) that such literary theory was not only without value, but literally counterproductive. Rather than attempting to make sense of literary works under any methodological framework whatsoever, the deconstructionists dedicated themselves to undermining others' claims about meaning in literary works—and indeed, undermining the very possibility of declaiming upon meaning at all. Rather than building anything up, the deconstructionists were dedicated to tearing things down, or so the complaint went.

Additionally, Derrida's notion that "there is nothing outside the text"—that there is no metaphysical demarcation between inside and outside—opened the world at large to literary analysis. If one prong of post-structuralism's approach involved the radical uncoupling of sign and referent, the other prong involved critiquing the worldly relations of power that in theory bestowed value and meaning on literary works to the extent that any such thing is feasible.

Post-structuralist theory thus ended up making two complementary claims. The first claim was that language cannot be a system of symbols whose meaning is generated by correspondence with the objects of the world and the logical rules for relating these symbols. It was such a claim that led some, such as de Man, to forego the pursuit of extralinguistic *meaning* entirely. The second claim was that, to the extent that literary works have anything like "meaning," such meaning is produced in virtue of the particular social arrangements—the cultural context—in which a literary work is embedded. Because of this second claim in particular, literary criticism sometimes began to take on the form of political activism, seeking to lay bare the ways in which literary works served to reproduce the status quo, especially with respect to hierarchies of class, gender, and race. In brief, for literary studies, the rise of post-structuralism put the pursuit of a work's meaning out of play by rendering "meaning" a logical impossibility, and it instead turned critical attention on the ideological labor that literature (and criticism) performs.

In the 30 years that have elapsed since post-structuralism's heyday, its startling success—in terms of its own prominence—remains the great trauma of literary studies and the humanities at large. For that reason, the post-structuralist moment is still a frequent touchstone for contemporary critics. Post-structuralism continues to be the theoretical nemesis against which emerging trends in criticism define themselves. Often, the first step in establishing a new theoretical framework is to take a swipe at the damage that post-structuralism has done to the humanities. William Giraldi, for instance, writing in 2015 in the *Virginia Quarterly Review*, blasts Derrida and de Man, whom he calls the "paladins of post-structuralist theory." In a neat and ungenerous synopsis of their position, Giraldi says, "Their deconstructionist shenanigans, their absurd and absurdist skepticism, posited that language doesn't really mean what it says, that language must always be a puzzle pointing to other puzzles" (Giraldi). Coupling this claim with the well-worn charge of "obscurantism," Giraldi accuses such thinkers of "assault[ing] everything you knew and admired about words," labeling the entire endeavor "a breed of nihilism born of cultural despair." Giraldi's words both foreshadow the rhetorical tactics of critics that I will investigate in greater depth and also justify my own decision to wrangle with certain aspects of post-structuralist theory. Deconstruction may no longer be the state of the art, but its effects are undeniably still with us: Giraldi's screed is startlingly hostile, given that its target has been so long out of favor.

Giraldi's screed also presents a lazy caricature of post-structuralism's central insight: that language cannot be adequately modeled as a closed system of interlocking logical symbols, and that meaning—of a sentence, of a work—cannot simply be divined by attending to formal structure alone. This was not necessarily to deny that language has meaning and to hurtle headlong toward a vapid relativism or solipsism, as is commonly assumed, even by luminaries who ought to know better.[2] Rather, it was to assert that language's meaning, the connection between signifier and signified, is not part of any logical system itself.

As far as the contemporary view of post-structuralism's second prong goes, Jeffrey Williams has recently recalled its "heyday" during the 1970s and 1980s in much the same way as Giraldi. In Williams's words, scholars of this earlier era "aimed to explode the foundation of Western metaphysics, foment a revolution of the sign, overturn gender hierarchies, and fight the class struggle" (Williams). Williams rightly conflates the deconstructionist revolution of the sign with the emancipatory political project I alluded to earlier: if the relation of signifier and signified is not logically given but rather is socially constructed, then asserting and defending the significance of a work is inescapably a political act. For some critical schools, exposing the canon's complicity in naturalizing a certain set of power relations, and subsequently combating those relations, became the principal aim of scholarship.

Giraldi and Williams are representative of those contemporary scholars who turn to defamatory portraits of post-structuralism in general and deconstruction in particular as a starting point in discussing recent trends in theory. Giraldi and Williams conveniently also typify the substance of the two main methodological arguments against post-structuralism: either it was an epistemologically nihilistic approach, as in Giraldi's article, focused on denying the very possibility of knowledge; or else it was not epistemologically oriented at all, as in Williams's article, aimed instead at the achievement purely political ends. In each case, these methodological criticisms are offered in order to disqualify post-structuralist scholarship *as* scholarship altogether.

Furthermore, especially in Williams's case, the articles evince a third trope: the use of a caricature of post-structuralism as the preamble for introducing a resurgent structuralism. This structuralism is rarely the (relatively) pure formalism of Richards or Leavis, though sometimes it is: in Williams's work, the methods he supports include "surface reading" and "distant reading." Surface reading certainly includes precisely that formalism, and distant reading, through trying to overcome literary scholarship's previous epistemological difficulties by using *all of the data,* seems particularly undeserving of the "new modesty" label that Williams gives it.[3] But these new forms of structuralisms all share the trait of *belonging* to the scholarly endeavor in just the ways in which post-structuralism's critics contend that it fails: these new structuralisms produce positive knowledge, and the character of such knowledge is pure and abstract, above the taint of politics or ideology.

One particularly irksome form of revitalized structuralism that has recently emerged in the study of both literature and history—and Shakespeare, in particular—seeks to combine evolutionary theory and cognitive psychology. I call this a form of structuralism because the general thesis of the scholars doing work in this area is roughly that our relation to literature in general and any given work in particular is ultimately reducible to the way we process representations of the world via our evolved brain physiology. Such approaches contend that discovering some fact or set of facts about how we are internally "wired" or evolutionarily predisposed to respond to our surroundings, including aesthetic works such as literature, will constrain or determine a given literary work's variety of possible meanings or senses. As a result, we will be able to say something true about the real meaning of a particular literary work. This particular subfield of literary scholarship includes the work of John Tooby and Leda Cosmides ("Does Beauty Build Adapted Minds?"), Tooby, Cosmides, and Spolsky ("Dialogue"), Dutton (*The Art Instinct*), Jonathan Gottschall (*Literature, Science, and a New Humanities*), Joseph Carroll (*Literary Darwinism*), Amy Cook (*Shakespearean Neuroplay*), Lisa Zunshine (*Why We Read Fiction*), and Brian Boyd ("Exhortation").

If this is so, then the aporetic conclusions of Derrida and other post-structuralists were certainly wrong: there *is* a final determinant of literary meaning, and exploring how the physiological properties of the brain underwrite the psychological aspects of navigating our representations of the world will pin those literary meanings down. It should therefore be completely unsurprising that many scholars working in this area take aim at post-structuralism as a first step.

This is as true in Shakespeare studies as it is everywhere else: Robin Wells's monograph, *Shakespeare's Humanism* (2005), opens by attacking the "anti-essentialism" common to all postmodern theory, including New Historicism, Cultural Materialism, Feminism, Lacanian psychoanalytic theory, and so on, and it concludes by suggesting "Neo-Darwinism" (which I will call "evocriticism" below) as a welcome solution, providing the bedrock for understanding the *essential* (and thus universal) nature of the human (Wells). Thus, evolutionary theory explicitly offers an antidote to the "relativism" and "anti-essentialism" of post-structuralist theory.

Similarly, in his own work on Shakespeare, Keith Oatley opens by taking issue with Rom Harré's post-structuralist thesis: "Psychologists have always had to struggle against a persistent illusion that in such studies as those of emotions there is something there, the emotion, of which the emotion word is a mere representation" (Oatley, "Simulation of Substance and Shadow" 16). Oatley, approaching Shakespeare from within the framework of cognitive psychology, understands Harré to deny the existence of something inner, of which language is a "mere representation," a denial that baldly affronts Oatley. Pointing to Proust, Bradley, and Stevenson, Oatley insists not only that the study of character, and particularly the emotions' role with respect to character, has long occupied a central position in literary study generally and in Shakespeare, specifically. Further, if the inner reality of character or emotion has ever seemed to be inaccessible, leaving us to study the symbolic representations of the same, this inaccessibility has been the result of inadequacies of scientific theory and method. As Oatley says in the same article,

> I propose that Shakespeare showed how pieces of literary art can model the world—especially the world within—and how, in the theatre, we can acquire distinctive and useful experiences of emotion as well as understandings of character. Bridges have recently been built between

cognitive science and literary theory (Hogan 2003a). I propose that these bridges allow approaches to these issues in Shakespeare, that do not lead to the dead ends to which the fingers of Derrida, Harré, and Cixous so accusingly point.

(Oatley, 16)

Oatley sees the post-structuralists as having too swiftly rejected the existence or the importance of extralinguistic referents altogether. In Oatley's view, the Romantics were looking in the right place—that is, exploring the idea of character—but were using with the wrong tools. Oatley's response to the post-structuralists is to reestablish notions of character and emotion as primary foci of study, but to ground those ideas in terms of updated scientific concepts and methods. For my purposes, Oatley's reaction to the post-structuralists is particularly useful, both in its dismissiveness of the findings of post-structuralism generally (a dismissiveness that post-structuralists would of course return in kind) and its representativeness of recent responses to the work of midcentury French theorists at large.

The vitriolic nature of the opposition to post-structuralist assumptions and their inheritors is representative of evocriticism, as it is to many contemporary takes on postmodern theory, as I suggested earlier. The "evocritics" or "literary Darwinists" that I listed earlier[4] position themselves as the saviors of literary scholarship at large, prepared and equipped to redeem literary studies from a dark age of anything-goes, nihilistic, obscurantist, or relativistic approaches to literature that alternately (or simultaneously) seemed to deny the existence of commonsense understandings of extralinguistic facts or the existence (or relevance) of anything extralinguistic at all.

Brian Boyd, for instance, is exemplary both in his hopes for a new "scientific turn" in literature and in his contempt for the work of his linguistic-turn forebears. For him, attempts to pinpoint a set of biologically essential features of human responses to literature are necessary to rescuing literary studies from their current reliance on "obscurantist dogmatism" and "coddled, preening radicalism" (Boyd, 2006, 19). Meanwhile, Jonathan Gottschall seeks to reverse the poles of literary scholarship's "nurturist commitment to theories of strong sociocultural constructionism," which he regards as an "epistemology strongly influenced by—if not based upon—post-structuralist antifoundationalism" (Gottschall, 2008, 6). In each case, these recent critics see the post-structuralists as having repudiated the very conditions of coherent scholarship. These critics view their denial of a metaphysical structure of determination as a repudiation of the scholarly impulse to search *for* something (something to say or to show) that would "light up a work," to borrow a phrase from Harold Bloom. In fact, intellectual historian Jennifer Ratner-Rosenhagen believes that Bloom shares this particular view of the post-structuralists: "It was efforts like the one in his friend and colleague Paul de Man's book *Allegories of Reading* (1979), in which de Man called off the search for an 'extralinguistic referent or meaning,' that led Bloom to conclude that deconstructionists had called off all quests altogether" (Ratner-Rosenhagen 280).

I have brought up the ongoing conflict between post-structuralism and various forms of structuralism mainly to underscore the *bipolarity* of the confrontation, particularly where the evocritics are concerned. The character of the commentary on all sides indicates the following epistemological assumption: either there *is* something metaphysically essential, and thus determinate of literary significance, a *foundation*—(whether this be a matter of "nature" or "nurture," or something imagined to be "inner" as in character or "outer" as in cultural forms)—or else there is *not*. Thus, all of our claims of grasping any determinate sense of a given work are at best naïve and at worst duplicitous.

On the strongest version of this latter view, which is the one Giraldi picks on, there is in fact *no* (true, single) meaning to be grasped. Thus, the project of reading literary works *does* or *ought to* do something other than what more traditional literary scholars envisioned.[5] In the former case, the task of literary scholarship is to investigate the (obviously existing) foundation or essence that binds together words and significance, and then to detail how this factor actually structures the meanings of particular works of literature. In the latter case, the task of literary scholarship is to reveal the ways in which radical indeterminacy reigns in readings of literature, or in which all readings are necessarily open-ended and undecidable. This version of critical work also remains alive and well in Shakespeare studies and is particularly visible in the "Presentist" response to New Historicism. Like the deconstructionists of an earlier era, Presentist scholars seek to puncture the image of criticism as a disinterested or objective enterprise, noting that contemporary concerns inevitably shape explorations of the past. And like the deconstructionists of old, this fact is not an occasion for epistemological despair but rather for joy: Grady and Hawkes call upon critics to "rejoice" in the resulting "indeterminacy" (Grady and Hawkes).

The central assumption shared by both structuralists and post-structuralists turns on a particular view of "essence," as Wells's work on humanism has already shown: post-structuralists are anti-essentialists, whereas humanists (along with structuralisms of all kinds, for that matter) "assume a core essence that unites people otherwise separated in time and social circumstance" (Wells). While the anti-essentialism of the post-structuralists seems to lead to relativism, in which (literary) meaning is always confounded by differences of time and space, and therefore true communication across time and space, however small, is impossible; the essentialist position holds the opposite view: a universal and transcendent quality exists (to the human or, say, to language) that guarantees the possibility of communication across time and space. On the one hand, the *denial* of a transcendent, general essence of any kind defeats the possibility of meaning; on the other hand, the *affirmation* of such an essence is taken to make meaning possible. In both cases, this metaphysical essence, transcending any and all particularities—any individual human, or any individual utterance—is imagined at least *necessary* to the possibility of linguistic significance. In its absence, solipsistic relativism reigns; in its presence, it explains the existence and parameters of linguistic meaning, and it sifts correct interpretations from incorrect ones.

On the evocritics' view, for example, biological essentialism refers to facts or features that are *common* to all humans, namely, evolutionary pressures and the very broad dispositions located in or reducible to the physiological (brain) structures that result. The exploration of these structures will reveal to us what beauty *really* is, why literature *really* appeals to us, what meanings are *really* available therein. If there *is* no such common or transcendent element, either biological or linguistic, as the post-structuralists claim, then all performance of determination, to the extent that anything is determined at all, is done *by* us, say by means of ideologically influenced interpretation. All meanings are up to us, a matter of radical personal choice or, more modestly, a matter of communal assent. This fundamental bipolarity, I will show, is based on an underdeveloped view of what an "essence" is and how it might work.

Specifically, this essence, which is linked to a *foundationalist* framework favored by Gottschalk and others, is envisioned as (1) a place, or an object, at which intrepid theorists arrive after an arduous journey; and (2) a sort of Rosetta Stone, or a spell, a formula that when applied to the messy business of existence will distinguish reality from deception, truth from lies, and so on. The quest for a foundation, or the application for purported theories of essence to works of literature, has just this type of triumph in view. Antifoundationalists are equally guilty of reifying this picture of essence: in (rightly) denying that any such thing exists, they also deny the ability to draw the sought-after distinctions at all, and precisely because they, too, see that only some foundational formula or essence could do such a thing. This shared picture can be conveniently and unoriginally labeled "the metaphysical picture of essence." Many theorists have acknowledged that this divide is overly simple and that this split in many ways fails to account for the ways in which we have the practices closest to us. But the relevant inferences from this insight seem only infrequently to have been drawn.[6]

The difficulty of dislodging this particular picture of essence, determination, and meaning in literature can hardly be overstated, and that is because, if each side of the divide seems inadequate to the other, the metaphysical picture they share is not *false* in any straightforward way. That is, human beings really do share biological commonalities; these biological commonalities can be cited in various contexts to explain certain aspects of what human beings are and what they are like. This fact should not imply that biological commonalities must therefore be the key to all understanding, but to some, it does. On the other hand, of course, human beings are not *only* biological, but are also embedded in cultures, in particular lifeways. If there are obvious commonalities across all human beings, there are also obvious differences across all humans and groups of humans, and such differences or particularities can be invoked to undermine the biologically causal explanations of any *particular* human action, predilection or decision. Obviously, however, because human beings are also not *strictly* products of their cultures, essentialist appeals to culture as an explanatory engine will also inevitably leave something out. Neither nature nor culture can adequately serve as a foundational and explanatory *essence* of the human.

Cavell often speaks of picturing Wittgenstein's notion of the human "form of life" along these very lines. In his reading, the "form of life" of humanity is imagined as the crossing of two axes irreducible to one another: one vertical and biological, one horizontal and ethnological. The upshot for research in the humanities is a certain limit to the project of accounting for human things by means of causal explanations, which is roughly what post-structuralism argues. However, against the most extreme forms of deconstruction, Cavell's reading of Wittgenstein does not denigrate the role of explanation in literary scholarship, nor the search for reasons—quite the opposite, in fact. It does, however, deny the possibility of turning to something *else*—say, biology or ideology—as a master explanatory framework. In short, denying the utility of a particular form of explanation is not to deny the utility of explanation altogether.

Put more emphatically, the absence of any such metaphysical framework of explanation does not free anyone from the responsibility for "seeing an explanation to its end somewhere." Rather, it ought to dissuade us from "wrongly addressing the goal (seeing the somewhere all explanations end)" (Cavell, *In Quest of the Ordinary*, 134). In this way, Cavell acknowledges the brute fact upon which structuralism turns: language in fact *works*. Determining the meaning of a remark, say, or a command is *obviously* possible: it happens every day. Elsewhere, Cavell affirms the obviousness of this possibility by noting that, "at each step, or level, explanation comes to an end." But Cavell further countenances the post-structuralist, anti-essentialist position by claiming that "there is no level to which all explanations come, at which all end" (Cavell, *This New Yet Unapproachable America* 116). Bringing explanations to an end—knowing and articulating the meaning to be found in any utterance or work—is thus figured as a labor that can and ought to be undertaken. It simply has to be undertaken in spite of (or rather because of) the fact that no one, sweeping theory will perform that labor for us.

Insofar as each side of the literary-theoretical oscillations I have described seize upon something that is undeniably true, it remains the case that neither position is *simply* wrong, such that either might be corrected by internalizing new facts: Humans are material, biological creatures; they share cultural features, but not limitlessly, and so on and so forth. Cavell seems to have such grand and exclusive worldviews in mind when he says that certain positions are "countered not by saying that a fact about the world is otherwise than you supposed, but by showing that your world is otherwise than you see. When you are wrong here, you are not in fact mistaken but in soul muddled" (Cavell, *The Claim of Reason* 180).

Cavell's readings of Shakespeare's tragedies return us in important ways to the moment in literary-theoretical history when the pivot was made from attending to character to attending to language, and his readings interrogate the fraught relation between the two. In these readings, Cavell suggests that much like scholars seeking to determine—or to undermine the very possibility of determining—the meanings of literary works, the characters of the tragedies themselves react poorly to an epistemological muddle, a muddle that more knowledge, more facts, can neither solve nor overcome. There is something crucial, these tragedies reveal, that the discovery and recitation of facts cannot do, or cannot do alone.

Instead, in Cavell's terms, meaning (or value, or significance, or relevance) must be *found* rather than *founded*, and the source of the potentially unsatisfying nature of this insight is that "foundation reaches no farther than each issue of finding" (Cavell, *This New Yet Unapproachable America* 114). As its present-continuous tense hints, finding is not the sort of once-and-for-all achievement typical of a given discovery in the natural sciences; it is rather a matter of ongoing work. This notion of *finding* does the determining work that the structuralists pursue, but it does so without positing the chimerical, self-interpreting metaphysical given, the type of mythological entity the post-structuralists successfully exploded. Both structuralists and post-structuralists, on Cavell's reading, reify "the truth of skepticism: that it names our wish (and the possibility of our wishing) to strip ourselves of the responsibility we have in meaning (or in failing to mean) one thing, or one way, rather than another (Cavell, *In Quest of the Ordinary* 135). The "impurity" of language, as Espen Dahl phrases it, naming the condition of language absent the support of metaphysical guarantee, is precisely what makes Cavell's "finding" a "responsible task" rather than a theoretical procedure, as a "founding" would be (Dahl 95). This finding-as-founding is at least as much a matter of *acknowledgment* as it is of knowledge, a movement of response, an acceptance or inheritance in addition to anything like a pure epistemological success.

1.2 SITUATING CAVELL'S READINGS OF THE TRAGEDIES

As I have indicated before, the ways in which the protagonists of *Lear* and *Othello* come to grief have particular resonance for both the assumptions of literary scholarship in general and for the ways in which the felicity of comedic resolution in Shakespeare might be understood. In exploring these two tragedies, Cavell takes aim at the grip of a particular sort of skepticism, which leads him to develop the important and novel notions of "acknowledgment" and "avoidance" as demarcating regions of knowing typically overlooked by modern epistemology.

Cavell's reading of *Lear,* titled "The Avoidance of Love," comes first, chronologically. Cavell's positioning of his reading of the abdication scene of *Lear* bespeaks the literary-scholarly concerns of the time. Specifically, he takes as his point of departure a 1963 essay by Paul Alpers, "*King Lear* and the Theory of the Sight Pattern," in which Alpers argues that, in contradistinction to several critics of his era, the many references to eyes and vision in the play do not produce—or rather, they do not *simply* produce—the conclusion that the characters of Gloucester and Lear, most importantly, arrive at "moral insight." Rather, Cavell suggests, these characters, and the references to their vision, illustrate the importance of "recognition," specifically the recognition of each other and their children. Cavell adopts most of Alpers's literary-critical assumptions,[7] but he seizes upon a weakness in Alpers's argument, precisely the point at which the arrangement of formal, symbolic devices—the pervasive eyesight imagery, in this case—is supposed to yield a particular thematic lesson. Cavell points out that, if Alpers's reading is correct, and the references to eyes and eyesight have something to say about the importance of sight, insight, or recognition, then "it becomes incomprehensible why or how these children have *not* been recognized by their parents; they had not become literally invisible" (Cavell, *Disowning Knowledge in Seven Plays of Shakespeare* 43).

This focus is characteristic of Cavell. He does not deny the value of the evidence that Alpers cites: repeated references to eyes and vision may indicate a central concern; this central concern may have to do with moral insight or with recognition (or with weeping or with agony). But if Alpers is correct in taking recognition as important to, and learnable from, the play, then appealing to symbol and image cannot account for the ways in which recognition has, until the end of the play, failed the characters. In other words, the link between references to eyes or eyesight and recognition or moral insight is not achieved by or entailed in the repeated symbolic references themselves. The move from symbolic order to significance is not produced algorithmically.

Cavell's response to the above incomprehension as to how these children have not been recognized will have to do with the relation of an avoidance-acknowledgment scale to the knowledge-ignorance continuum. This is simply to aver that no knowledge is lacking in this play: on Cavell's view, Lear knows full well, for example, and indeed never doubts the measure of Cordelia's love. If this is the case, then the elaborate demand for proof of filial love in the opening act performs a task that is not fundamentally epistemological. Cavell calls Lear's decision to stage the abdication scene's trial an act of *avoidance* whose epistemological form allows Lear to mask this avoidance (of the requirements of love) by transposing it into an intellectual register. The transposition—if Cordelia would only fulfill her role—would make Lear's recognition of her love a matter of simple proof, which, crucially, would allow him to remain objective, out of the emotional fray, safe.

For Cavell, this sort of distortion drives the tragedies: in his essay on *Othello* he singles out this distortion as "the cause of skepticism—the attempt to convert the human condition, the condition of humanity, into an intellectual difficulty, a riddle" (Cavell, *The Claim of Reason* 492). Recognition of the type Cavell sees at work in *Lear*—Lear's ultimate recognition of Cordelia's love for him—is not, or is not merely, produced by knowing. Acknowledging is something further.

Put briefly, Cavell's notions of acknowledgment and avoidance obtain in situations in which the circumstances exert—immanently, in their being what they are—a certain claim upon us, in virtue of our being who and what we are. Considering the classical epistemological problem of privacy, as expressed in the question of whether we have the same experience as another (say the experience of pain, which always comes down to how we would *know* that we can have, or could *say* that we have, the same experience as another), Cavell follows a Wittgensteinian befuddlement at the expression, "I know that I am in pain." It is an expression that Wittgenstein asserts cannot be said, except as a joke. Here Cavell disagrees with Wittgenstein, finding a live situation in which those words could sensibly and seriously be uttered; but, where they are uttered seriously, they could not be an expression of *certainty* or *knowledge*.

Rather, as Cavell notes, these words would then be an expression of exasperation, or more directly, an *expression* (to another) of pain: "it is the exhibiting of an object about which someone (else) may be certain," but this does not make it an expression of one's own certainty with respect to this object. Claiming in the third person that "I know he is in pain" may be a statement of certainty; it may also be an expression of exasperation. But the example that Cavell seizes upon to demonstrate the concept of acknowledgment, the case of saying "I know you are in pain," the second person, cannot be imagined as both, though here too, exasperation is also possible. "I know you are in pain" is first and foremost an expression, Cavell emphasizes, of "*sympathy*"

> But why is sympathy expressed in this way? Because your suffering makes a *claim* on me. It is not enough that I *know* (am certain) that you suffer—I must do or reveal something (whatever can be done.) In a word, I must *acknowledge* it, otherwise I do not know what "(your or his) being in pain" means. Is.
> (Mulhall, "The Cavell Reader" 68)

Cavell here points to one particular case—knowing another's pain—an imagined product of having defeated other-minds skepticism—in order to reveal how traditional methods of overcoming the philosophical problem of other minds come up short of the effects they are imagined to imply. The appropriate *responsiveness* of acknowledgment is not entailed even in perfect certainty, and, as countless generations of human beings demonstrate, no *perfect* certainty—if the notion is even coherent—has thus far been necessary to any such responsiveness.

That another's suffering makes a claim upon us, as Cavell continues with this example, means also that such a claim can be refused or deflected. Cavell calls this sort of refusal a "failure of acknowledgment," or simply *avoidance*, and this avoidance is to be distinguished from plain ignorance. In this instance, too, a focus on certainty or knowledge misses the mark. As Cavell says,

> The claim of suffering may go unanswered. We may feel lots of things—sympathy, *Schadenfreude*, nothing. If one says that this is a *failure* to acknowledge another's suffering, surely this would not mean that we fail, in such cases, to *know* that he was suffering? It may or may not. The point, however, is that the concept of acknowledgment is evidenced equally by its failure as by its success. ... A failure to know might just be a piece of ignorance, an absence of something, a blank. A failure to acknowledge is the presence of something, a confusion, an indifference, a callousness, an exhaustion, a coldness.
> (Cavell, *Knowing and Acknowledging* 69)

In "The Avoidance of Love," Cavell homes in on the opening scene of *King Lear* in which Lear partitions his kingdom among his children in accordance with their relative abilities to demonstrate their love for him. The tragic events are set in motion when Lear rewards the dishonest flattery of Regan and Goneril while disinheriting the one daughter who truly loves him. Cavell notes that Lear's error here has been the focus of much critical attention, calling out, as it does, for an explanation.

> The usual [contemporary] interpretations follow one of three main lines: Lear is senile; Lear is puerile; Lear is not to be understood in natural terms, for the whole scene has a fairy tale or ritualistic character. ... My hypothesis will be that Lear's behavior in this scene is explained by—the tragedy begins because of—the same motivation which manipulates the tragedy throughout its course ...: by the attempt to avoid recognition, the shame of exposure, the threat of self-revelation.
> (Cavell, *Disowning Knowledge in Seven Plays of Shakespeare* 57–58)

Cavell's emphasis on "the shame of exposure" links his hypothesis for the character's conduct to his philosophical concerns: "Shame," Cavell later says, "is the most isolating of feelings ..."

> but it is also the most primitive of *social* responses. With the discovery of the individual, whether in Paradise or in the Renaissance, there is the simultaneous discovery of the isolation of the individual; his presence to himself, but simultaneously to *others*.
> (Cavell, *Disowning Knowledge in Seven Plays of Shakespeare* 58)

The problem that shame poses, or the one it reveals, is one of isolation, or ineradicable privacy, and this problem emerges from one's exposure to and separateness from others. As is true of his work on other-minds skepticism in general, Cavell takes any successful being with others in Lear's situation to depend upon overcoming the threat of perennial isolation that manifests itself in the "shame of exposure." Given, a priori, "the discovery of the individual" as a condition of (modern, Western) humanity, acknowledgment and avoidance, rather than knowledge and ignorance, represent the proper terminology for the responses appropriate to the task of overcoming this virulent sense of one's isolation.

The "traditional interpretations" of *Lear* that Cavell mentions seem to follow from the failure to view acknowledgment and avoidance as separate regions of, or as at all distinct from, the axis of knowledge and ignorance. Cavell casts the plausibility of these interpretations into doubt ("Lear is puerile? Lear senile?") by contrasting the face value of these claims with the abundant evidence of Lear's "powerful, ranging mind." Cavell asks how we are to understand such a mind to honestly believe that Regan and Goneril offer love, or proof of love, while Cordelia simply withhold it. He takes the "traditional interpretations" as responding to this jarring discrepancy: "We imagine that Lear *must* be wildly abused (blind, puerile, and the rest)" in order to account for the seeming fact that he accepts these false beliefs. There is nothing wrong with this view, on Cavell's reading, "*if*, that is, we assume that Lear believes in Goneril and Regan and not in Cordelia. But we needn't assume that he believes anything of the kind" (Cavell, *Disowning Knowledge in Seven Plans of Shakespeare* 60).

To counter the notion that Lear must be either blind or puerile, tragic and therefore exceptional from the outset, Cavell notes that the abdication scene "doesn't *begin* badly." Rather, the scene pictures something quite ordinary: a father bribing his children for some of the putative fruits of filial love. Hendrik Hartog, in a study of inheritance law in the nineteenth-century United States, indicates the quotidian nature of this issue by pointing precisely to what he calls the "King Lear problem: If property were transferred too quickly, too finally, too securely, then one placed oneself at the mercy of one's children. Nothing protected one. One could not trust to love or duty alone" (Hartog 55). Cavell's point is that, with respect to "true love," one is always already at the mercy of the objects of one's love and commitment, and that no such exchange of goods can purchase or secure *love itself*. What Lear's bribe attempts to buy is *merely* what Hartog calls "the labor of care," which is notably distinct from love.

For Cavell, the traditional interpretations of Lear's wild abuse are necessitated by a view on which Lear genuinely believes that his kingdom buys love. Cavell himself, meanwhile, takes seriously the possibility that Lear only desires Hartog's "labor of care" under the appearance of love:

> Lear knows it is a bribe he offers, and—part of him anyway—wants exactly what a bribe can buy: (1) false love; and (2) a public expression

of love. That is: he wants something that he does not have to return *in kind*, something which a division of his property fully pays for. And he wants to *look* like a loved man—for the sake of his subjects, as it were. He is perfectly happy with his little plan, until Cordelia speaks. Happy not because he is blind, but because he is getting what he wants, his plan is working.

(Cavell, *Disowning Knowledge in Seven Plays of Shakespeare* 61–62)

Cordelia, as Cavell further points out, disrupts Lear's plan by "putting a claim on him he cannot face. She threatens to expose both his plan for returning false love with no love, and expose the necessity for that plan: his terror of being loved, of needing love" (Cavell, *Disowning Knowedge in Seven Plays of Shakespeare* 62). The specific danger that Cordelia poses for Lear lies in the threat of making what Cavell will later call the "partiality" or "dependence" of his own existence unavoidable—and it is precisely what Lear seeks to avoid.

In his reading of *Othello*, Cavell takes a similar tack: Cavell opens his essay by drawing a parallel—not an uncommon one—between *The Winter's Tale* and *Othello*. He asks, specifically, "how it is that we are to understand ... Hermione's reappearance as a statue" and "how it is that we are to understand Leontes' acceptance of the 'magic' that returns her to flesh and blood, and hence to him" (Cavell, "Epistemology and Tragedy: A Reading of *Othello*" 32). *Othello*, it seems to Cavell, traces an opposite path, from flesh and blood to stone. As Othello enters the bed chamber to kill his wife, he says, "Yet I'll not shed her blood; / Nor scar that whiter skin of hers than snow, / And smooth as monumental alabaster" (5.2.3–6). The monument Othello makes of Desdemona is linked through highly conventional imagery to purity, even virginity (Cavell, *Disowning Knowledge in Seven Plays of Shakespeare* 131–134). A wife's association with a statue in each play, Cavell suggests, amounts to a repudiation or denial of each heroine's flesh-and-blood humanity. Cavell would suggest, I believe, that this transformation of a human other to stone also requires—or is produced by—a sort of magic, or spell, namely the impulse to a skeptical denial of our fundamental relation to the world and to others, a retreat in the face of the (unbearable) demands of the human condition.

Importantly, Cavell notes that his notion of repudiation or *denial*, particularly with respect to Othello, but also with respect to Lear, does not "mean something requiring psychoanalytical, or any other, theory. I mean merely to ask that we not, conventionally but insufferably, assume that we know this woman better than this man knows her" (Cavell, *Disowning Knowledge in Seven Plays of Shakespeare* 133). If we do not hazard such an assumption but instead assume that Othello knows Desdemona at least as well as the readers or audience do, then "however far Othello believes Iago's tidings, he cannot just believe them; somewhere he also *knows* them to be false. This is registered in the rapidity with which he is brought to the truth" (Cavell, *The Claim of Reason* 488).

Cavell links Othello's denial of his wife's humanity with Othello's refusal of his own humanity, as well—that is, with a denial altogether of the very "condition of humanity." The way in which Othello's "stoning" of Desdemona is related to his own monumentalization is indicative of the particular kind of avoidance that Cavell has in mind. As Cavell explains toward the end of his discussion, "A statue, a stone, is something whose existence is fundamentally open to ocular proof. A human being is not." This is one articulation of what he calls "the truth of skepticism," expressed here in the fact that once Desdemona's relation to Othello is held up to skeptical doubt, and can, by fiat, as it were, only be returned by the epistemological procedure of Othello's "ocular proof," it is simply lost altogether. In this reading, skepticism seizes upon the true fact of our true separateness but treats it as a problem that knowledge or certainty might—indeed, must—overcome.

Cavell, however, argues that there is nothing that any refutation of skepticism can do for Othello in this case: "What [Othello] lacked was not certainty. He knew everything, but he could not yield to what he knew, be commanded by it" (Cavell, *Disowning Knowledge in Seven Plays of Shakespeare* 141). Cavell characterizes Othello's demand for certainty in the case of Desdemona's fidelity as an attempt to go beyond the limits of the human, and he tethers it to the notion of tragedy generally and Othello's tragedy in particular:

> The failure to acknowledge a best case of the other is a denial of that other, presaging the death of that other, say by stoning or by hanging; and the death of our capacity to acknowledge as such, the turning of our hearts to stone, or their bursting.
> (Cavell, *Disowning Knowledge in Seven Plays of Shakespeare* 138)

In each of the tragedies considered here, Cavell interprets the protagonist as appealing to the truth of skepticism under the conditions of avoidance. The language of avoidance (or acknowledgment) becomes necessary when one views the protagonist as adopting a skeptical stance in *denial* of something the protagonist cannot fail to know, which for Cavell manifests a failure to take on one's education. With respect to *Othello*, Cavell frames the matter as follows:

> Nothing could be more certain to Othello than that Desdemona exists; is flesh and blood; is separate from him; other. This is precisely the possibility that tortures him. The content of his torture is the premonition of the existence of another, hence of his own, his own as dependent, as partial. According to me further, his professions of skepticism over her faithfulness is a cover story for a deeper conviction; a terrible doubt covering a yet more terrible certainty, an unstatable certainty.
> (Cavell, *The Claim of Reason* 493)

In each tragedy, then, Cavell sees the protagonist as motivated to escape or deny a crucial element of the human condition, or the condition of humanity. In Lear's case, Cavell calls it "his terror of being loved, of needing love." In Othello's case, the "terrible certainty" the Moor flees has similarly to do with his own existence "as dependent, as partial." The fantasy that each protagonist entertains is that of complete autonomy, the self's independence from any and all others; Cavell interprets the two tragedies as arising from what might be called confusing the *separateness* from others inherent in individuality with this very idea of absolute *independence* from all others. On such an understanding, Lear and Othello both attempt to perfect their independence, to respond to the fact of their separateness from others by making it, in one way or another, absolute and final. Dependence upon others, in both of these tragedies, is imagined to be mutually exclusive of the fact of separateness; given the fact of human separateness, their logic leads these tragic heroes to aspire to independence.

But in Cavell's diagnosis of the shared tragic pathology that misinterprets separateness as independence, and in calling this misinterpretation a "failure of acknowledgment," there remains the implication that *successes* of acknowledgment are likewise standing possibilities. Earlier, I quoted Cavell's claim that "the tragedy is that comedy has its limits," by which Cavell means to express the ineradicable nature of our human separateness from one another: "Join hands as we may, one of the hands is mine and the other is yours" (Cavell, *Disowning Knowledge in Seven Plays of Shakespeare* 110). It is once again my contention that the primary movement of Shakespeare's comedies, with respect to the threat of skepticism—figured here as the confusion of separateness with independence, a view on which mutual dependence, or being-together, is imagined to be predicated upon the relative possibility of dissolving this separateness—involves the dramatization of skepticism's deflation. If tragedy is the drama of avoidance, Shakespeare's comedies can be read as the drama of acknowledgment.

Recall once more the scene of Beatrice and Benedick facing each other at the altar. The scene of public repudiation is momentary but telling. Each protagonist asks the other to declare his or her (inner) feelings of love, to which each might then safely respond in kind. This is a demand—for a fact, let us say, on the basis of which each might be justified in reciprocation—a demand that each in turn (skeptically) refuses. The raising of evidence at this point, Hero and Claudio's intervention with pilfered sonnets, seems to resolve the matter and prove to both Benedick and Beatrice that each in fact does love the other.

Benedick's response to this intervention, as I have said, is presciently half-right: "A miracle! Here's our own hands against our hearts" (5.4.94). It is, in a manner of speaking developed at the end of the next chapter, miraculous. But I will wonder in what sense these sonnets—produced under the conditions of a deception just now exposed in each lover's repudiation—can be taken as evidence of either lover's true (inner) feelings. It is a question as to what kind of problem we understand Beatrice and Benedick to have faced. Is it an empirical one, solvable, as in §109 of Wittgenstein's *Philosophical Investigations*, through "new discoveries," namely, the discovery of the facts contained in the sonnets? If, on the other hand, we cannot take the sonnets to provide *new* information to anyone in the scene, given that the mutual love between the protagonists has long been obvious to everyone, including the lovers themselves, then how do we understand the poems to perform their miraculous evidentiary work? If the conversion of the denial of a particular truth to its acknowledgment proceeds by some other means than the discovery of anything *new*, then it seems to point to a sort of learning that might occur instead, as Wittgenstein suggests, "by assembling [*durch Zusammenstellung*] what we have long been familiar with" (*PI* §109).

In making this contention with respect to the comedies, a great deal depends on the nature of what one "cannot fail to know" and what "we have long been familiar with," for this is what is to be either avoided or acknowledged. In the case of Othello, Cavell has characterized the character's avoidance in terms of an inability to "yield to what he knew, be commanded by it," and the consequences of his denial testify to the difficulty of such yielding. Assembling what we have long been familiar with ought not to be conceived as easy work. The scenes of avoidance in the tragedies—the arisings of the skeptical threat—are obviously scenes of crisis. The scenes of acknowledgment, for which I am provisionally suggesting that Beatrice and Benedick's interaction serves as an example, also respond, albeit differently, to moments of crisis, the threat of repudiation or withdrawal from the world.

But both acknowledgment and avoidance, therefore, presuppose a sort of ordinary and unproblematic getting-around in something like an objective world shared with others. It is against a background of such ordinary or everyday functioning that crises show up as exceptional situations. In having suggested that Shakespeare's tragedies and comedies alike explore responses to such moments of impasse or crisis, and in having suggested that the opposing poles of literary theory mirror these (tragic) responses to an aspect of "the world withdrawn before skepticism," seeing the task of (scholarly) reading as *differently* productive—as taking literature also as a site of acknowledgment beyond knowledge—will require an account of how and in what sense this background understanding is something that we "cannot fail to know" and that "we have long been familiar with," and something that is furthermore public a priori, such that it is possible to teach and to learn by means of reminding ourselves and others of the knowledge that we already have. This is the subject of the next chapter.

NOTES

1. Appeals to a "practical" or "defactoist" view ought not to be confused with "pragmatism," at least not as that particular philosophical position has been consolidated in the works of John Dewey, Charles Sanders Peirce, William

James, and, to an extent, Richard Rorty. There are points of similarity, of course, but pragmatism classically restricts itself to the reframing of truth conditions around a consequentialist pivot. James, I believe, says that "truth happens to an idea." Defactoist considerations are less concerned with the ability to predicate "truth" and "falsity" of ideas, period; defactoism attends to the practical (rule-following, language-use, mathematical proofs) as a way of understanding what sort of thing "truth," among other concepts (knowledge, certainty, confidence), is. This is more similar to Nietzsche's "mobile army of metaphors" formulation in "On Truth and Lying in an Extra-Moral Sense" than to anything in later pragmatism.
2. Such as Bruno Latour (Latour).
3. Williams's source for "surface reading" is the introduction to a 2009 work by Stephen Best and Sharon Marcus, and it is important to note that "surface reading" takes many forms, some of which—"surface as a practice of critical description" and "surface as affective and ethical stance" (9–10)—are surely very close to the practice I inherited from Cavell. Others—narratological and linguistic—are not, as it seems to me, immediately different from "symptomatic reading": each begins with a theory of how literature *works* and then strives to see *through* the text(s) to the truth of that theory.
4. This is not a perfect name for this group of critics associated with the scientific turn in literary studies, as they are not all equally committed to precisely the same view of evolutionary theory itself or to the role of evolutionary thinking in the development of mind, or even to the same philosophy of mind. They are united, however, in the view that science can uncover the facts about ourselves that explain our relation to the world in general and to literature in particular, whether these facts are based in (or in any way related to) evolutionary theory or whether these facts are purely neurological or cognitive in nature. "Evocritics," as a label, therefore, is merely shorthand and is not meant to mislead.
5. I take Nick Bromell to be on the right track in suggesting the aims of this way of reading literary works, or doing scholarly work in the humanities at large: "As I write, many colleagues in my home discipline of literary and cultural studies have come to believe that imagination is just a myth or fantasy. Because an earlier generation of critics writing seventy years ago seemed to depoliticize the work of criticism by banishing history from it, my generation has committed itself to bringing history back in. Many of us are now convinced that because we can think only what our history has made possible, the very word imagination is naive, misleading, and even dangerous—promising as it seems to an escape from history that simply is not possible. Consequently, literary and cultural studies today are energized by a largely—almost exclusively—critical energy. For thirty or more years now, these fields have been motivated mainly by an obligation to critique the world as it is, to question authority, to demystify ideology, and to train students in critical thinking. All this is well and good. All this is indispensable. But what about imagination? What about vision?" (Bromell 149–150)
6. Judith Butler, for instance, says, speaking of identity, "For an identity to be an effect means that it is neither fatally determined nor fully artificial and arbitrary" (Butler 187), which Jennifer Schell notes "opens up a middle ground—where identity is neither externally imposed nor freely chosen" (Schell 49). Similarly, Hubert Dreyfus describes Samuel Todes's view of

the "creative discovery" as one in which "the world reveals a new order of significance which is neither simply discovered nor arbitrarily chosen."
7. The assumptions, as I read them, are standard fare for New Criticism: that Shakespeare and his characters are best read as poetry; that the complexity of poetry and literature in general encodes messages or philosophies (from authors); that this complexity consists primarily in the formal properties of poetic language (symbolism, imagery, paradox, tension); and that close reading can decode and translate the encoded message for wider dissemination. Cavell does not adhere strongly to the formalism of New Criticism, but his reading certainly is "close" nonetheless. His close reading, one might say, is the close reading of characters.

REFERENCES

Beckwith, Sarah. *Shakespeare and the Grammar of Forgiveness*. Cornell University Press, 2011.
Best, Stephen, and Sharon Marcus. "Surface Reading: An Introduction." *Representations* 108.1 (2009): 1–21. Web. 7 January 2015.
Boyd, Brian. "Exhortation: Getting It All Wrong: Bioculture Critiques Cultural Critique." *The American Scholar* 75.4 (2006): 13–18. Print.
Bromell, Nick. *The Time Is Always Now*. New York: Oxford University Press, 2013. Print.
Butler, J. "Gender Trouble." (1999): n.p. Web. 5 April 2013.
Carroll, Joseph. *Literary Darwinism: Evolution, Human Nature, and Literature*. New York: Routledge, 2004.
Cavell, Stanley. *Disowning Knowledge in Seven Plays of Shakespeare*. London: Cambridge University Press, 2003. Print.
———. "Epistemology and Tragedy: A Reading of Othello." *Daedalus* 108.3 (1979a): 27–43.
———. *In Quest of the Ordinary*. Chicago: University of Chicago Press, 1988. Print.
———. *Little Did I Know: Excerpts from Memory*. Stanford, CA: Stanford University Press, 2010. Print.
———. *The Claim of Reason*. New York: Oxford University Press, 1979b. Print.
———. *This New Yet Unapproachable America: Lectures After Emerson After Wittgenstein*. Chicago: University of Chicago Press, 2013. Print.
Cook, Amy. *Shakespearean Neuroplay: Reinvigorating the Study of Dramatic Texts and Performance Through Cognitive Science*. New York: Palgrave Macmillan, 2010.
Dahl, Espen. *Stanley Cavell, Religion, and Continental Philosophy*. Bloomington, IN: Indiana University Press, 2014.
Dutton, Denis. *The Art Instinct: Beauty, Pleasure, and Human Evolution*. New York: Bloomsbury Press, 2009.
Fischer, Michael. *Stanley Cavell and Literary Skepticism*. Chicago: University of Chicago Press, 1989. Print.
Giraldi, William. "On Loving Literature." *Virginia Quarterly Review* 91.1 (2015): n.p. Web. 10 January 2015.
Gottschall, Jonathan. *Literature, Science, and a New Humanities*. New York: Palgrave Macmillan, 2008.

Grady, Hugh, and Terrance Hawkes. *Presentist Shakespeares*. Vol. 2006. New York: Routledge, 2006. Print.
Hartog, Hendrik. *Someday All This Will Be Yours*. Cambridge, MA: Harvard University Press, 2012.
Latour, Bruno. "Why Has Critique Run out of Steam? From Matters of Fact to Matters of Concern." *Critical Inquiry* 2004: 225–248.
Miller, J. Hillis. "The Critic as Host." *Modern Criticism and Theory*. Ed. David Lodge. New York: Longman, 1988. Print.
Mulhall, Stephen. *Stanley Cavell: Philosophy's Recounting of the Ordinary*. New York: Oxford University Press, 1998.
———. *The Cavell Reader*. Malden, MA: Blackwell, 1996: n.p. Print
Oatley, Keith. "Simulation of Substance and Shadow: Inner Emotions and Outer Behavior in Shakespeare's Psychology of Character." *College Literature* 33.1 (2006): 15–33.
Ratner-Rosenhagen, Jennifer. *American Nietzsche*. Chicago: University of Chicago Press, 2012. Print.
Schell, Jennifer. *A Bold and Hardy Race of Men: The Lives and Literature of American Whalemen*. Amherst, MA: University of Massachusetts Press, 2013.
Tooby, John, and Leda Cosmides. "Does Beauty Build Adapted Minds? Toward an Evolutionary Theory of Aesthetics, Fiction and the Arts." *Substance* 94/95 (2001): 6–27. Print.
Tooby, John, Leda Cosmides, and Ellen Spolsky. "Dialogue." *Substance* 30.1/2 (2001): 199–202.
Wells, Robin Headlam. *Shakespeare's Humanism*. New York: Cambridge University Press, 2005.
Williams, Jeffrey J. "The New Modesty in Literary Criticism." *Chronicle of Higher Education*. n.p., 2015. Web. 23 January 2015.
Zunshine, Lisa. *Why We Read Fiction: Theory of Mind and the Novel*. Columbus, OH: Ohio State University Press, 2006. Print.

2 A Defactoist Practice of Literary Scholarship

In the previous chapter, I raised the issue of "the truth of skepticism," associating it with the fact of our separateness or isolation, both from the world and from others. I also quoted Cavell as claiming that this fact can neither be effaced by providing new information nor put off by understanding it as a sort of curse. To do either would be to confuse a "metaphysical finitude" with an "intellectual lack," or at any rate something that stands in need of overcoming, that might be overcome (Cavell, "Knowing and Acknowledging" 68). I have further indicated that the bipolar conflict between various forms of structural determination in literary studies and its opposite in deconstruction share a metaphysical picture of essence, and that the epistemological task that follows from this is a matter of being "in soul muddled" rather than being "in fact mistaken." In this chapter, I wish to pursue the implications of these observations for literary studies as a means of grounding my readings of the comedies in the coming chapters.

Stephen Mulhall most succinctly captures the sense in which the foundational epistemological assumption underwriting the broad variety of approaches to literary criticism expresses a muddled soul:

> The truth in skepticism is not exactly a truth. … The truth of the matter is rather that this fundamental relation to the world (the human creature's basis in the world as a whole) is not one of knowing; but, as the tenacity both of the sceptical [sic] impulse and of the impulse to oppose scepticism in epistemological terms makes clear, nothing is more human than the compulsion to characterize this relation in that way.
> (Mulhall, *Stanley Cavell* 106)

The soul of literary scholarship is muddled to the extent that it (mis)conceives its relation to its subject matter, and to the world at large, in terms of either a rationalist sort of knowing or a straightforward refutation thereof. Despite being so usefully succinct, the above quotation calls for a good deal of explanation. How can this be? How might our "fundamental relation to the world" be better characterized? How might that fundamental relationship be connected to the project of literary scholarship? What does Shakespearean comedy have to say about any of it?

Mulhall, following Cavell and Wittgenstein, views the distortions visible in the extreme positions occupied by the evocritics of the Introduction, as well as those they take themselves to be responding to, as arising from feeling the need to provide a general refutation of skepticism as a fundamental condition of entering claims about, specifically, intentionality or motivation in literary characters. Put simply, the theoretical edifices constructed with an eye toward studying works of literature assume that we must account for the way in which an approach to literary works manages to solve an epistemological riddle. Works require *approaching*, on this view, and their fundamental estrangement from us—like the estrangement of the world at large, like the estrangement of others—implies that the task of studying them requires a means of effacing that epistemological distance.[1] On what basis can we know, finally, that a character *has* the sort of motivations or dispositions that he or she *seems* to or that a work *really* means what some assembly of evidence suggests?

The view shared among the collection of theorists on whom I will rely for support is that questions of this nature—questions, that is, that take this estrangement from the world and from literary works as a necessary starting point—*produce* the distortions to which I allude precisely because the form of the question requires that any acceptable answer present itself in terms of a specific, and erroneous, view of what *knowing* amounts to in this case. So, various theoretical candidates present themselves; if any or all are defeated or revealed to be inadequate to the task of explanation, it becomes uncomfortably easy to suppose that we do not know anything at all in the sense we imagined, that our public applications of words to the world or to other minds lack the sort of regularity or certainty or conviction that we (merely) imagined them to have.

The consequences of such defeats seem inescapable to the poststructuralists: since there are no transcendent means of fixing our symbols to objects, or of establishing certainty as to the existence of some object "emotion," to recall Harré's example, it follows that our use of symbol-systems is plainly groundless. As such we are radically free to create, reclaim, or reshape the meanings and appropriate contexts of words, and thus radically free to author ourselves, as it were. Meanwhile, the evocritics I have cited earlier represent a different sort of response, one that insists that the brute fact that we *do* know what words mean and can use language with one another as easily as we in fact do entails of necessity that there *must* be some *thing* that accounts for the regularity of, and our ability to learn, language-use at all, and they set off in search of this thing.

Both responses are illustrative of the major claim above: they share the assumption that the implicit problem of knowledge requires a particular sort of answer before any fruitful progress in areas involving language, including literary studies, can hope to commence. If no such answer is forthcoming, if the problem of knowledge is insoluble, then the proper work of literary studies is simply to disabuse us of our illusions of meaning and significance, or reveal their true sociopolitical underpinnings.

But the conclusion, or moral, suggested by Wittgenstein's investigations and the work of like-minded philosophers is that (a) nothing recognizable as an answer to the question so posed could in principle achieve the results that such an answer is thought to entail, and that (b) no such answer (no *such* answer) is necessary to our use and knowledge of language. Cavell's particular contribution to this line of thinking, particularly where literary scholarship is concerned, emphasizes the importance—the necessity—of undertaking the difficult labor of *making sense* of literary works as we would make sense of one another.

The ways in which this moral relates to the bipolar vacillations of literary theory is of crucial importance: it agrees with and acknowledges the deconstructionist insight that accounting for the significance of language or literature by means of structural determination is impossible. It likewise agrees with and acknowledges the source of the evocritics' umbrage: the simple fact that we *do* understand language, that literary works *have* meaning or significance, is obvious on its face, and so post-structuralist attempts to overstate the ramifications of ambiguity in language look like erudite chicanery, to put it nicely. Accommodating both facts at once—language's iterability or malleability, on the one hand, and our ordinary competence in grasping and discerning meaning on the other—is what a *defactoist* perspective offers. Both post-structuralism and evocrticism rest their arguments upon the denial of something that seems plainly obvious; Wittgenstein's investigations, and their development in Cavell and others, attempt to do justice to the truths of both sides, such as they are.

What is propounded in a Wittgensteinian or Cavellian view, I will argue, is not a theory of knowledge as such, nor any outright repudiation of Cartesian epistemology. Wittgenstein and his exegetes offer instead something like an alternative view of knowing that centers upon the activities or scenes of *teaching and learning*. Although these concepts are obviously related to the traditional epistemologist's picture of knowledge, they are hardly, as I will show, coextensive with it. In a paradoxical phrase: What we "cannot fail to know" and "what we have long been familiar with" are not simply available to us at birth—they can and must be taught and learned—but this does not mean that everything that one teaches and learns can be explicitly *known*, that is, known explicitly or formalized. Allowing for this insight leads Cavell and Wittgenstein to consider what happens in, and what is necessary for, the sort of teaching and learning that allows a child, for example, to grow into membership among a people. Acknowledgment and avoidance must be taken into account precisely because the traditional epistemologist's view of *knowing* mischaracterizes "our fundamental relation to the world." A Wittgensteinian/Cavellian picture of teaching and learning holds salutary import for the field and aims of literary scholarship.

2.1 THE PLACE(S) OF SKEPTICISM AND DOUBT IN OUR LIVES WITH WORDS AND OTHERS

I have suggested that something goes awry when we picture our relation to the world and to others as in all cases being a relation of *knowing*.

Wittgenstein raises problems for such a view in a number of places in his later work; indeed, one might regard the overarching strategy of the *Philosophical Investigations* as extended variations on this very theme. David Stern (*Wittgenstein's Philosophical Investigations*), for example, takes Wittgenstein to be following to their dead ends in logical paradox various traditional accounts of coming to know or to be able to do things with words that presuppose a representational view of mind and language.[2] Starting with Augustine's depiction of "ostensive definition"—in which elders fix names for objects in the minds of children by pointing to the object and speaking the name—Stern finds Wittgenstein raising paradoxical problems also for traditional views of the role of "explanation," "rule-following," and "private ostentation." Ultimately, none of these traditional views can be successfully invoked as an account of how we come to have the sort of everyday understanding that we regularly demonstrate.

Robert Fogelin groups these several paradoxical problems together under the label of "the paradox of interpretation" (Fogelin 17), since in each example of explaining, of rule-following, or of ostentation, a mediating component, an interpretation or a judgment, is posited in order to bring the concept (rule, definition, name) and the world (object, action, meaning) together. One way that Wittgenstein, as read by Fogelin, attacks the invocations of interpretation in service of this explanatory account is by pointing out the *impossibility* of foundationally grounding the link between concepts and objects or between minds and worlds. Such a mediating interpretation would *itself*, as deconstructionism suggests and as structuralism of all kinds abhors, be groundless, or "abyssal" (Glendinning 102). As Wittgenstein demonstrates in the *Blue Book* and the *Investigations* in particular, to view rule-following or language-use as in every case invoking, however implicitly, an act of interpretation leads to an infinite regress, "as if each [interpretation] contented us at least for a moment, until we thought of yet another lying behind it" (Wittgenstein, Anscombe, and Hacker, *Philosophical Investigations* §201b, henceforth abbreviated *PI*). If acts of interpretation—judgments of how to apply rules, or whether to affix just this concept to just this object in this particular situation—are recruited to defeat the possibility of doubt, or otherwise to account for the conviction or the certainty with which we act when we act with ordinary and unreflective correctness, no mediating component can successfully accomplish this task because it is always possible to raise a doubt at the level of the interpretation itself. This suggests that an epistemological theory that begins, along Cartesian lines, with the radical separation of mind and world cannot succeed in bringing the two together.

But Fogelin, in particular, along with Cavell, Mulhall, and Hubert Dreyfus, brings out Wittgenstein's often-overlooked insistence that "there is a misunderstanding here," that "what we thereby show [by means of the regress] is that there is a way of grasping a rule which is *not* an interpretation" (*PI* §201b). In other words, a second mode of response to these paradoxes is to point out that no such mental or cognitive interpretation is *necessary*. As Dreyfus has it, in his account of the failures of symbolic Artificial Intelligence to reproduce the varieties of intelligent or skilled human behavior along the lines of traditional epistemology,

> What hides the impasse [this misunderstanding] is the conviction that the commonsense knowledge problem must be solvable, since human beings have obviously solved it. But human beings may not normally use commonsense *knowledge* at all. What commonsense *understanding* amounts to might well be *everyday know-how*.
> (Dreyfus and Dreyfus, *Mind over Machine* 99)

This everyday know-how to which Dreyfus alludes also arises in Mulhall's reading of Wittgenstein, in which Wittgenstein notes that such know-how is neither had nor available in terms of any explicable or formalizable interpretation, since "the practical know-how we are thereby drawing upon is such that any attempt to state it in words will produce an utterance that anyone who possesses that know-how will recognize as itself nonsensical" (Mulhall, *Wittgenstein's Private Language* 7). Practical know-how emerges as an alternative to the sort of representational knowledge that Fogelin and Wittgenstein call "interpretations" in the application of rules. Mulhall and Dreyfus suggest that such know-how is central to ordinary getting around in the world and is also, in principle, "on pain of regress," nonformalizable, such that any attempt at formalizing it results in "nonsensical" propositions.

That know-how can be invoked in this way suggests a disjunction between the conviction or certainty with which we ordinarily act in the world and the sorts of things we take as generally necessary to dispelling doubt in highly abstract epistemological investigations. Put differently, our acting-with-certainty in ordinary circumstances is not as snugly tied to our ability to defeat skeptical questions as we are prone to imagining. For just this reason, any *inability* to defeat skeptical doubts at a general level (How do we learn the meanings of words? How do we know we are not hallucinating?) has no *necessary* bearing on our everyday actions in the world.[3]

If practical know-how is an accurate way of accounting for our most basic relation to the world and to others,[4] as Mulhall and Dreyfus have it, and if our ordinary uses of language and our everyday interactions with people are not in every case produced by or reducible to formalized or formalizable knowledge, as traditional epistemology demands, then it will be obvious that our ordinary or everyday activities are also not generally answerable to the kinds of highly abstract doubts that other-minds or external-world skeptics often raise. Nor, as we have already seen—and have also pictured in the Shakespearean examples of Othello and Lear—could we expect any answers we might conjure for such doubts to be able to restore the sense of engagement or involvement in the world that we, in point of fact, live out from day to day.

Wittgenstein's writings are suggestive of this conclusion, particularly in the following example, with respect to other minds. In what was formerly known as Part II of the *Investigations*—which is now called *Philosophy of Psychology—A Fragment* (henceforth *PPF*)—Wittgenstein reframes the typical answer to the Cartesian "evil-demon problem." Considering how we can claim to know that this or that other person *is* a person rather than an automaton—is another like oneself—Wittgenstein's response attacks the implicit premise that *knowing* that a person is this or that kind of thing captures the nature of the relation between people: "My attitude towards him," says Wittgenstein, "is an attitude towards a soul. I am not of the *opinion* that he has a soul" (*PPF* 22). The sort of comportment toward another as an other like oneself is irreducible to a recognition of any particular features shared in common; it is not a matter of abstract knowledge but of practical know-how, practical coping.

Taking a similar approach to problems associated with external-world skepticism, and in this case invoking the paradox of rule-following, Wittgenstein first heads in the direction of a regress of rules and then makes a *defactoist* move:

> Speaking of the application of a word, I said that it is not everywhere bounded by rules. But what does a game look like that is everywhere bounded by rules? Whose rules never let doubt creep in, but stop all the gaps where it might?—Can't we imagine a rule regulating the application of a rule; and a doubt which *it* removes—and so on? But that is not to say that we are in doubt because it is possible to imagine a doubt. I can easily imagine someone always doubting before he opened his front door whether an abyss did not yawn behind it, and making sure about it before he went through the door (and he might on some occasion prove to be right)—but for all that, I do not doubt in such a case. (*PI* §84)

Here the insistence is that the *possibility* of a doubt's arising does not necessarily commit anyone to foreclose upon that doubt in order to go on. The thrust of his position here, as Fogelin, in particular, emphasizes, is that under ordinary circumstances no doubt arises at all. *In fact*—the defactoist gesture—our going out the door in the morning does not require any assurance that no chasm gapes in the front yard. The attention to the everyday and the ordinary, to what happens as one prepares to leave one's house, is meant not to defeat this indefeasible doubt, but merely to show that this doubt does not *in fact* ordinarily apply as generally as is seemingly threatened.

When and where to raise or cope with the threat of skepticism is therefore not something that one might posit *generally*. But various circumstances do solicit various kinds of doubts, which will require various kinds of responses. And growing up entails the teaching and learning of what counts as a reasonable question or a sufficient response to a particular demand in any number of different cases. As any parent of any three-year-old will attest, the limits to the reasonable asking of "why" do not come hardwired in any child's brain.

I have been urging throughout this and the previous chapter that (literary) theory's attempts to locate or postulate a general refutation for skepticism, a general epistemological account of our relation to language or to the objects of the world or to others, which is always an attempt to foreclose in the widest possible sense on the grounds for doubting or to provide an abstract means of overcoming such doubts, will fail, just as a matter of historical fact, such theories have always failed so far. But no radically postmodern conclusion—that meanings and facts are simply up to us or are *merely* "social constructs" in the derogatory sense with which such words are uttered—follows from this, as such a conclusion turns on the same assumption about the relative existence of any *general* set of conditions for claims to knowledge. Rather, any particular knowledge claim is entered in response to a particular call for justification or explanation, and what will make that claim sufficient to its particular task is a matter of Dreyfus's "commonsense understanding," which he grounds in our "*everyday know-how*."

In particular, I hope to have drawn into question the tacit assumption that in order to enter a claim about something like literary meaning, or indeed the meaning of any piece of language, we require a *general* theoretical understanding of mind or of language. Describing the "resolute" reading of the *Tractatus*'s strategy, which he (and others) see also at work in the *Investigations*, Mulhall says that the *Tractatus*

> mobilizes a certain kind of practical knowledge, a know-how possessed by anyone capable of speech, in the service of overcoming certain philosophical illusions—in particular, the illusion that our everyday understanding of language, and hence of the distinction between sense and nonsense, is in need of the support or authority of a philosophical theory.
> (Mulhall, *Wittgenstein's Private Language* 7)

My intention in raising these considerations with literary scholarship in mind is motivated by a very persistent and apparently wide frustration with the results or products of literary studies: we see just such a frustration in the evocritics' denunciations of the methods and results of post-structuralism as evidencing a "coddled, preening radicalism" and consisting of "obscurantist dogmatism." It is as though such scholarship has never yet provided (but always promises to be on the cusp of providing) the sort of findings—or truths, or advances—that we expect research to produce.

At the same time, every research paradigm that produces demonstrable, empirical, and coherent results seems to leave the ordinary experience of grasping the meanings of a Shakespearean comedy, for example, completely untouched. The simple suggestion here is that asking the wrong sorts of questions is producing unsatisfying responses. Providing satisfying answers will require, as Wittgenstein says, "turning our whole inquiry around. (One might say: the inquiry must be turned around, but on the pivot of our real need)" (*PI* §108). I simply assert without argument that the ability to conduct serious conversations around the meanings of particular literary works constitutes a real need of literary studies.

2.2 ON TEACHING AND LEARNING AS TRAINING OR INITIATION

I was saying earlier that, rather than any epistemological theory, Wittgenstein and his acolytes draw out a particular view of *teaching* and *learning*. Having already shown, by pointing to the paradox of interpretation, the fatal problems associated with the idea that learning to use language is generally a matter of forming the correct representations of a collection of facts about the world; and having further assayed the claim that the sort of *knowledge* embodied in, for example, "an *attitude* towards a soul" amounts to "commonsense understanding" or "everyday know-how," I want to say something about the nature of the *common* in the commonsense, as well as about how teaching and learning proceeds in the absence of any hypothetical third man, any mediating component. Bringing out Wittgenstein's view of teaching and learning will be particularly important inasmuch as it reveals generally underappreciated subtleties in terms of the stakes and possibilities involved in handling literature in a scholarly way.

Wittgenstein's examples, across many of his works, of coming to know how to "go on" in a given context—how to continue a series, how to apply concepts in new situations, and so on—explicitly picture scenes of teaching and learning. In *Remarks on the Foundations of Mathematics*, Wittgenstein describes a student–teacher interaction when he says, "The only criterion for [anyone's] multiplying 113 by 44 ... is his doing it in the way in which all of us, who have been trained in a certain way, would do it" (Wittgenstein, *Remarks on the Foundations of Mathematics* 58). In the *Investigations*, Wittgenstein asks,

> How do I explain the meaning of "regular", "uniform", "same" to anyone?—I'll explain those words to someone who, say, speaks only French by means of the corresponding French words. But if a person hasn't yet got the *concepts*, I'll teach him to use the words by means of *examples* and by *exercises*.—And when I do this, I do not communicate less to him than I know myself.(§208)

In considering how it is possible that rule-following should get off the ground at all, Wittgenstein and his interlocutor have the following conversation:

> Let me ask this: what has the expression of a rule—say a signpost—got to do with my actions? What sort of connection obtains here?—Well,

this one, for example: I have been trained to react in a particular way to this sign, and now I do so react to it. But with this you have only pointed to a causal connection; only explained how it has come about that we now go by the signpost; not what this following-the-sign really consists in. Not so; I have further indicated that a person goes by a signpost only in so far as there is an established usage, a custom. (§197)

These three examples highlight two important aspects of teaching and learning, aspects that both Fogelin and Cavell underscore, albeit with different emphases. Both philosophers point, first of all, to this view of teaching and learning's inherent publicness, its commonality; to the fact that in order for there to *be* anything to be taught or learned, there must be "an established usage, a custom." Parenthetically, this particular requirement could also be fulfilled by some kind of universal access to a transcendent or abstract rule. But Cavell and Fogelin also, secondly, point to Wittgenstein's reliance upon *training* ("initiation" in Cavell's parlance), which sidesteps the (impossible) demand to meet the requirement via an appeal to anything abstract. Fogelin's gloss of the talk of usages, customs, "stage-setting" (*PI* §179), and training emphasizes what such learning explicitly *does not* include, particularly in §208 above:

> Here the person doing the teaching possesses certain skills and abilities. She can give examples of uniformities and nonuniformities. She can employ the concept in a variety of contexts. In her teaching, she is trying to imbue her student with these same skills and abilities. She is not holding anything back. She is not in possession of a secret key that she is trying to pass on to her student that, when successfully transmitted, will successfully complete the training.
>
> (Fogelin 37–38)

This sort of training need not produce an abstraction or a representation of any particular rule or custom, since it is entirely unclear that the one doing the teaching has any such thing herself ("When I do this, I do not communicate less to him than I know myself"). Elsewhere, Fogelin describes Wittgenstein's view on teaching and learning still more simply:

> Wittgenstein says that the only criterion for the student's multiplying correctly is conformity to public practice. Those who do the training have themselves been trained. The student who cannot conform to their training is dismissed as a hopeless case—a lunatic. There is nothing more to it than that.
>
> (Fogelin 36)

Regardless of a teacher's or a student's ability to formulate something like a rule after the fact, any such formulation of any such rule cannot be involved in the actual *practice* of the skill (rule-following, concept-application, signpost-following) that the learner and teacher share, at least insofar as such involvement is imagined on the model of making a kind of internal appeal, precisely because of the infinite regress that both Dreyfus and Fogelin discuss. In fact, as Fogelin says, immediately following the passage quoted above:

> In particular, the training need not produce a mental intermediary (a third thing) in virtue of which the student, in concert with members of his community, is able to multiply correctly. Or rather, even if training did produce some such mental intermediary, it would not provide a justification of the student's performance. Appeals to it would simply raise the paradox of interpretation anew.
>
> (Fogelin 36)

Earlier I argued that the evocritics and their post-structuralist opponents go astray in the same manner—namely, by making their arguments about whether we can really know anything about language or literature depend upon the issue of whether or not we have access to any third thing, any metaphysically or naturalistically determinative essence. Fogelin's paragraph provides a concise restatement of my position with respect to these schools of thought.

Once more, we can see that reliance upon any such "third man" in questions of establishing knowledge in terms of language or literature, following a rule, or continuing a series is, as Stern says, both "unnecessary and impossible. It [is] unnecessary because we do not need an unmoved mover in order to follow a rule. It [is] impossible because nothing could perform that task" (*Wittgenstein on Mind and Language* 116). Cavell makes this point, too: "universals are neither necessary nor even useful in explaining how words and concepts apply to different things" (Cavell, *The Claim of Reason* 187). "Training" or "initiation" in a given practice—even in mathematics and language—tends to produce in the learner the correct responses to other, similar situations. The paradox of interpretation shows that this cannot occur in virtue of the internalization of any general theory. The *fact* that this learning occurs anyway indicates that no such theory is necessary.

But simultaneously, and contra Fogelin, Cavell points out that it is not as harmonious as the "there is nothing more to it than that" formulation might imply. Specifically, Cavell focuses on the implications of the many passages in which Wittgenstein discusses the possibility of a student *failing* to learn, the places in which the teacher's willingness or ability to teach, or the student's willingness or ability to learn, come up short. Cavell's emphasis on the student's *acceptance* of training or initiation has important ramifications for the *public* aspect of "commonsense understanding" and is deeply implicated in Cavell's understanding of comedy and tragedy.

If such training is the nonformalizable and thus nonsensical ground of the rationality or regularity directly manifest in shared human practices of whatever kind, then part of the effect of Wittgenstein's many illustrations of this point is the lengthy shadow cast by the fact that "there is *nothing more* to it than that." If such training proves insufficient to compel a student or an initiate to continue the series in the way that we do, to multiply in the way that we do, to apply this or that concept in a new context as we would, then nothing *else* will achieve that end or perform that labor. If training or initiation is all that there is, and if one can attempt to train another, then the other can also *fail* or *refuse* to accept this training. Wittgenstein considers this possibility explicitly, as Fogelin summarizes: "The student who cannot conform to their training is dismissed as a hopeless case—a lunatic."

The *personal* stakes in teaching and learning are thus considerably higher on this view than on any traditional picture: when a student fails to understand the lesson, it is not some *thing* that she fails to grasp, some rule, but much more profoundly, it is *her people* that she cannot comprehend, *her place* with respect to a community that she fails to occupy, *herself* that remains in some sense unrecognizable, both to herself and to others. Nothing other than entering into and accepting such training can undergird the practical regularity in continuing series or using language, and if this is refused or defeated, then the would-be teacher and the would-be student stand helpless in their isolation from one another. The sort of knowledge that "training" or "initiation" confers is fundamentally practical, and thus it cannot be forced upon anyone in virtue of any abstract notion of correctness.

The activity of teaching and learning depends upon students and teachers extending toward one another, assuming without final justification their mutual intelligibility. (The educational psychology literature calls the space into which each extends "the zone of proximal development.") But this mutual extension itself can be neither compelled nor guaranteed. It is no coincidence, I will suggest, that the would-be student and the would-be teacher figured above in their helpless isolation from one another recall the helpless isolation of Beatrice and Benedick at the altar.

These notes hint in the direction of Cavell's unique contribution to this discussion: if practical know-how, or what Dreyfus calls "background practices," are invoked to account for the actual bringing together of concepts and objects, mind and world, that we in fact live out in our ordinary lives, then attempting to step outside of this everyday know-how in order even to attempt a theoretical explanation of a practical ability, as both structuralists and post-structuralists are wont to do, is to make anything like practical ability vanish, which is also akin to what Mulhall memorably calls "the world go[ing] dead for [us]." There is suddenly nothing *there* to be investigated, as whatever a theory successfully represents or formalizes or explains is by definition not the practical know-how that was supposed to be its object.

For this reason, it can sometimes seem that our everyday practical commitments in the world stand on shaky ground, as though the sort of conviction with which we act and feel and live cannot bear close examination, a situation that roughly restates (and understates and motivates) Othello's condition. Indeed, this intimation might be taken as another formulation of the "truth in skepticism." We seek to better (theoretically) grasp the nature of our practical engagement with the world *in order to* shore up our shaky ground. But in stepping outside of our practical engagements, or by, in Wittgenstein's words, "assum[ing] the abrogation of the normal language game," we cut ourselves off from *any* ground, for suddenly we again face the paradox of interpretation. To conclude Wittgenstein's above sentence: once we have attempted an objective explanation of our ability to express pain, we "need a criterion of identity for the sensation; and then the possibility of error also exists" (*PI* §288).

The truth in skepticism is precisely that the practical know-how undergirding our everyday relation to the world and to others, once disengaged from its ordinary functioning and made answerable to skeptical scrutiny, cannot perform the sort of engagement that such practical know-how in point of fact and under ordinary circumstances achieves. From such a perspective, just as the skeptic fears, we *really are* cut off from the world and from others.

When Cavell perceives the threat of failure, denial, or avoidance in learning the meanings of words or how to follow a rule, this threat arises from the *dual* facts (1) that commonsense understanding is nonformalizable in principle, which means that a teacher can hit bedrock with a student, and vice versa, beyond which there is no further appeal to be made; and (2) that the existential discomfort produced by this situation, the discrepancy between the felt certainty of our ordinary relation to the world and our literal inability to explain it to ourselves, provokes an irresistible temptation to *come up with* a formalized account, which would (and does), only *confirm* the skeptical insight that motivates the quest for foundations in the first place by *actually* driving an unbridgeable gap between ourselves and anything else.

Sarah Beckwith, in her recent similarly oriented study, *Shakespeare and the Grammar of Forgiveness*, brings the above point to bear specifically upon Shakespeare and upon the movements in literary scholarship already discussed:

> Part of the crisis and difficulty in this understanding is that [in skepticism] we lose sense of ourselves and our communities together, in one and the same movement of self-exile from shared words and shared expressions. Once we see those words and expressions not as showing but as hiding us, we lose touch with our only means of self-knowledge and contact with others. It is this chapter that motivates the predicament that gives rise to the sense of this split. It is my belief that much contemporary criticism inhabits this very split, and so the therapeutic and diagnostic power of Shakespeare's dramaturgy is unavailable to it.
>
> (Beckwith 9)

I will return to the points expressed in the above passage. In the meanwhile, Cavell's contributions to understanding the extent, importance, and nature of what he calls "initiation" draw upon the Wittgensteinian notions of "agreement" and "forms of life." These concepts are necessary to grasping the sense in which a background practical know-how is by its very nature, as Beckwith hints in speaking of our "shared words and expressions," both common and public.

2.3 "AGREEMENT NOT IN OPINION, BUT RATHER IN FORM OF LIFE"

Wittgenstein introduces the notion of "form of life" (Ger. *Lebensform*) very early in the *Investigations*. In §19, he notes that "to imagine a language is to imagine a form of life." In §23, he says that "The word language-*game* is used here to emphasize the fact that the *speaking* of language is part of an activity, or of a form of life." The nature of my appeal to Fogelin, Dreyfus, and Mulhall earlier in this section underlines the importance of the connection between the notions of "an activity" and a "form of life": a form of life is, on this view, an embodied or practical matter, a matter of sharing practices, a sharing possible within the limits of both biological and ethnological constraints. In §30, Wittgenstein further emphasizes the practical nature of the stratum underlying language that a form of life is by asserting that "one has already to know (or be able to do) something before one can ask what something is called." The logical space of any object—the *grammar*, as he will come to call it, of any given concept—is prepared (or the stage is set; cf. §179) by practical know-how, or by Dreyfus's "commonsense understanding." This entails some oft-misunderstood consequences.

In *PI* §§241–242, Wittgenstein's "voice of temptation" (Cavell, "The Availability of Wittgenstein's Later Philosophy" 92) has the following conversation with the "voice of correctness":

> 241. "So you are saying that human agreement decides what is true and what is false?"—What is true or false is what human beings *say*; and it is in their *language* that human beings agree. This is agreement not in opinion, but rather in form of life.
> 242. It is not only agreement in definitions, but also (odd as it my sound) agreement in judgements [sic] that is required for communication by means of language. This seems to abolish logic, but does not do so.

Connecting language once more to "form of life," and tying both of these notions to "agreement in judgments," Wittgenstein again stresses the practical know-how undergirding even the regularity of logic, which the necessity of agreement in judgment does not abolish.

These passages are frequently misunderstood as advocating a sort of relativistic and communitarian epistemology—something that reader response theory inferred, for example—which misses the point.[5] In particular, these passages are often understood to make the correctness or incorrectness, truth or falsity, of any given action or proposition answerable to community assent, but this is too superficial of a reading. Fogelin brings out in one way the importance of distinguishing the operative notion of *agreement* in Wittgenstein from any sort of mental or cognitive *decision* effected at any particular moment, and he connects it once more to the notion of training:

> Wittgenstein is not saying that an individual's interpretation of a rule is correct to the extent that it squares with the community's interpretation of it. In rule-following, we join a consensus in *action*—a consensus grounded in the kind of training that we, as humans, *can* successfully undergo and the kind of training that we actually *do* undergo in the community in which we are reared.
>
> (Fogelin 28)

Here form of life is pictured, just as Cavell pictures it, as involving both and at once a cultural articulation ("training that we actually *do* undergo in the community in which we are reared") and a natural or biological articulation ("training that we, as humans, *can* successfully undergo"). Harking back once more to the evocritics and their "sociocultural constructionist" opponents, Wittgenstein's "form of life" defies reduction to, or explanation in terms of, *either* a natural or cultural essence alone, as it involves both simultaneously.

Fogelin's depiction of rule-following (continuing a series, applying a concept) as *joining* a consensus in action points to the presupposition of an already existing consensus, but it also underscores the fact that the consensus is directly (and only) manifest in action, as opposed to "opinion," and it emphasizes that the coming-to-agree with this consensus is itself a matter of activity, a matter of *joining* the consensus, as opposed to any purely cognitive achievement of internalizing the algebraic expression of a mathematical rule, for example. To agree in form of life *means* to do what others would do in this given or any similar situation, nothing more—but also, and crucially, nothing less.

Where this agreement breaks down, where students simply fail or refuse to learn at this level, or where a would-be teacher fails to recognize a student as one who ought to be trained in the ways of this community, nothing *else* can step in to reinstate or repair it—nothing, that is, except the sort of groundless extending toward one another that teaching and learning is, the entering into a certain kind of relation to another, the pretentious claim to speak with and for others.

In such breakdown situations, Wittgenstein pictures attempts at appealing to fundamental reasons or justifications for following a rule or drawing an inference as ineluctably futile: in *PI* §217, he notes that "Once I have exhausted the justifications, I have reached bedrock, and my spade is turned. Then I am inclined to say: 'This is simply what I do.'" The implication for Fogelin, Cavell, and Dreyfus, of course, is that the practical know-how that undergirds the regularity and rationality of our agreement is not itself available in terms of propositional reasons or justifications. It is important that Wittgenstein notes that his temptation, upon hitting bedrock with a student, is to gesture to himself, to fall back on what *he* does as representative of what *one* does. This may or may not turn out to be enough. When justifications give out, one still has oneself; but the use of oneself as an example that ought to be accepted depends upon the ungrounded assertion of mutual intelligibility.

To return at last to Cavell's dramatization of the stakes involved in teaching and learning under this notion that teaching and learning must result in the "joining [of] a consensus in *action*" that "agreement in form of life," in point of fact *is*, one must therefore picture this idea of "joining" in terms of the "acceptance" of something to which Wittgenstein often alludes. In the *PPF*, for example, Wittgenstein says: "What has to be accepted, the given, is—one might say—*forms of life*" (*PPF* §345). Cavell now draws out the necessity of a student's acceptance of training or education in *The Claim of Reason*:

> Our ability to communicate with him depends upon his "natural understanding", his "natural reaction", to our directions and our gestures. It depends upon our mutual attunement in judgments. It is astonishing how far this takes us in understanding one another, but it has its limits; and these are not merely, one may say, the limits of knowledge but the limits of experience. And when these limits are reached, when our attunements are dissonant, I cannot get below them to firmer ground. The power I felt in my breath as my words flew to their effect now vanishes into thin air. For not only does he not receive me, because his natural reactions are not mine; but my own understanding is found to go no further than my own natural reactions bear it. I am thrown back upon myself; I as it were turn my palms outward, as if to exhibit the kind of creature I am, and declare my ground occupied, only mine, ceding yours.
> (Cavell, *The Claim of Reason* 115)

Here at last is the crucial moral to which all of this preparatory ground points: the threat of refusal, of the discovery of one's isolation, of one's powerlessness to convince or compel, is *standing*; this possibility, in virtue of what human beings are, is ineradicable. The *fact* of the matter is the fact of human separateness; that this is not *always* a bar to teaching and learning, or to a sense of belonging to a common world, belonging with others, indicates that Wittgenstein's attitudinal comportment to another as a person has practical traction; that our separateness always *can* bar these kinds of belonging indicates that the threat to such belonging is not defeasible in any ultimate sense.

The practical grounding of rationality or intelligibility is *given*, as Wittgenstein says, but it must also be *accepted* in order to take effect, and this acceptance cannot be ensured or enforced by anything else at all. What it means, however, to repudiate or to refuse such agreement is to sacrifice one's intelligibility to oneself, as much as to others. All knowledge, grounded in "everyday know-how," is thereby established on the inherently public grounds of shared human practices.

2.4 SKEPTICISM, AGREEMENT, AND INHERITANCE

To explore Cavell's understanding of Wittgenstein's scenes of teaching and learning is to picture the givenness of logic, intelligibility, and reason as *literally* given. But the consequence of this literal picture is the understanding that such gifts can also be refused, denied, or misunderstood. Cavell reads Wittgenstein's many deconstructions of traditional accounts of language and the mind as explorations of the ways in which we would and do deny this literal sense of givenness, "Which is to say," as he puts it, "that language is not only an acquirement but a bequest; and it is to say that we are stingy in what we attempt to inherit" (Cavell, *The Claim of Reason* 189).[6]

Although such inheritance can be refused or can fail to take effect, this agreement in form of life binds us in ordinary circumstances to others and to the world. As such, agreement amounts to joining a consensus in action; it is practical, embodied, lived. For this reason, as I quoted Mulhall as saying much earlier, "the truth of the matter is rather that this fundamental relation to the world (the human creature's basis in the world as a whole) is not one of knowing." Taking *knowing* to be our fundamental relation to the world is the crucial mistake (*PI* §308: "The decisive move in the conjuring trick has been made, and it was the very one that seemed to us quite innocent"); it renders the practical agreement in forms of life that we can readily see completely irrelevant: we close ourselves off from all that the fact of this agreement might reveal. The move of taking our fundamental isolation or estrangement from the world as our default condition turns out to be the very move of *estranging* ourselves from a world to which we are not, for the most part, strangers. From this estranged position, it seems suddenly that there is something we *cannot* do, something like bridging a gap between ourselves and the world. This supposition leads to conclusions such as Kant's, that appearances are all that we might access, and that things in themselves are forever out of reach.

Cavell's view of teaching and learning repudiates this compromise, as he lays out what a Wittgensteinian grammar amounts to:[7]

> To summarize what has been said about this: In "learning language" you learn not merely what the names of things are, but what a name is; not merely what the form of expression is for expressing a wish, but

what expressing a wish is; not merely what the word for "father" is, but what a father is; not merely what the word for "love" is, but what love is. In learning language, you do not merely learn the pronunciation of sounds, and their grammatical orders, but the "forms of life" which make those sounds the words they are, do what they do—e.g., name, call, point, express a wish or affection, indicate a choice or an aversion, etc. ... Instead, then, of saying either that we *tell* beginners what words mean, or that we *teach* them what objects are, I will say: We initiate them, into the relevant forms of life held in language and gathered around the objects and persons of our world.
(Cavell, *The Claim of Reason* 177–178)

The skeptical impulse, one might say, seizes upon the standing possibility of disavowal or refusal of the forms of life that are bequeathed to us, and it makes this standing possibility, or rather the disavowal or refusal itself, *characteristic* of our relation to the world and to others, the rule and the starting point rather than an exceptional or extraordinary circumstance. Skepticism figures each of us as facing one another, palms outward, pathologically unreconciled—Beatrice and Benedick, once more. Such a view sends us off "in pursuit of chimeras" (*PI* §94), some general guarantor of reconciliation, which will also be a general explanation of the ordinary agreement we exhibit in our everyday practices. Such a pursuit directs our attention to the general or the transcendent, and it prevents us from attending to particular cases, "which alone could have helped [us] understand the usage of the general term." (Wittgenstein, *Preliminary Studies for the "Philosophical Investigations" Generally Known as the Blue and Brown Books* 19).

But for Cavell, as I hinted earlier, the skeptical impulse has much more serious and profound consequences than simply throwing theorists off the correct path. In being thrown off (in hurling ourselves off) the correct path, we destroy our lived relation to the world and to others, just as Beckwith notes. It is not an *academic* error: once we require our everyday know-how to present itself in theoretical form, "the world" as Mulhall puts it in one place, "goes dead for [us] and recedes from [our] grasp" (Mulhall, *Stanley Cavell* 154). Once we have repudiated the means by which, for example, the inner states of others are available to us—our everyday capacity to say, and with accuracy, that "he looks sad"—once we have denied the *effects* of training or initiation embodied in our ability to use language ordinarily, then there are no *others* anymore to whom our knowledge might apply, nor even, in any relevant sense, a self.

Precisely because only chimeras will satisfy our skeptical search, we imagine that we have to discover something new, something sublime, something we have never laid eyes upon, something that will return to us that which we unproblematically had before a general doubt came over us. The divergent positions of the post-structuralists and the evocritics express a fundamental disagreement as to the existence of this sublime, chimerical thing. But in a deflationary move, Cavell notes that, far from repudiating the possibility of human knowledge,

> My contrary sense was that Wittgenstein was articulating what human assurance amounts to, that it does not stop short of conviction in the world, but that we ourselves become restive with this assurance, and we have the power to undermine ourselves in the name of an, as it were, unachievable or rather illusory rationality.
> (Cavell, *Little Did I Know* 376)

Wittgenstein clarifies the distinction in his own words: we do not need to "hunt out new facts; it is rather of the essence of our investigation that we do not seek to learn anything *new* by it. We want to *understand* something that is already in plain view. For *this* is what we seem in some sense not to understand" (*PI* §89b).[8] Attempting to find some hidden or latent guarantor of our connection to the world is in this light a fool's errand for a number of reasons, not the least of which is the way in which it distracts us from the difficult and necessary task of understanding something in plain view.

In Heidegger and especially in Wittgenstein, that which we would understand lies perfectly open to view. As Wittgenstein likes to say, "nothing is hidden": the knowledge that we seem to seek in metaphysical explorations is already and visibly at work in the regularity of our everyday dealings in the world. This sort of knowledge—what Cavell calls the "tak[ing] on [of] our education" (Cavell, *Little Did I Know* 374)—is achieved when we adopt a certain (practical) stance toward ourselves and toward others. Wittgenstein says,

> The difficult thing here is not, to dig down to the ground; no, it is to recognize the ground that lies before us as the ground.
> For the ground keeps on giving us the illusory image of greater depth, and when we seek to reach this, we keep on finding ourselves on the old level.
> Our disease is one of wanting to explain.
> (Wittgenstein, *Remarks on the Foundations of Mathematics*, VI 31)

Beckwith, along with Wittgenstein and Cavell, characterizes succumbing to the skeptical urge as something that forecloses upon Shakespeare's "diagnostic and therapeutic power." Here Wittgenstein also characterizes the temptation to explain (by means of "subsuming phenomena under general causal laws" (Cahill 154)), as a sort of an illness. And if we can fall ill, then we can also recover. But as with any other illness, recovery here is hardly a foregone conclusion.

2.5 "ESSENCE IS EXPRESSED IN GRAMMAR": COMEDY, BELONGING, AND EDUCATION

A defactoist means of dissolving skeptical problems, both in literary studies and in other domains, requires repeated reminders of the ordinary and the everyday, the way in which things are for us. Wittgenstein's examples of learning for the first time how to apply names to objects or how to follow a signpost, as well as his earnest attempts to imagine the problems of classical skepticism emerging in the contexts of daily life, keep alive a powerful tension between two opposing truths—on the one hand, the indefeasibility of skepticism by means of any recourse to reason, justification, or causal explanation; and on the other hand, the infrequency of skeptical crises in the course of ordinary or everyday life.

Although "defactoism" is Fogelin's term for Wittgenstein's invocations or reminders of our ordinary practical abilities as a defense against or as a cure for the temptations of skepticism, my use of the term in the context of literary scholarship seeks to inflect this particular notion of defactoism's "therapy" with Cavell's heightened sensitivity to the ultimate incurability of skepticism, the ways in which the ordinary is perpetually unsatisfying, or the occasions on which we come to find our worlds strange, or to estrange ourselves from them.

On such occasions, the therapeutic power of defactoism's recitations alone is severely circumscribed, since our "criteria," in such moments, "are dead" (Cavell, *The Claim of Reason* 84). The way we use words in real life, the ways in which we carry out our regular practices, become in these instances precisely the *question*, and so mere *reminders* (or *mere* reminders) that we simply *do* so cannot obviously or simply be imagined to function as answers to skeptical doubts, if they were ever so imagined. For this reason, Cavell often figures criteria as "disappointing" in virtue of their inability to "assure that my words reach all the way to the pain of others. [Criteria] just do not do the very thing they were meant to do" (Cavell, *The Claim of Reason* 79), which only expresses once more the "truth in skepticism." As he says in another place, considering one's effort at approaching the "world withdrawn before skepticism," "there is no nearer for him to get, since he is already there; somehow that itself is what is disappointing, that this is what there is" (Cavell, *This New Yet Unapproachable America* 108). Reminders of our criteria, or the simple citations alone to the ordinary functioning of daily life, cannot restore us to the world, nor it to us. And yet these reminders are the only saving power available.

Criteria may be disappointing in their very nature, but they do not *always* disappoint, and this is shown in the fact that even the great skeptical epistemologists of the modern era—Descartes by his fire, Hume in his study—managed in point of fact to get on with their lives. Hume describes his "avocations"—including dining, conversing, and being merry with his friends—as "cur[ing]" him of his "philosophical melancholy," as "obliterat[ing] these chimeras," such that when he returns to "these [skeptical] speculations, they appear so cold, strained, and ridiculous that [he] cannot find it in [his] heart to enter into them any further" (qtd in Burton 100). These "avocations," which, especially in their publicness, offer a contrast with the figure of the isolated philosopher attempting to make sense things by his lonesome, apparently suffice to reanimate the world, to loosen or shed the grip of skeptical worries.

If, as I said before, skepticism is *ultimately* incurable, this is so only in the sense that nothing, including any given recitation of or pointing to criteria, can cure us of skepticism once and for all; but Hume's example serves to show that skepticism can nevertheless *perpetually* be cured—that is, it can be cured on any particular occasion, or at least given rest, returned to dormancy. The publicness, or the community, in Hume's example strikes me as crucial.

Reminders or criteria alone prove disappointing in their ability to assure our connection to the world in any general or necessary sense, but *reminding* and *being reminded* of our criteria, *recalling* the grammar of our concepts—reminders imagined as actively *given* and *accepted*, that is—can in any given instance suffice to quell the skeptical impulse. Another expression for "reminding and being reminded of our criteria" might be "taking on our education," or understanding what we know. The movement of acknowledgment, I suggest, is necessary to the animation of our criteria and is constituted in accepting a recitation of what we say or do as a *reminder*, in understanding oneself as *being reminding* of something we cannot fail to know. Without this form of acknowledgment, citations and recitations of criteria are mere propositions, mere statements; they are as inanimate as they are unanimating.

Teaching and learning, the taking on of our education, is not, for this reason, exhausted or even well described when one pictures education in terms of the transmission of knowledge to one who is ignorant. Wittgenstein's examples of education point more ordinarily to the inculcation of rules, usages, or customs *within* a community; they point to members of a community engaging in "serious communication" with one another. Thinking of education as *reminding* and *being reminded* allows one to recognize that, even within the environs of our own communities, our teaching and learning is ever ongoing; we are ever initiating others, and in the process we ourselves are ever being initiated into our "relevant forms of life." Cavell is also highly sensitive to this fact: "The anxiety in teaching, in serious communication, is that I myself require education" (Cavell, "The Normal and the Natural" 45). As he says in still another place, considering this view of teaching and learning in terms of criticism, "[Wittgenstein's] signature mode of criticism is one that is simultaneously turned toward oneself and toward one's contribution to the communal" (Cavell, "Philosophy as Education" 145). This mode of criticism holds promise for literary studies as well: criticism as an education, which means the personal hazarding of one's reading in the attempt to change another's way of looking at things.

This most radical notion that Cavell learns from Wittgenstein deserves to be stated clearly: In order to participate in "serious communication," skeptical worries have to be set aside rather than either defeated or surrendered to. Setting aside the skeptical urge is a sensible rather than defeatist course both because skepticism is not exactly the kind of impediment that skeptics believe it to be and because this "setting aside" is nothing at all like offering a shrugging "oh well" in the face the unprovable existence of the external world, say. Instead, this setting aside occurs in turning toward others as a means of understanding matters of common concern, which is to acknowledge (rather than prove or establish) both the concern's reality and its publicness. Offering oneself as representative, or acquiescing to another's representativeness, is also an inflection of this move. That is, turning toward another, whether in need or in support, is to acknowledge that other, to acknowledge that the other has something like standing with respect to the particular problem—thus, one offers oneself as both resource and pupil.

I have already traced Cavell's understanding of Shakespeare's tragedies as *failures* of this sort of acknowledgment. The turning-toward movement of acknowledgment as I have figured it above surfaces explicitly in Cavell's later work on Emerson and on filmic comedies. There, Cavell equates "the recognition of the other" with "acknowledgment of a relationship," and he notes that "Emerson does not much attempt to depict such a relationship (film may call it marriage, philosophers have usually called it friendship), but the sense I seek to clarify is that Emerson offers his writing as an other for his reader" (Cavell, *Conditions Handsome and Unhandsome* 31). In this succinct statement, Cavell underscores (a) the way in which acknowledgment binds individuals together into an "us"; (b) the way in which acknowledgment finds its apotheosis in what film calls marriage, which will be of somewhat obvious importance as we witness Shakespeare's comedic protagonists grapple with skeptical temptations; and (c) the way in which scholarly reading—reading to learn—also partakes in this pattern. If the groundwork of all learning is relational and predicated on acknowledging another as in the position to teach or to learn, then scholarly reading of literature will be both more difficult and more fruitful than simply applying a theory to a work. This is Cavell's contribution to literary studies.

Adopting a view of literary scholarship akin to such a picture of teaching and learning might provide a way out of the double bind figured in the exchanges between the evocritics and their post-structuralist interlocutors. It is in this light that I would like to recall and re-collect some earlier themes, to revisit these scholarly exchanges, and Cavell's treatment of *King Lear* and *Othello*, as a means of more directly introducing a defactoist way of conversing about Shakespeare's comedies.

To take up one evocritical example, Keith Oatley's attention to the cognitive psychology of emotion as the center of character in Shakespeare, as this attention is featured particularly in his study of *Othello*, is meant as an announcement of a certain foundation of what we call "character."

Oatley specifically opposes this sort of foundation to the sweeping skepticism voiced in the antifoundationalism of the post-structuralists. But the above discussion and exegesis of Wittgenstein's work on rule-following, language-use, and public practice serves to show that it is both unnecessary and impossible to simply refute a post-structuralist sort of skeptical antifoundationalism by positing a *general* foundation for the motivating power of the emotions and the emotions' relation to character. In Oatley's work, this is borne out in two ways.

The impossibility of Oatley's particular refutation reveals itself in the highly selective use he makes of textual evidence, in the first place. He supports the claim, for instance, that Iago understands the "character" of his protagonists by taking single lines pertaining to Othello's "free and open nature" and Desdemona's "disposition," where it is described as "so kind, so apt, so blessed," as unproblematically, uncomplicatedly, or simply accurate (Oatley 21). But in taking these statements in this way, Oatley ignores contradictory evidence. Desdemona's bawdy beachhead exchange with Iago, for instance, shows that she is *at least* more than simply kind, apt, and blessed. But this complication means that an unaccounted-for interpretation, one that sifts lines reflecting essential characteristics from those voicing inessential properties, has intervened in Oatley's understanding of Desdemona. This interpretative judgment will require its own foundation, and with this realization we head for the same infinite regress that Wittgenstein has already drawn out. Oatley's cognitive-psychological foundationalism cannot by itself refute the post-structuralist antifoundationalism he would overturn.

Further, it is immediately obvious that no such foundational cognitive psychology is *necessary* to arrive at the reading of *Othello* that Oatley recites, one in which Othello is jealous and gullible, Desdemona pure, and Cassio concerned with his reputation. Oatley leans on a computationalist view of the mind in order to account for the ways in which Iago manipulates the other characters, but his account must be understood as supporting the particular philosophy of mind at work, rather than this particular reading of the play. Othello's jealousy, Desdemona's purity, and the rest have been taken as the essential features of these characters since at least Coleridge's work on the subject. In terms of reading the play and understanding its characters, Coleridge's ability to see into the minds and essences of characters proves equally incisive to Oatley's model. Whatever utility acquiring Oatley's "new facts" about theater as the simulation of emotion might have, it is not at all clear that such utility lies in the generation of new understandings of particular literary works. No new reading is on offer at all in Oatley's version of *Othello*.

As I return to the notion of taking teaching and learning as central to the concerns of literary studies, I want to point out that part of the problem with Oatley's work pertains to the way in which he apparently understands the findings of literary scholarship to function, which is characteristic of the evocritics and their post-structuralist counterparts alike. By understanding the purpose of such scholarly products as establishing, developing, or evincing some sort of foundational truth, or by simply rejecting the possibility of foundations, period, both kinds of critics neglect (or implicitly reject) the importance of Cavell's notion of "serious communication," the simultaneous orientation of such findings toward oneself and toward the communal. The sort of (anti)foundationalism visible in the proclamations of the evocritics and the insights of the post-structuralists either takes the ordinary fact that the world is animated, assumes that this animation is a matter of causal necessity, and then attends to the mechanisms involved, which is one way of avoiding the truth in skepticism; or else it seeks to demonstrate that the in-principle failure of all such structural mechanisms must mean that something like the objective world really is inaccessible and beyond reach, which denies that brute fact of the regularity of our practices with others and in the world at large.

A Cavellian or defactoist practice of reading bears several affinities with certain of Oatley's assumptions, which is among the factors that raises Oatley for consideration here. Cavell, like Oatley, takes literary characters and their motivations as central to the pursuits of literary scholarship, for instance. For Cavell, however, it would be (has been) a disastrous mistake to think of a focus on character or motivation *as opposed to* a focus on language. Rather, the words a character speaks under certain conditions, before certain audiences, are *expressions* of character, expressions of what one might call a character's inner life. A defactoist literary criticism, like the New Critics Cavell refers to and whom Oatley cites, will thus require a form of close reading; in this respect, a Cavellian or defactoist reading also partakes of what Jessica Pressman has called "the aesthetics of difficulty" (Pressman 78–79).

But for Cavell the closeness of the close reading is not necessitated in virtue of any inherent encodedness of an underlying message and thus is not geared toward exploring or disentangling paradoxical formal features that hide a work's true meaning. Nor is it necessitated in virtue of any general theory according to which language-use masks any foundational notion of "character," which would be the real object of investigation, as in Oatley. Rather, the closeness of the close reading responds to another kind of difficulty, one that exists precisely because of the truth in skepticism, the absence of any *general* foundation.

In short, the work of reading closely is difficult because it is never clear beforehand, in any foundational way, exactly what the stakes of a work will be, what will require explication, or what will matter. As Cavell says, "the way to overcome theory correctly, philosophically, is to let the object or the work of your interest teach you how to consider it" (*Pursuits of Happiness* 10), which one ought to think of as a gloss on Wittgenstein's attention to particular cases. Cavell refers to the challenge posed by a close reading in light of the truth in skepticism as "the difficulty of seeing the obvious"

(Cavell, *Must We Mean What We Say?* 310). Joseph Schwab puts this in a slightly different way: "This is difficult because we normally only see what we are instructed to look for and we are instructed by theory" (Schwab 496). Understanding the work, and others, as capable of instructing us—understanding ourselves as in a position to learn in public, as it were—is at the center of a Cavellian or defactoist critical practice. The obviousness requires expression because it may not be, but might become, so obvious to others; what is obvious, in brief, must be *found*. Rather than a defiant, skeptical antifoundationalism, we have *founding* in *finding*.

My primary concern in this book pertains to the places in Shakespeare's comedies where the temptation toward skeptical disavowal and repudiation arises, the ways in which the temptation to appeal to something below or beyond the everyday that might ground or verify or return one's relation to ordinary existence threatens to cut characters off from the world and rob them of their happiness. I have noted that Wittgenstein sometimes frames such temptations in terms of illness; I have also noted that the grammar of illness includes the concept of recovery. Cavell's study of the tragedies shows us that such recovery *need* not occur, that skepticism can be (literally) fatal. The comedies, I will contend, not only reveal that recoveries *can* occur, but they also provide examples—make themselves exemplary—of such recoveries.

Such a focus, such readings, will also be a matter of taking on one's education, of teaching and learning, of allowing a work to remind us—and allowing ourselves to be reminded of—the sorts of things that matter to us, the words and gestures in which we succeed or fail to make ourselves known, or unknown. The criticism that this mode of close reading produces ought also to be seen in such an educative light, not, once more, as in the transmission of a true interpretation, *proven* with various types of evidence, but rather as instances of exemplarity, an offering of a particular axis of relevance and of an invitation for reciprocation and response; an attempt, most basically, in the direction of mutual intelligibility.

Such close reading may also help to bridge the growing divide between the findings of literary scholarship and the general public: on a defactoist view, the regularity and relative ease of our everyday language proceeds on just such an ungrounded assumption—or rather, a wager—of mutual intelligibility, which regularly is, in spite of its ungroundedness, successful. Beckwith invokes an important vector of this discussion in asserting that although mutual intelligibility "seems too insecure a foundation, too liable to breakage," mutual intelligibility can be—and in point of fact is—"forged anew and through each conversation. This is the miracle in an age where all miracles are past" (Beckwith 5). The citation to the miraculous is revelatory.

In the "Lecture on Ethics," Wittgenstein considers the relation to the miraculous in related terms, speaking of the limits of language and logic with respect to "the absolute good" or with respect to matters of aesthetics or religion:

> Now I am tempted to say that the right expression in language for the miracle of the existence of the world, though it is not any proposition *in* language, is the existence of language itself ... for all I have said by shifting the expression of the miraculous from an expression by means of language to the expression by the existence of language, all I have said is again we cannot express what we want to express and that all we say about the absolute miraculous remains nonsense.
> (Wittgenstein, "A Lecture on Ethics" 11)

Thinking back to the various movements in literary theory over the previous century, and particularly to the evocritics' insistence on opposing themselves to the post-structuralists and "sociocultural constructionists" that came before, these many movements have been united in the view that in order to say anything meaningful about, for example, Shakespearean comedy, we first require an account of how literature *makes* or *has* or *conveys* meaning, how words represent objects, and so on. Even the New Critics, such as Richard Henze, whom I will take up in the next chapter, approach Shakespeare on the assumption that the plays smuggle coded lessons or truths about human nature; that these can be discerned and explicated by attending to the interplay between formal elements of the text; and that once decoded, these ciphered truths can be made publicly available.

Taking literature according to the defactoist sensibility of Wittgenstein's writing, as this perspective or sensibility is developed by Fogelin and Cavell, deflates the assumption that any theoretical account of language's representative ability is either possible or necessary to any given discussion of significance in literary works: for all the results of these various theoretical ways of approaching the meaning or significance of literature, when scholars keep their gazes fixed upon it, amount simply to nonsense. Where such approaches yield results with sense, they of necessity miss their mark; they are *about* something else (history, psychology, biology, etc.). In this case, once more, they are "not in fact mistaken but in soul muddled."

Pivoting from a view on which we require theories of knowledge and language in order to go on with literary scholarship to a view on which going on with literary scholarship is most basically a practical matter of teaching and learning resists the pitfalls involved in falsifying our fundamental relation to the world and to others. Toril Moi ("The Adventure of Reading") has argued that, just as one person can teach something to another, or can change her way of looking at things, literary works can do the same with respect to a given reader. Channeling de Beauvoir, Moi calls this simply the "adventure of reading."

Taking teaching and learning as the center of literary studies returns to us our ability to speak with one another about *significance* in literature without being merely naïve. Additionally, it defuses the drive to chase chimeras under the misguided assumption that by capturing or securing something *else* we can come to understand, stabilize, control, or fix the objects of our study. The desire to speak with the dead, which Stephen

Greenblatt famously voices, signifies both aspects of this drive in simultaneously positing a theoretical (historical, contextual) means of fixing meaning and also expressing a certain chimerical wish that dramatically understates the difficult work of conducting "serious communication" with the living.

The notion that any attempt to say something about the absolute miraculous yields nonsense ought merely to suggest that the point of miracles is not to *say* anything about them, at least not in the way that literary scholarship has traditionally proceeded. Taking up Shakespearean comedy from the practical perspective of teaching and learning might show us, instead, how to *do* things with miracles; or putting it better, perhaps, how to inherit the miracle of the existence of the world.

NOTES

1. I owe this formulation of the issue of "approaching" literature to David Rudrum, whose work I quote at length in the Coda.
2. That is, the rationalist picture of the mind. As Dreyfus describes it: "Rationalists such as Descartes and Leibniz thought of the mind as defined by its capacity to form representations of all domains of activity. These representations were taken to be theories of the domains in question, the idea being that representing the fixed, context-free features of a domain and the principles governing their interaction explains the domain's intelligibility. On this view all that we know—even our general know-how for getting around in the world and coping with things and people—must be mirrored in the mind in propositional form" (Dreyfus, *What Computers Still Can't Do* xvii).
3. This is not to assert, of course, that the need to overcome doubt about the existence of this or that object, for example, is *never* necessary, but simply that, as a matter of ordinary practical dealings, we do not seem to need to prove to ourselves before we sit down that we are not merely hallucinating a chair.
4. This is also a way of taking the moral of Heidegger's analysis of the hammer in *Being and Time*, that a detached or objective view of the world is derivative of a more basic, more involved, mode of being in the world, one characterized by practical coping.
5. In fact, the way in which this point is missed is *precisely* the same way in which the import of Nietzsche's notion that truth is a "mobile army of metaphors" is missed in "Truth and Lying in an Extra-Moral Sense." It *seems* to "abolish logic but *does not do so*."
6. I read the later Heidegger's insistence that "the current view" of language has gone astray in imagining language to be "the audible expression and communication of human feelings," which are "accompanied by thoughts" (Heidegger and Hofstadter 190) as also emphasizing this point. When Heidegger famously declares that "language speaks. Man speaks in that he responds to language. This responding is a hearing" (Heidegger and Hofstadter, *Poetry, Language, Thought*, 207), and when he notes that "What is spoken is never and in no language what is said" (Heidegger and Hofstadter 11), I take him to be highlighting the same defactoist points that the other thinkers discussed here have been urging: (1) there

is, in point of fact, something *said*; (2) what is said is irreducible to "what is spoken"; (3) the grasping of the said depends upon occupying a position of inheritance with respect to language; (4) inheriting a language is a matter of practical activity, which means both that it has to be *done* and that the *doing* of it can be avoided, deflected, refused, or failed. Like Cavell, Wittgenstein, Fogelin, and Dreyfus, Heidegger regards "the current view" of language as just such an avoidance or denial of our inheritance; and once that inheritance is refused, nothing *else* can restore our connection to the world or to others.

7. Somewhere Cavell has hilariously said something to the following effect about the Kantian bargain with Cartesian skepticism: "Thanks for nothing. Or more accurately, no thanks for everything."
8. I take Heidegger to once more make a very similar point in this respect, as he attempts to resist the temptation to depart from our ordinary practical circumstances in order to seek a theoretical explanation, a departure that will ineluctably cut us off from what we seek to know: "We do not want to get anywhere. We would like only, for once, to get to just where we are already" (Heidegger and Hofstadter 188).

REFERENCES

Beckwith, Sarah. *Shakespeare and the Grammar of Forgiveness*. Ithica, NY: Cornell University Press, 2011. Print.

Burton, John Hill. *Life and Correspondence of David Hume*. Edinburgh: W. Tait, 1846. Print.

Cahill, Kevin. *The Fate of Wonder: Wittgenstein's Critique of Metaphysics and Modernity*. New York: Columbia University Press, 2011. Print.

Cavell, Stanley. *Conditions Handsome and Unhandsome*. Chicago: University of Chicago Press, 1990. Print.

———. "Knowing and Acknowledging." *The Cavell Reader*. Ed. Stephen Mulhall. Malden, MA: Wiley-Blackwell, 1996. Print.

———. *Little Did I Know: Excerpts from Memory*. Stanford, CA: Stanford University Press, 2010. Print.

———. *Must We Mean What We Say?*. Cambridge, UK: Cambridge University Press, 1969. Print.

———. "Philosophy as Education." *Stanley Cavell and the Education of Grownups*. Ed. Naoko Saito and Paul Standish. New York: Fordham University Press, 2012. Print.

———. *Pursuits of Happiness*. Cambridge, MA: Harvard University Press, 1981. Print.

———. "The Availability of Wittgenstein's Later Philosophy." *The Philosophical Review* 71.1 (1962): 67–93.

———. *The Claim of Reason*. New York: Oxford University Press, 1979. Print.

———. "The Normal and the Natural." *The Cavell Reader*. Ed. Stephen Mulhall. New York: Blackwell, 1996. Print.

———. *This New Yet Unapproachable America: Lectures After Emerson After Wittgenstein*. Chicago: University of Chicago Press, 2013. Print.

Dreyfus, Hubert L. *What Computers Still Can't Do: A Critique of Artificial Reason*. Cambridge, MA: M.I.T. Press, 1992. Print.

Dreyfus, Hubert L, and Stuart Dreyfus. *Mind over Machine: The Power of Human Intuition and Expertise in the Era of the Computer*. New York: Free Press, 1986. Print.

Fogelin, Robert J. *Taking Wittgenstein at His Word: A Textual Study*. Vol. 2009. Princeton University Press, 2009. Print.

Glendinning, Simon. *On Being with Others*. New York: Routledge, 1998. Print.

Heidegger, Martin, and Albert Hofstadter. *Poetry, Language, Thought*. New York: Harper, 1971. Print.

Moi, Toril. "The Adventure of Reading: Literature and Philosophy, Cavell and Beauvoir." *Literature and Theology* 25.2 (2011): 125–140.

Mulhall, Stephen. *Stanley Cavell: Philosophy's Recounting of the Ordinary*. Oxford University Press, 1998. Print.

———. *Wittgenstein's Private Language: Grammar, Nonsense and Imagination in Philosophical Investigations*. New York: Oxford University Press, 2006. Print.

Oatley, Keith. "Simulation of Substance and Shadow: Inner Emotions and Outer Behavior in Shakespeare's Psychology of Character." *College Literature* 33.1 (2006): 15–33.

Pressman, Jessica. *Digital Modernism*. New York: Oxford University Press, 2014. Print.

Schwab, Joseph J. "The Practical: Arts of Eclectic." *The School Review* 79.4 (1971): 493–542.

Stern, David. *Wittgenstein on Mind and Language*. New York: Oxford University Press, 1995. Print.

———. *Wittgenstein's Philosophical Investigations: An Introduction*. New York: Cambridge University Press, 2004. Print.

Wittgenstein, Ludwig. "A Lecture on Ethics." *The Philosophical Review* 74.1 (1965): 3–12. Print.

———. *Preliminary Studies for the "Philosophical Investigations" Generally Known as the Blue and Brown Books*. New York: Harper, 1958. Print.

———. *Remarks on the Foundations of Mathematics*. Cambridge, MA: MIT Press, 1983. Print.

Wittgenstein, Ludwig, G E M Anscombe, and P M S Hacker. *Philosophical Investigations*. 4th ed. Malden, MA: Wiley-Blackwell, 2009. Print.

3 Much Ado about Nothing

It will hardly be new or revolutionary to suggest that the happiness of *Much Ado*'s happy ending is afforded by the principal characters' having learned something important, say a lesson, over the course of the play. The view of teaching and learning developed in the previous chapter, however—a view that emphasizes the role of reminding and being reminded of a kind of knowledge that is best pictured not as lacking but as denied or avoided—will, I hope, alter the tenor of the assertion that learning facilitates *Much Ado*'s eventual felicity.

I wish to demonstrate that the characters in this play confront in various places the threat and temptation of skepticism, occurring here in insistences that love or marriage depend upon, or proceed upon the (causal) condition of, several kinds of deeper facts pertaining to purity or to the truth of another's emotions. The skeptical threat or temptation manifests itself in the characters' tendencies to treat the possibility of disproving these deeper facts—or the impossibility of establishing them beyond doubt—as threatening the reality or veracity of love.

In contrasting the expressions of love to which characters give voice under love's spell, if I can call it that, with the views of loving that emerge on occasions of doubt, I hope to show that the felicitous endings of this play are not the simple *effect* of having learned any particular and theoretically abstract lesson. This is once again to insist that the type of learning that occurs in this comedy actively involves adopting a specific stance with respect to another, the understanding of another as in a position to call one back to oneself. The implication of such a demonstration would be that what one might claim characters to have "learned" over the course of the play—to have come to know—cannot be anything like new facts. Rather, the movements from engagement in the world to skeptical withdrawal and back again to engagement trace a pattern of learning as the recovery or acknowledgment of that which one cannot fail to know.

Much Ado's comedic outcome explores the ramifications of the unstable truth of Hero's diagnosis: "loving goes by haps" (3.1.108).[1] The means by which Don John dupes Claudio not once but twice highlights the frailty of the foundational grounds from which the play's characters and later literary scholars alike, operating under the temptations of skepticism, imagine reason and rationality to unerringly proceed. This foundational frailty is no less evident in this play for Don John's eventual failure than it is manifest in *Othello* through a similar plot's success. Additionally, Beatrice and Benedick's particular relationship will require investigation: each of them, in forswearing love and marriage completely in the play's early scenes, do so by taking their criteria for falling in love to be something like necessary and sufficient conditions—as though failing to satisfy these conditions would preclude the possibility of falling in love, where satisfying them will simply entail the emergence of love, as if by natural law or contractual obligation. That their forswearing takes this particular form, as though each knew in advance what love would require of them and vice versa, I will claim, makes this particular forswearing also an expression of skepticism. That the love they eventually find seems unrelated to the discovery of any such conditions (which is not to claim that the criteria go unsatisfied) draws into question a view of loving that depends upon aprioristic knowledge.

In taking the protagonists of this comedy as capable of teaching and learning—learning from one another, that is, and educating an audience or reader in addition to other characters—it will once again be necessary to offer a direct contrast with other critical endeavors that have sought to achieve roughly the same ends. Specifically, I wish to contrast my reading with certain New Critical approaches, most directly that of Richard Henze. Henze offers an analysis of "right" and "wrong" deception in *Much Ado* (Henze, "Deception in *Much Ado About Nothing*"), under the assumption that the structure and action of the play contain an encoded and formalizable lesson for the audience. In a similar vein, Carl Dennis has provided a study of "wit and wisdom" in the play, which superficially bears some strong affinities with what I would like to say (Dennis, "Wit and Wisdom in *Much Ado About Nothing*"). Maurice Hunt occupies similar ground (Hunt, "The Reclamation of Language"), and his analysis also points to the characters' linguistic relation to real knowledge of events and circumstances. However, the differences between what these scholars and I take as the theoretical ground from which our work proceeds, as well as the differences between what we take as the end goals toward which our work aspires, I think, remain significant, and I must open this exploration of the play by drawing these distinctions explicitly, particularly with regard to Henze's work.

3.1 DISQUIETUDES AND PROBLEMS

In calibrating my own reading of this work, it will be helpful to part company with others who have taken up similar concerns. A number of critics have addressed the two most problematic aspects of the play's plot, both of which are bound up in the play's ostensibly happy ending: the role of the seeming death and resurrection of Hero, which absolves her of her supposed sin, and which has the salutary effect of drawing attention away from

Claudio's own faults; and also the bald-faced deception designed to bring Beatrice and Benedick together. In order to read the play's conclusion as happy, one must take both matches as occasions for genuine happiness, which has been no mean feat for scholars' powers of justification, given the scandal in the former case and the duplicitous grounds of loving in the latter. I will suggest that the justificatory labor that other critics embark upon is at once responsive to the genuine difficulty posed by the twin specters of Claudio's public shaming of Hero and the questionable, not to say false, basis of Benedick and Beatrice's union, but that these projects of justification or explanation mischaracterize the nature of the difficulty posed by these two issues.

Celebrating the union of Claudio and Hero requires dissolving or overcoming the substantial problem raised by Claudio's vitriolic rejection of Hero and the equally vitriolic responses to it by her loved ones. As Henze says of Claudio's behavior here, in a great understatement, "Claudio is cruel, shamefully cruel. However well, according to some concept of 'honor' he may be acting in trying circumstances, he is not acting well according to the more general standards of human decency" (Henze 194). Claudio, having discovered Hero's supposed infidelity, waits until the wedding day to publicly denounce her, labeling her a "rotten orange" (4.1.32) and "an approvéd wanton" (4.1.44) as he throws Hero back upon her father. The spectacular nature of Claudio's repudiation reverberates expansively: Hero falls in a swoon, and her father calls out for his own death, crying, "Hath no man's dagger a point for me?" (4.1.109). In the aftermath, as the Friar casts doubt on Hero's guilt, Leonato's passion is undimmed: "If they speak but truth of her / These hands shall tear her. If they wrong her honor, / The proudest of them shall well hear of it" (4.1.192–194). He and Antonio threaten to revenge themselves murderously upon Hero's wrongers in no fewer than four instances in this scene. Beatrice, too, lusts for vengeance upon Claudio: "O God that I were a man! I would eat his heart in the marketplace" (4.1.308).

The fury in all of these words is both palpable and authentic. Hero somehow takes no righteous exception to her own slandering or her father's threats against her life, an aspect of her character's gendering, and a point on which many other scholars have remarked (Scheff, "Gender Wars"; Cook, "The Sign and Semblance of Her Honor"; Williamson, "Doubling, Women's Anger, and Genre"; Friedman, "Hush'd on Purpose to Grace Harmony"). But even if Hero herself demands no penance from Claudio in her own name, the chasm opened by Claudio's slander is a wide one. Death presents itself immediately as the best available remedy—for Leonato himself in his call for the point of some man's dagger, for Hero's honor under the Friar's plan, and for Claudio's misdeed in Beatrice's exhortation to Benedick: "Kill Claudio." Yet in the space of a single act, marriage rather than death sets things right. Critics have long found themselves drawn to this particular issue, and with good reason. The bridging of this chasm is no small matter; the fact of its happening demands attention.

Similarly, celebrating the marriage of Beatrice and Benedick seems to require papering over certain incongruities that are at the very least a struggle to reconcile. In the first place, each of the lovers has professed an eternal aversion to love and marriage outright, and in the strongest of terms. The dissonance involved, then, in simultaneously witnessing the reversals of such proclamations and delighting in equally eternal proclamations of love and marriage at the end of the play presents something of a difficulty. More than that, however, the proximate cause of the protagonists' newfound professions of eternal love also wrinkles the brow. That each comes to love the other on the basis of an elaborate conspiracy to deceive—that each is at least initially tricked into loving the other—inspires no great confidence in the authenticity of the bond that they share.

In fact, the truth of their love in the face of these inconvenient facts seems most glaringly to call for a defense, and the distinction that Henze draws between "right" and "wrong deception" is meant in part to ameliorate these (merely) apparent issues and ground the authenticity of their love on something like the level of the real. If these incongruities seem problematic, in other words, it is only because we have not yet grasped the appropriate and subtle difference between "right" and "wrong deception." Similarly to the brief analysis of Oatley's *Othello* in the previous chapter, I will show with respect to Henze's reading that the foundational distinction he draws cannot and need not work as pictured.

In saying that I wish to part company with such critical approaches to the play, I express my deep suspicion both of the assumptions that they make and of the conclusions that they draw. Importantly, however, I do not wish to quarrel with what they take as the object of their investigations nor with the evidence that they cite, by and large. The striking movements from death to resurrection, from slander to plaudit, from trickery to truth—to say nothing of the degree of easy felicity that accompanies them—seem at the very least counterintuitive. Addressing these obvious "disquietudes" (*Beunruhigungen*, in Wittgensteinian and early Heideggerian parlance) is a fit task for literary criticism. But I would like to insist on the appropriateness of the term "disquietude" in characterizing that which invites a response in these plays, and in parting company with my predecessors, I wish to make evident the ways in which these earlier approaches incorrectly understand a disquietude as a species of *problem*, and so amenable to a specific kind of solution, a means of securing or grounding the truth of the happiness that attends the play's conclusion.

The primary distinction that Henze draws is indeed offered as an explanatory solution to the perceived problems of the speedy resurrection and reconciliation involved in Claudio and Hero's marriage plans, and to the duplicitous means by which Beatrice and Benedick come together. Henze asserts his primary claim straightforwardly at the article's opening:

> Deception in *Much Ado* is of two sorts. One deception leads to social peace, to marriage, to the end of deceit. The other deception breeds

conflict and distrust and leads even Beatrice to desire Claudio's heart in the market place. Wrong deception occurs when one trusts appearances and not one's intuition or "soul," when one depends on eavesdropping and circumstantial evidence instead of careful study, when one has too little trust in human nature.

(Henze 188)

Farther along, Henze accounts for the play's celebratory ending in similar terms:

> The play is finally much ado about nothing because a sufficient bedrock of trust exists to support social harmony. Appearances do not deceive, at least not importantly, if one trusts one's friends. Just as every man should know Dogberry is an ass because he has proved himself so, so every man should know Hero for a chaste woman and Don John for a villain.
>
> (Henze, 199)

It is important to keep one's eye on Henze's claims as *responses* to the particular problems that he perceives: the nature of these perceived problems, evidenced by the nature of his responses, clearly bespeak certain New Critical assumptions about the nature and function of literature, most evident in the methodology involved in his seeking to discover the "theme" of the work, and to explicate the structural means by which that theme emerges. In fact, Henze says in his introduction that "while all critics do not agree the major theme is deception ... most do agree that deception or improper noting is an important factor." He also proposes to illuminate the way that the "major images" in the play "reflect the double theme," and he wishes to "place Claudio ... in this context of theme and image" (188–189).

Post-structuralist developments in critical methodology reject as a first principle most of the assumptions that undergird Henze's analysis—in particular, the privileged position of formal structure, as well as the (feasibility of the) goal of uncovering a work's theme. Having already discussed those arguments in some measure earlier, I do not need to retrace them again. Rather, I aim to put those questions aside and focus instead on the adequacy of Henze's argument insofar as its ability to respond to the difficulty he perceives in the play is concerned.

His response is oriented toward *solving* a particular problem by asserting a distinction between two kinds of deception: "right" and "wrong deception." Once one sees the difference clearly, one will presumably be in a position to see the self-consistent mode in which the distinction works its way through the drama, driving the plot and ensuring the happy ending. Henze's response, I argue, treats the fact of the happy ending as something that calls for an explanation in causal terms; the distinction between two types of deception is meant to account for both the appearance of a near-disaster in the repudiation scene and the necessary reality of the happy conclusion. But it is not immediately obvious that, conceptually speaking, deception is categorically divisible into "right" and "wrong" varieties, as Henze argues, even in the specific context of *Much Ado,* and Henze's discussion of the matter invites some unpacking.

With regard to the match of Claudio and Hero, Henze attempts to distinguish the way Don John deceives Claudio into believing Hero to be "no maid" from the way the Friar and Hero's entire clan fool Claudio into thinking Hero dead.[2] The first, Henze claims, is "wrong deception"; the second, "right deception." In terms of Beatrice and Benedick, he also glimpses these two types of deception at work: first, the obvious way in which each of the principals is caught with tickling, so to speak—allowed to overhear and thus come to love one another on the basis of contrived falsehoods—represents a "right deception"; but this tickling is taken to overcome a more basic, wrong deception, namely, the *self*-deception perpetrated by each, in which each professes at the outset of the play not to love the other (or indeed any of the other's sex).

Henze's attempt to posit a (real, transcendent) distinction between two varieties of deception, to trace the working of these varieties throughout the course of the play, first runs into trouble in its effort to treat Beatrice and Benedick's case as symmetrical with Claudio and Hero's in terms of this distinction. Simply put, the claim that Benedick and Beatrice's movement from the rejection of love to its acceptance at the end of the play is best characterized in terms of awakening from self-deception to the truth is quite a stretch, from an evidentiary standpoint, whereas to claim that Claudio's acceptance of Hero's maidenhood occurs as the result of undoing a deception (by means of "new facts") is not nearly so problematic. We in the audience really do know because we are privy to the secret plotting of Don John, the Friar, and the conspirators against Benedick and Beatrice, respectively, (a) that Hero is belied, (b) that Hero does not in fact die, and (c) that Benedick and Beatrice's love emerges from the straightforward lies of their friends. But the fourth claim—the one that would make these cases fully symmetrical—claim (d), that Beatrice and Benedick actually love each other throughout, despite their protestations to the contrary, rests on substantially less self-evident ground.

In fact, Henze's fourth claim begs the question, assuming the truth of its conclusion in its premises. We can only call Beatrice and Benedick's biting remarks against each other a form of self-deception if we already know that the two love one another in Act 1. Yet the only evidence of their mutual affection lies in hearing those biting remarks *as* false, a falsity that appears in contrast to the truth that they really do love each other, and so on in circular fashion.[3] The stretching of this claim unravels the basic tenets of Henze's argument. In the Hero-Claudio plot, one deception certainly leads to discord while the other serves to patch things up. Does this imply that there are two categorically different varieties of deception, distinguishable according to criteria involving "intuition" as opposed to "appearances"? Henze's attempt to locate an echo of the Hero-Claudio deception dichotomy in the Beatrice-Benedick story is intended to shore up this claim. However, rather than affirming the Hero-Claudio example, as it is meant to do, the dubiousness of the Beatrice-Benedick argument rather invites us to reexamine the primary example instead.

Claudio's public rejection of Hero and its aftermath in 4.1 provide Henze with the material to explore how "wrong deception" functions, as well as the means by which it might be opposed with "trust." In one telling passage, Henze denounces Claudio in strong terms for getting it wrong in 4.1, and he simultaneously lauds Beatrice and the Friar for getting it right. Henze first contrasts Don John's banal evil with Claudio's more condemnable qualities: "The dangerous one is Claudio, who conceals a huge and active suspicion behind a mask of virtue and fidelity. One can anticipate Don John's villainy; one does not expect Claudio's suspicion" (Henze 193). In the next breath, Henze further contrasts Claudio's duplicitous "suspicion" to Beatrice's more noble nature: "If everyone were like the Friar and Beatrice—disinclined to accept slanderous accusations without clear proof—Don John would have no success whatever" (Henze 193).

The argument here is that Beatrice's disinclination to accept slander without proof protects her from being taken in by "wrong deception," while Claudio's suspicious nature renders him vulnerable to precisely this kind of trickery. Elsewhere, too, Henze praises Beatrice's skeptical nature, casting it positively as intuitive trust: "[Beatrice] knows intuitively that Hero is innocent. The Friar adds to that intuition a careful study of the evidence. This combination of intuitive trust and careful observation seems to be the one the play recommends" (Henze 194).

These arguments overlook two important facts. In the first place, "clear proof" and "careful study of the evidence" are not unequivocal. Claudio no more lacks clear proof of Hero's wantonness than the Friar has evidence of her innocence. Claudio has his very own eyewitness account (an account seconded by Don Pedro) of a woman, dressed in Hero's clothing, as Borachio notes (5.1.229), in Hero's room, responding to the name "Hero" during the throes of sexual passion. Given this fact, it seems strange to fault him for taking this woman to be Hero or to deride him on this basis as overly credulous.

Meanwhile, Henze's depiction of the Friar's "careful study" picks out the way the Friar notes and assimilates the "evidence" of Hero's blushing, which the Friar takes for the sign of true innocence. He marks "a thousand blushing apparitions" that steal across Hero's face, and he also sees "a thousand innocent shames / In angel whiteness beat away those blushes" (4.1.161–162), on the basis of which he proclaims her "guiltless." Henze therefore reaches the conclusions that "the Friar and Beatrice assure themselves, on the basis of human evidence that Claudio ignores, that Hero is guiltless" (Henze 195). Henze casts Claudio as so eager to believe Don John's word that he overlooks or "ignores" the "human evidence" of Hero's purity.

But Claudio does not ignore this evidence. These are precisely the same blushes and whitenesses that Claudio points to as supporting the very opposite conclusion earlier in the same scene: "Behold how like a maid she blushes here! / Oh, what authority and show of truth / Can cunning sin cover itself withal!" (4.1.34–36). The Friar's proof of Hero's deep guiltlessness is also Claudio's evidence of her underlying "cunning sin." It therefore seems extremely facile to assert that the Friar's "study" of the evidence is somehow more "careful" than Claudio's, as the two note identical features of Hero's reaction.

The second important fact that Henze's argument overlooks is the resemblance between the suspicion with which Beatrice and the Friar approach Claudio's "slander" and the skepticism for which Henze condemns Claudio himself. Claudio's "huge and active suspicion" marks him as "the dangerous one" in Henze's reading. Henze frames Claudio's suspicion as a failure to fulfill his nobility: "The problem is that Claudio, who should measure up to an expectation of nobleness, conceals beneath his noble appearance a lack of trust, a lack of soul" (Henze 195). Henze also characterizes this "lack" as a problem of a merely *apparent* fidelity: "Claudio's faithfulness has to be deceptive in order for Don John's plan to work" (Henze 193), while Henze paints Beatrice and the Friar as invested with a ground-level attitude of intuitive trust. The power of suspicion reigns unchecked, Henze says, "until someone notes evidence carefully, as the Friar does, and contrasts [Claudio's] suspicion with trust" (Henze 194). Henze thus contrasts the qualities of authentic faith and trust, embodied in Beatrice and the Friar, to the dangerous suspicion that Claudio represents. As I have already quoted, Henze sums up the point: "This combination of intuitive trust and careful observation seems to be the one the play recommends" (Henze 194).

But the positive qualities of "trust" that Henze attributes to Beatrice are demonstrated by her *skeptical* stance toward Claudio, as Henze also explicitly notes. In other words, while Henze praises Beatrice's willingness to accept Hero's innocence in spite of the apparent evidence—which he characterizes as "slander"—leveled against her, this level of "trust" comes out in her refusal to accede to Claudio's account, which Henze characterizes as her "disinclin[ation] to accept slanderous accusations without proof." Accepting Hero's guiltlessness is immediate, a matter of trust, while accepting Claudio's accusation is taken to require mediating proof in order to overcome a certain default belief in Hero's innocence. Beatrice's character makes both of these movements at once—the extension of trust and its deferral pending evidence—and so it cannot be the case that she simply "has" some sort of trust or faithfulness that Claudio "lacks."

Claudio's complexity is equally evident in the play, as well as in Henze's own article. Henze faults Claudio as much for his credulousness as for his faithlessness: "His 'love' for Hero is much too shallow to preserve him from doubting both his friend Don Pedro and Hero. When told that Don Pedro loves Hero, Claudio instantly believes 'Tis certain so'" (Henze 193).

Doubting Don Pedro and Hero is constituted in this case in his trusting of Don John's false report. As Beatrice does with Hero's innocence, Claudio immediately extends his trust to the assertion that Don Pedro intends to woo Hero for himself. In one case, this immediate and intuitive trust is a saving grace; in the other, it is damnable sin. Where Beatrice is right to trust Hero, Claudio is wrong to trust Don John's accusation. Where Beatrice is right to doubt the evidence against Hero, Claudio is wrong to doubt Hero's simple professions of her innocence in the face of overwhelming evidence. Though Henze moralizes the action as a simple contest between a faithful inclination to trust and a faithless inclination to doubt, it is obviously no such simple matter.

Inasmuch as Henze attempts to locate a foundational lesson that the play strives to impart—a lesson communicable through and embedded in the play's formal interactions among theme, character, and image—his reading of the play does not reach any foundational level. Henze locates the happiness of the play's conclusion in the triumph of "right" over "wrong" deception. He distinguishes between "right" and "wrong" deception primarily by means of their distinct outcomes: "One deception leads to social peace, to marriage, to the end of deceit. The other deception breeds conflict and distrust and leads even Beatrice to desire Claudio's heart in the market place" (Henze 188). But in an assumption that remains uninterrogated, in his paper, he imagines that these distinct outcomes must be the *results* of distinct *causal conditions,* namely, Claudio's intrinsic "suspicion" in the latter case and Beatrice's "intuitive trust" in the former. That is the sense in which, as Henze asserts, the play "recommends" a particular approach to the world.

As my analysis makes evident, though, "intuitive trust" is not only insufficient to secure the desired outcome, but is positively complicit in the near-success of its opposite. It is an identical matter with skeptical "suspicion," which supposedly causes disaster, but which also proves instrumental to avoiding catastrophe.

Henze's explanatory schema omits a significant determining factor: *to whom* one extends trust and *from whom* one withholds it are matters of genuine, indeed decisive, import. In fairness, Henze does allude to this factor when he adds a caveat in the article's conclusion: "Appearances do not deceive, at least not importantly, as long as one trusts *one's friends*" (199, emphasis added). But this, too, only works in Beatrice's case. She trusts her cousin and doubts Claudio, and she turns out to be right. Claudio, meanwhile, also trusts in his friends, and he turns out to be wrong. Claudio, like Beatrice, requires evidence before he will believe slander: with his own eyes, and with his friend, Don Pedro, at his side, he witnesses what he takes to be Hero's wanton transgressions. If it is a matter of trusting one's friends, Claudio's reliance on his friend(s)[4] at best proves incapable of resisting the "deception" of "appearances."

It would have been right to trust Hero even in the absence of evidence, even to the point of rejecting the evidence that speaks against her. It would have been right to suspect Don John in the absence of evidence,[5] even to the point of rejecting the evidence that speaks in his favor. That much is obvious in retrospect. But must we therefore assume that it is, if not obvious, then at least discoverable from Claudio's perspective in Act 3? A simultaneous question, focused on the positive: on what basis does one imagine that the matter was obvious or discoverable to Beatrice in Act 3? How is it that Beatrice knows her true friends while Claudio does not?

I raise these questions with no intention of answering them, but rather in the interest of vivifying the flaws inherent in what Henze understands his literary explorations to *seek out*—in order to show the problems, in other words, with *any* answer to such questions that Henze or any other critic might discover. Henze takes the happiness of the play's end, the "social harmony," as a basic fact. He also understands that it might have been otherwise, should Don John's plot have succeeded, and he emphasizes the nature of Claudio's character and its vulnerabilities in allowing for this virtual, darker ending. Why, ultimately, does one thing occur rather than the other? Henze answers that "social harmony" is secured by a "bedrock of trust." But one immediately encounters the objection that Claudio's trust in Don John is precisely what makes him susceptible to evil (not unlike Othello's faith in Iago, it might be added; or Gloucester's in Edmund). To his earlier formulation, Henze appends the qualification that one must extend trust to not just anyone, but "one's friends." Of course, as the rhetorical questions that conclude the above paragraph bring out, the matter cannot rest there. It then becomes a further problem of establishing the knowledge required to distinguish true from false friends, which will immediately engender further problems, and so on once more into a logical regress.

This looming regress remains the central problem, not only for Henze in particular but also for other foundational or structuralist critical endeavors as well. One asserts truth or knowledge claims about literature in general or certain works in particular and then supports the assertions with some evidence imported from the work (or an element of its context or history, or evolutionary biology, or psychology, or philosophy, among other domains). In all cases, the nature of the critic's claim is one of (universal) validity, which also comes with an attendant ought-claim: reasonable people ought to agree with the validity (if not the truth) of the conclusion. But this constructs such agreement or acknowledgment as produced by logically rigorous *knowledge*, as a mediate matter of transcendently indisputable proof, which, as the Henze example suggests—along with the entire project of the post-structuralist critics—is never in fact sufficient to *ground* that knowledge or, by extension, that agreement.

What remains at the end of *Much Ado*, however, is the uncomfortable co-presence of the happiness that *is* and the misery that *might have been*: this is the disquietude that compels attention. Henze, in a manner typical of New Criticism, treats this discomfiture in the proximity of outcomes as something like mere appearance. In his reading, the disquieting shadow of near-disaster masks the necessity of the happy outcome, given the ways in which characters turn to "right deception" in order to counter its opposite. Dispelling the discomfort, for Henze, requires an explanation of the necessity of the happy ending. But it is not at all clear that things *must* have ended happily, that an audience is simply incorrect—but does not yet see how—to feel the disquieting shadow of the tragedy that almost was alongside the comedy that in fact takes place.

The play's action, it is worth noting, bears certain resemblances to *Othello* and to *The Winter's Tale*. If Othello and Leontes can have their faith in their wives shaken, and in one case returned, why must we consider Claudio to be *simply* deceived rather than in some sense driven mad? Why, to put it another way, ought we to take Claudio's deception to be *simple*?

It is striking, in the suggestion that Claudio might be taken as an object of comparison with Othello or Leontes, to note the place of the resurrection sequence in *Much Ado About Nothing*. If one takes Claudio's rejection of Hero to be a consequence of simple deception, and if such deceptions can be undone by some form of ocular or testamentary proof—testamentary proof that Borachio's confession amply provides—what use does Hero's (supposed) death and resurrection serve, since it is entirely superfluous to undeceiving Claudio? To what need does it respond?[6]

3.2 A MIRACLE!

Henze's most problematic assumption, to my mind, comes out in a claim of his that I quoted earlier: "Claudio's faithfulness has to be deceptive in order for Don John's plan to work" (Henze 193). The assumption is that true—as opposed to "deceptive"—faithfulness is simply unshakeable, that this is what makes it "true." Given the fact that Don John's plan indeed shudders Claudio's faith in Hero, Claudio's faith must be deceptive and is thus indicative of a character flaw, visible in an inadequate attention to evidence and a pessimistic credulity of slanderous and false reports. True faithfulness in this matter is embodied in Beatrice, whose attitudes toward evidence and slander directly oppose Claudio's, in Henze's reading. Henze's flawed account of the necessity of the play's happy ending is partly underwritten, as I have said, by the very assumption that it is *necessity* at work, that *Much Ado* has a formalizable lesson to impart to its audience or readers.

In considering Claudio's case in light of Cavell's reading of *Othello*, on the other hand, one might come to see Claudio's doubt of Hero—the way he takes up Don John's misrepresentations of events—as the movement of skepticism, which, for Cavell, is an indefeasible aspect of the condition of humanity. Taking the threat of skepticism as *standing*, rather than as something conquerable by appeals to rational evidence, allows one to make a different sort of sense of the play's happy ending. Additionally, it provides a more compelling way of understanding the Beatrice-Benedick narrative than Henze's unconvincing but highly conventional view that Beatrice and Benedick simply move from the darkness of ignorance to the dawning of the truth over the course of the play.

Contra Henze, Claudio's faithfulness does not have to be "deceptive" in order for Don John's plot to work: the grammar of faithfulness includes the losing of one's faith, or having it shaken, or put to trial. It also includes the concepts of finding one's faith and of that faith's restoration. To see Claudio's narrative as one of *returning* to faithfulness rather than simply *acquiring* it helps to make sense of the resurrection scene, and it does not require Henze's faulty assumptions about the role of evidence in the dispelling of error.[7]

In order for the ending to be legitimately happy, Claudio, whose relation to Hero has come to be marked by a skepticism that he hopes to defeat by means of rational evidence, must recover his original stance with respect to his marriage prospects. Similarly and simultaneously, Beatrice and Benedick, who have been tricked into loving each other by means of false evidence, must likewise cope with a skeptical threat that the revelation of their evidence's falsity raises. Both movements suggest that, despite Henze's picture, the "intuitive trust" that he associates with Beatrice is less a *characteristic* than a *movement*, an extension toward the world, something like acknowledgment. It is, in other words, an active achievement. For that reason, what Henze describes as Beatrice's "trust" cannot be arrived at via what Kevin Cahill (citing Jim Conant) calls a "reflective detour." The extension of such intuitive trust need be no mental act, and in fact cannot be explained in such terms, an assertion that recalls Wittgenstein's distinction between the "*Einstellung zur Seele*" and any sort of "*Meinung, dass er eine Seele hat*" (*PPF* 22). Claudio's movement from skepticism to intuitive trust, as well as Benedick and Beatrice's rejection of skepticism, affords critics a means of "making evident" the quieting of the skeptical impulse.

Claudio and Hero

The triumph over skepticism makes itself apparent in contrasting Claudio's attitudinal dispositions toward his commitments in the world in Act 3 with the ones he evinces in Act 5. In the third Act, the skeptical lure presents itself to Claudio in the form of Don John's framing of the evidence. Anthony Dawson claims that "the appeal of Don John in *Much Ado*'s world of masks and mistaking is that he offers *certainty*—what Othello will later call 'ocular proof.' He promises 'further warrant' for his slander of Hero in III. ii, and challenges Claudio and Pedro with the words 'If you dare not trust that you see, confess not that you know' (III.ii.115–116)" (Dawson). Dawson is certainly correct to gesture to the way in which Don John suggests that Claudio's love for Hero ought to be based on certain knowledge of her virtue, and that this knowledge itself ought to be founded upon certain facts, or disprovable in like manner.

But Dawson exaggerates Don John's "promise" of the wholeness of meaning or direct certainty, as the malcontent offers no such thing. Rather, the discord that Don John sows relies on establishing *doubt* of Hero's virtue: without making promises of any kind, he rather induces Claudio to treat his relation to Hero as subject to verification. This is the skeptical temptation. In taking up Don John's hint that Hero is disloyal, Claudio holds himself apart from his love for Hero until he might possess certain facts that would banish the doubts that have been raised against them. The posture he adopts is what Dreyfus calls the "detached attitude" (Dreyfus, "Overcoming the Myth of the Mental" 60). Don John presents Claudio with a picture of his love for Hero wherein love depends upon or follows from certain conditions—namely, in this case, her virtue, something subject to knowledge or truth claims.

This picture distorts, and is notably distinct from, Claudio's depiction of his initial attachment to Hero. In the play's opening scene, Claudio recounts to the Prince and to Benedick how his affections for Hero have erupted:

> When you went onward on this ended action
> I looked upon her with a soldier's eye
> [....]
> But now I am returned, and that war-thoughts
> Have left their places vacant, in their rooms
> Come thronging soft and delicate desires,
> All prompting me how fair young Hero is,
> Saying I liked her ere I went to wars.
>
> (1.1.280–288)

In Claudio's description, "soft and delicate desires" have "come thronging" to him, and these thronging desires "prompt" him to see "how fair young Hero is." His words present precisely the opposite of the idea that Claudio loves Hero *because* of her fairness or any other characteristic, including her virtue. Rather, the disposedness to love comes first. Claudio experiences the "thronging" of "soft and delicate desires" as something external to himself; he experiences his love for Hero as simply given from without; it is beyond his control, including his approbation. The attitudinal comportment toward Hero as toward one beloved precedes any recognition of her "fairness" as a predicate. Nowhere in this scene is there any mention of Hero's virtue or honor.[8]

In other words, the love that Claudio finds for Hero emerges irrespective of any judgment of her moral qualities. Thus, when Don John frames Claudio's relation to Hero (and the world itself) in conditional terms—"*If* you love her then, tomorrow wed her" (3.1.104), and "*If* you dare not trust that you see, confess not that you know" (3.1.109)—he holds up an altogether different picture of Claudio's connection to the world, one in which love and confession straightforwardly require articulable or verifiable truth as a precondition. This is the sense in which Don John distorts the original phenomenon of Claudio's love, wherein no such conditional terms arise. Don John speaks of Claudio's relation to Hero as if these conditions were *implicit* in the original phenomenon, but Claudio's description of his own experience in Act 1 makes it at the very least doubtful that this is so.

In taking up Don John's picture of things, along with the picture's skeptical assumptions, Claudio transforms the phenomenon of loving into something new and different. Don John's conditional language drives an epistemological wedge between Claudio and Hero, and the way in which Claudio comes to treat his love for Hero as necessitating the fulfillment of these conditions—the overcoming of specific doubts—constitutes Claudio's taking of the skeptical bait. The maneuver here is identical to Othello's. Claudio's Act 1 depiction of discovering his love for Hero is precisely one of "yield[ing] to what he knows, be[ing] commanded by it" (Cavell, *The Claim of Reason* 496). Adopting Don John's view of the matter amounts to the opposite.

Of crucial importance to my reading of the comedies in general is the fact that, unlike the intransigence of skepticism in *Othello*, for example, the above movement of renunciation is undone, and the powerful skeptical temptation is returned to (temporary) dormancy: happiness is achieved not by *defeating* skepticism, but simply by turning away from it, that is, re-turning to the world, at once converting and reverting to a certain position with respect to the facts of the world, so to speak. This sense of the matter accounts for the need to which *Much Ado*'s resurrection scene responds. Borachio's confession alone is sufficient to defeat the particular worries about Hero's fidelity that Don John originally raised, the specific doubt that the malcontent posed. Re-turning from a skeptical position in general, though, requires something further, something that the resurrection scene makes available.

In order to be authentically happy, following the horrific events of the previous day—which include Claudio's public repudiation of Hero, Hero's ostensible death, multiple threats against Claudio's life (including one from his best friend), and so on—Claudio's love for Hero must return to its original character. Many critics regard this process as one of Claudio's "redemption," more or less explicitly in Christian terms (Findlay, "Much Ado About Nothing"; Lewalski, "Love, Appearance and Reality"). But this type of journey from sin to redemption, whereby one does penance for one's sin and is thereby—that is, on the basis of behavior signifying the payment of a debt—reintegrated into a fold of one kind or another, seems insufficient to account for the general absence of any ill-will in the play's final scene. This is not at all to suggest that understanding the scene as a form of redemption has no value; it is simply to suggest that the scene's value is not exhausted in such a view. Rather than, or in addition to, restoring Claudio's intrinsic virtue or his standing within the community, which compels forgiveness, I take Claudio's actions in Act 5 in the sense of returning him to the world, and the world to him. Conceiving of Claudio in terms of a return enables the *forgetting* necessary to the play's happy conclusion.[9] Claudio's error cannot simply be paid for; it must be undone. Or, to put it perhaps more accurately, Claudio's original experience of love must be *re*-done.

Despite using the language of sin and redemption himself, Claudio rejects the idea that he has committed a moral transgression, and he simultaneously labels his fault correctly in begging Leonato's pardon: "Impose me to what penance your invention can / Lay upon my sin. Yet sinned I not / But in mistaking" (5.1.265–267). Contrary to the insights of readers like Henze, Claudio does not misperceive in uncommon fashion any sort of factual knowledge about certain objects in the world; rather, he mistakes his world as merely objective, one founded upon and explicable in terms of detached knowledge in the first place. Correcting his mistake requires that he re-take the world as it formerly gave itself to him.

Claudio's actions in Act 5 bear out the notion of re-taking the world on its original terms rather than merely doing a penance in the repayment of sin. Leonato requires that Claudio, in making amends to him, personally, marry instead a nonexistent cousin of Hero's, "and so dies [Leonato's] revenge" (5.1.284). Claudio "embraces" the offer immediately, without hesitating or naming conditions. The following morning, Leonato challenges Claudio: "Are you yet determined / To marry with my brother's daughter?" (5.4.36–37), to which Claudio replies, "I'll hold my mind, were she an Ethiope" (5.4.38). The "determined" state to which Leonato refers, and which Claudio affirms, is an engaged one, one that brooks no doubt or any dependency upon abstract conditions. Claudio in fact notes a certain quality—beauty—that might in some instances affect one's detached calculus, but he excludes its relevance in the immediate case. His determination precedes all other factors. He further affirms his engagement or determination by eventually asking, "Which is the lady I must seize upon?" (5.4.53). This seizing-upon likewise bespeaks the aprioristic nature of his commitment in the matter. Finally, though, when he once again voices this commitment—"Well then, she's mine"—and asks his bride-to-be to lift her veil, Leonato intervenes, insisting that before she remove the veil, Claudio "take her hand / Before this Friar and swear to marry her" (5.4.56–57), which Claudio straightway does.

Claudio's reference to the qualification of beauty in this scene bears mention. In protesting that he would marry his mysterious bride, *even if* she were "an Ethiope," he indicates a level of determination that would overcome some negative fact. But the task of re-taking the world is still more difficult: the woman he will marry wears a veil, under which conditions he can no more wed her *despite* any ugliness than he can marry her *because* of any beauty. He must take her in the *absolute absence* of factual knowledge. Leonato's protestation that the bride remain veiled is in one sense easily explained by the fact that he knows that the bride he offers is Hero. But he also forces Claudio to leap, as it were, into the total unknown.

If Claudio's error in the play lies "in mistaking" (and if my reading has it right in suggesting that this mistaking pertains to taking his relation to Hero as one dependent upon verifiable facts about Hero's virtue), then Leonato's challenge has the effect of ensuring that Claudio takes up this new relation neither in spite of some negative fact nor because of any positive virtue, but rather simply irrespective of factual knowledge, which is to say, precisely in the manner according to which Claudio experienced this relation to Hero in Act 1. Claudio originally seeks to dispel his doubt with facts, but his true task lies in returning to the pre-reflective experience of loving.

Claudio's foray into skepticism—the inclination to doubt everything that exists until proof can give it back untainted by doubt, as it were—distorts the nature of love in this case.[10] It is significant, I suggest, that the Friar insists that it be given out that Hero has died. I connect this insistence with Cavell and Mulhall's considerations of the ways in which skepticism causes the world to "go dead" for us. From this perspective, Hero's resurrection figures the returning to life of the world as a whole, achieved simultaneously with Claudio's returning to it. While Claudio's doubt can be fed with evidence—and everything is evidence to the doubter—it cannot be killed with starving, or even with the mere defeat of any particular skeptical worry. Only engagement in the world, in the form of a response to the felt demands of the world, can give rest to doubt.[11] The ritual of resurrection, featuring Claudio's unconditional attitude toward his veiled bride, returns characters and the world simultaneously to one another. Seeing Claudio and Hero's narrative in this light will also help to make sense of the more confounding Benedick and Beatrice plot.

Benedick and Beatrice

Henze is correct to see in the Beatrice and Benedick plot some salient reflections of the movements in the Claudio and Hero story, but his stretching of the claim about the self-deception that Beatrice and Benedick perpetrate upon themselves reveals that his focus is misdirected. Thinking of what Henze refers to as their "self-deception" on the model of Claudio's skeptical disengagement from his love for Hero affords a more palatable understanding of the matter. Benedick and Beatrice, I would like to say, face the same skeptical temptations that Claudio does, make the same movements of renunciation and repudiation, and ultimately make the same sort of return to the original experience of their love for one another, a return that neither requires nor could be achieved within the domain of reason and knowledge, upon which Henze's mode of argumentation assumes that it must depend.

Another way of articulating the sense that Henze stretches his claim about Beatrice and Benedick's self-deceptions is to note that the acknowledgment-avoidance axis is even more readily visible in their case than in the case of Claudio and Hero. In the latter instance, it was something of a painstaking matter to demonstrate that Don John's duping of Claudio could not operate by *mere* deception, that is, by deception alone. In the example of Beatrice and Benedick, the very concept of self-deception, imagined, as in Henze, along the lines of deceiving another person, falls flat.

Self-deception must always be a denial of what one in fact knows, of what one does not and could not under ordinary circumstances doubt. Don John's deception of Claudio, if it were mere deception, really could be straightened out with "new facts"—for example, that it was Margaret and not Hero that Claudio had seen at Hero's window. No new information, by contrast, could in principle solve a self-deception, since the very fact that one deceives *oneself* indicates that one already has all the relevant information, including whatever might be necessary to undo the lie. For that reason, a self-deception cannot be conceived as plain ignorance of any facts. If it is a kind of ignorance, it must be conceived as *willful* ignorance, which Cavell appropriately describes as avoidance, a failure of acknowledgment. Where ignorance, or a failure to know, is "an absence" or "a blank," as Cavell has said, "a failure to acknowledge is the presence of something, a confusion, an indifference, a callousness, an exhaustion, a coldness" (Mulhall, *The Cavell Reader* 69). If one can be said to deceive oneself, this cannot be imagined on the model of deceiving another, say by means of withholding facts or providing false information. In deceiving oneself, one must reject, repudiate, or deny certain facts that one already has.

If Beatrice and Benedick appear to have the wrong facts, or to be ignorant of the right facts, this confusion is made possible by the fact that their early denials of love in general and of each other, especially, proceed in the form of reasoned argumentation. It appears that their arguments are valid. But the same sort of validity, I will show, attends the arguments of each as they reason their way toward loving one another; when *these* premises are shown by the exposure of the conspirators' plot to be baseless, each faces the disheartening prospect of the evaporation of the love that they had been so thrilled to recognize. They are saved, as I noted in the Introduction, by the sonnets that Claudio and Hero bring out. But the poetry's *performance* of this salvation cannot be achieved by thinking of their contents as containing or providing justificatory facts.

Benedick and Beatrice both, and separately, set out their refusals to marry as the logical consequences of holding impossible or paradoxical conditions for appropriate candidates to meet: Beatrice will have neither a man with a beard nor one without because "He that hath a beard is more than a youth, and he that hath no beard is less than a man: and he that is more than a youth is not for me, and he that is less than a man, I am not for him" (2.1.31–34). Benedick, meanwhile, says that because he will not do women "the wrong to mistrust any, I will do myself the right to trust none; and the fine is, for which I may go the finer, I will live a bachelor" (1.1.227–230). These statements represent the apotheosis of the skeptical position. Benedick couches his virtue in terms of trusting no woman because, for him, worse than the withholding of trust altogether is a single instance of unwarrantedly extending trust. Because he can apparently see no (abstract) method of drawing distinctions correctly between people—women, specifically—who deserve trust and those who perhaps do not, he simply refuses to distinguish at all. Beatrice does little better in drawing distinctions, grouping men into two sets according to the single criterion of facial hair, and then disqualifying each set in turn.

This is precisely what Mulhall points to as the danger in skepticism: Benedick and Beatrice hold themselves apart from the world of human affairs, and each treats this stance as a virtue, Beatrice by claiming to protect those who are "less than a man" from discovering the fact that "[she] is not for him," and Benedick by claiming to do no woman "the wrong to mistrust any," thus doing himself the "right to trust none." Cavell characterizes this stance as a manifestation of avoidance in response to skeptical doubt. Benedick's words are especially acute in this regard: he repudiates his ability to properly predicate certain meaningful qualities of any individual woman, and so he withdraws the very conditions of his engagement with all women, completely. Like Beatrice's repudiation, Benedick's is offered in response to specific suggestions about the possibility in his life for romantic love, or marriage—it is offered, in short, as a (successful) way of rejecting that possibility.

It is worth noting that Benedick's refusal to individuate women according to quality seems *only* to arise in this context, that is, in the context of the possibility of his own romantic engagement. Thirty lines after those quoted above, Benedick comments on Hero in response to the possibility of Claudio's "buying her": "Why, i'faith, methinks she's too low for a high praise, too brown for a fair praise, and too little for a great praise. Only this commendation can I afford her, that were she other than she is she were unhandsome" (1.1.158–159). Though obviously possessing the ordinary ability to predicate relevant concepts of individual women, Benedick bases his stance against marriage or romance on the denial of this obvious fact, which amounts to a withdrawal of his criteria from the objects of the world, and thus his own withdrawal. In the structure of their arguments, Benedick and Beatrice make finding a spouse a matter of identifying certain conditions in a person—trustworthiness, for example; or, in Beatrice's case, a certain man-youth superposition. In other words, both claim that they will not love *because* they cannot know particular things with certainty: for them certainty becomes a prerequisite for loving.

It is therefore easy for Henze to confuse the nature of the conspirators' trap for Benedick and Beatrice, primed, as we are, to see the matter of love as dependent upon a kind of knowledge. Put briefly, Beatrice and Benedick *do* love one another at the play's end, and they do not *know* one another any better than they did in Act 1 (at least as far as their articulated criteria go), and so, because love seems to depend on knowledge, one might reasonably conclude that they loved one another all along, or at least that the *necessary and sufficient conditions* were always in place, just waiting to be seen. Such a view treats their love as *always present* but heretofore hidden.

But just such a view ignores or suppresses the fact that no new (true) information is discovered over the course of the play, which is to say that the concept of their love's "hiddenness" makes no sense in this context: the sense in which one might say that their love for one another was "hidden" is not one that can be countered simply by uncovering it. The sense in which the necessary and sufficient conditions, as one might call them, were "just waiting to be seen" ought therefore to be understood in terms of the kind of "recognition" that Cavell explores in *Lear*, the acknowledgment of facts already present. In taking as my clue the everyday fact of witnessing Benedick and Beatrice arrive at loving one another at the end of the play without either of them knowing anything further about the other, the picture of love as depending upon knowledge falls apart dramatically, revealing instead something similar to what Claudio's happy marriage to Hero depends upon: the stilling of skeptical doubt by means of acknowledging, accepting, or inheriting that which one "cannot fail to know."

If Claudio must experience the "prompting" of "strong desires" that come "thronging" from without, the external source of loving manifests itself plainly and bodily in the case of Benedick and Beatrice. Scene 3 of Act 2 offers a juxtaposition of Benedick's skeptical stance on love, where loving is imagined to proceed from certain causal conditions, and the responsive acknowledgment by which his love for Beatrice in fact emerges. At the scene's opening, Benedick, by way of musing about Claudio's recent transformations under the spell of love, attempts once more to lay out the qualities that could cause him to become "the argument of his own scorn" (2.3.10), including qualifications pertaining to wealth, wisdom, virtue, beauty, and wit (2.3.29–34). While one could assay the argument that Beatrice in fact meets these criteria, such a claim misses the point: if Beatrice does meet all of these criteria, the criteria have not, to this point, been sufficient to mark Beatrice as a candidate for Benedick's affections. This note raises once more the question I posed in the Introduction: what kind of problem do we understand Beatrice and Benedick to face at the altar? Cavell's distinction between countering various positions by claiming that "a fact about the world is otherwise than you supposed" and asserting that "the world is otherwise than you see" will be important in answering the above rhetorical question.

Henze's reading, meanwhile, takes up a version of the former view, that self-deception is corrected through the application of new knowledge. But if Beatrice does indeed meet Benedick's criteria, as he lays them out in Act 2, then it is unclear that any further facts could bring him to see what he thus far has failed to countenance. That Benedick's criteria cannot pick out, or have not picked out, Beatrice as the home of his concept of love is another expression of what Cavell calls the "disappointing" nature of criteria: in the *Claim of Reason*, he says, "there is something they do not do. It can seem essential. I have to know what they are for. I have to accept them, use them" (Cavell, *The Claim of Reason* 83). Such acceptance or use is not, as we have seen, itself a consequence of formalizable knowledge. This suggests that the problem confronting Benedick and Beatrice is one of seeing the world aright, requiring an acknowledgment of the world as otherwise than they see.

Earlier in the aforementioned speech, Benedick couches the matter in just these terms, marveling at Claudio's amorous affliction and wondering, "May I be so converted, and see with these eyes?" (2.3.21–22). Of primary importance in this sentence is the sense in which "conversion" ought to be understood as reacting to a shift in the ground, or as the acceptance of and going on with a converted world, which Cavell links with the Emersonian and Heideggerian understanding of the importance of "reception" (Cavell, *Conditions Handsome and Unhandsome* 39). The differences between the causal conditions that Benedick names at the opening of the scene as necessary for his conversion and the language in which he discusses the conversion that in fact takes place allow one to see the limits of the detached or disengaged posture that Benedick and Beatrice each purport to hold.

Having heard in Act 2 the conspirators falsely describe how Beatrice "falls, weeps, sobs, beats her heart" and so on out of love for him, Benedick emerges from his hiding place to say, "Love me! Why, it must be requited" (2.3.212–213). Far from anything resembling a realization that Beatrice meets the criteria he has specified a few lines prior, Beatrice's (rumored) love itself elicits his direct responsiveness. No fulfillment of articulable criteria is thus aprioristically necessary to his love, as he imagines earlier. Further, as I have suggested, if Beatrice does indeed meet the requirements of beauty, wit, and so on, then no *mere* fulfilling of criteria proves capable of engendering his love. Responsiveness, reception, and conversion come first. He feels an external demand in the form of the conspirators' misinformation, and *must* requite Beatrice's love—that is the specifically appropriate response immanent in his immediate situation, his immediate experience.

Benedick's language in this scene highlights instances of the world be(com)ing otherwise. Benedick admits that he may have some "remnants of wit broken on" him as a result of his previously steadfast position against love and marriage, "but doth not the appetite alter? A man loves the meat in his youth that he cannot endure in his age" (2.3.226–227). His rationalization refers simply to the "appetite alter[ing]," as if by idiopathic processes. The appetite itself alters intransitively, independent of causal conditions. In responding appropriately to Beatrice's love, Benedick further posits as a ground the "career" of one's "humour," which he implies should be proof against the "paper bullets of the brain" (2.3.228–230). Benedick experiences the irruption of his love for Beatrice as a *response* to her purported love, an understanding that *happens to* him, that he undergoes. In short: a conversion that he finds himself capable of accepting.

His earlier attitude, which treats love as a certain state of being, has already been indicated in the way Benedick imagines any sort of "conversion" he might undergo as a shift from one solid state to another by means of causal conditions denoted in the criteria of wealth, wisdom, and the like. His new attitude comes out in this post-hoc view of his own conversion, in which he imagines conversion as a standing and ongoing possibility irrespective of any predictable causal conditions. Here is another occasion to note the intersections of Shakespeare's comedy and tragedy: if the threat of skeptical withdrawal cannot be ultimately put to rest, the conversion from skepticism, a return to the world, is nevertheless also a standing possibility.

Beatrice, meanwhile, evinces striking similarities to Benedick in this regard. Upon her own gulling, she, like Benedick, abhors the vision of herself that she confronts in her friends' report, and she bids "audieu" to "pride," "scorn," and "contempt," the expressions of her skeptical disengagement from the world (3.1.108–109). She also, like Benedick, experiences her love in the responsive terms of requiting, as she soliloquizes in apostrophe: "And Benedick, love on; I will requite thee, / Taming my wild heart to thy loving hand" (3.1.111–112). Beatrice is, however, explicit on the responsive dependency of her love: "If thou dost love, my kindness will incite thee / To bind up our loves up in a holy band" (3.1.113–114). Like Benedick, then, Beatrice's love responds to the (imagined) truth of his love for her, which hardly resembles her formerly abstract qualifications for suitors. The mutual responding that she here depicts—her love as a response to the condition of his love, his "binding" of the two of them as incited by her kindness—speaks to the degree of departure from her characterization of the world and her relation to it that she laid out earlier.

The responsiveness witnessed in each character—and in particular the immediacy thereof, its conviction—underscores the important contrast between learning as coming into possession of a new fact about the world and learning as coming to understand something that is already in plain view, which I have earlier linked with the idea of "taking on one's education." The distinction is crucial in this case because it looks for all the world as though whatever "learning" is achieved in each protagonist's overhearing the conspirators could be constituted by assertions of fact—Beatrice is in love with Benedick, Benedick is in love with Beatrice—and that therefore what each protagonist does in overhearing these rumors is to internalize this new (and false) information, upon which their responding is logically grounded. What is learned from these rumors, though, cannot be facts on the model of the criteria that Beatrice and Benedick have posited earlier. What is taken from these rumors differs in significant ways from learning that Beatrice is (or is not) virtuous, is (or is not) wise, and so on. Instead, one might say, Benedick learns to *apply* these criteria *to Beatrice,* which is a matter irreducible to factual knowledge.

That each responds to just this "fact"—the fact, that is, that each is beloved of the other, that *this* rumor is capable of inciting their responsiveness—suggests at least that the knowledge-based model of loving to which they have both so far adhered, on which the fulfillment of certain a priori conditions will result in love, is simply idle. The finding of this epistemological model's impotence and irrelevance with respect to love cannot itself be conceived as coming to know an additional fact. It is only in responding to *this* learning that Benedick comes to engage his existing criteria with the particular person of Beatrice: "They say the lady is fair. 'Tis a truth, I can bear them witness. And virtuous—'tis so, I cannot reprove it" (2.3.218–220). Benedick cannot be imagined simply to have been ignorant to this point of Beatrice's beauty or virtue or wit, and it is entirely unclear how, when imagined as a *fact*, the assertion that Beatrice loves him entails his recognition of these other facts, much less the necessity (the "must") of requiting her love.

Beatrice's existence in the world, her beauty and her virtue, were already facts that Benedick knew. The felt necessity of requiting her love amounts to *understanding* what he knows, taking on a certain education. This is simply to say that neither protagonist *infers* love from a series of facts. The rumor that Beatrice loves him rather *animates* Benedick's criteria, gives them life and directionality. Benedick's application of criteria to Beatrice, from whom they had formerly been withheld, is the movement of acknowledgment.

Both Beatrice and Benedick experience love as a response to a similar offering from the other, and they likewise reveal a converted relation to the world by way of this responsiveness. In glossing Samuel Todes's notion of the "creative discovery," Hubert Dreyfus understands the matter like so:

> When a man falls in love he loves a particular woman, but it is not that particular woman he needed before he fell in love. However, after he is in love, that is after he has found that this particular relationship is gratifying, the need becomes specific as the need for that particular woman, and the man has made a creative discovery about himself. He has become the sort of person that needs that specific relationship and must view himself as having lacked and needed this relationship all along. In such a creative discovery the world reveals a new order of significance which is neither simply discovered nor arbitrarily chosen.
> (Dreyfus, *What Computers Still Can't Do* 276)

Benedick neither chooses to love Beatrice, nor can he be said to have discovered for the first time her beauty or her virtue. His love for Beatrice is produced by the conversion signaled in the world's "new order of significance." The world takes on a "new order of significance" along with something Benedick "has found," which ought to recall Cavell's association of founding with finding.

While Dreyfus notes that the man's "creative discovery" is "about himself," the world's new order of significance means that this discovery cannot simply be a *fact* about himself. An idea of Cavell's sheds light on Benedick's situation here: "Knowing oneself is the capacity, as I wish to put it, for placing-oneself-in-the-world" (Cavell, *The Claim of Reason* 107). Both this way of characterizing self-knowledge and my earlier claim that Benedick has learned to apply his criteria to Beatrice bespeak a *practical* sort of knowledge, what Cavell calls here "a capacity" to do something, namely, to place oneself *in* the world. Previously, Benedick has wielded his criteria as a means of speaking either about an *abstract* woman ("rich she shall be, that's certain") or about women *in general* ("I will not do them the wrong to mistrust any ..."). That is, his criteria have previously served to distance himself from the world; they have served the purpose of *refusing* to individuate particular women. Because of the very fact that "there is something [criteria] do not do," because, in other words, their incorrect application is always possible, he has heretofore refused to apply them at all: "I will do myself the right to trust none."

Benedick's creative discovery, I am claiming, is not voiced in his "Love me!" exclamation—that is, it is not a discovery of the fact that Beatrice loves him, whether true or false. It is rather voiced in his next breath: "Why, it must be requited." The logical necessity of requiting Beatrice's love as a matter of course is not itself a fact about the world; nor is it simply entailed in the (false) fact that she loves him. As Cavell says, "What I take as a matter of course is not itself a matter of course. ...I cannot *decide* what I take as a matter of course any more than I can decide what interests me; I have to find out" (Cavell, *The Claim of Reason* 122). What Benedick learns in the gulling scene is literally nonsense: he learns that he is bound by what Wittgenstein calls "the rigidity or inexorability of logical inference" (Wittgenstein 198) to love Beatrice. But this logical necessity is *found* along with his discovery of the world "as otherwise" than he had heretofore seen. He has always had, in the abstract, many reasons for loving Beatrice—including her wit and her beauty; that he is now inclined to *point* to those facts *as* reasons constitutes his finding of this logical necessity.

I noted earlier that the felt necessity of requiting Beatrice's love has not been and cannot be inferred from a series of facts; Benedick's love for Beatrice, like hers for him, does not therefore come to rest upon facts. To recall Cavell's discussion of finding as founding, the creative discovery made by each lover, in which they find the world to have taken on a new order of significance, is all the founding that their love requires. Their mutual recognition of facts that neither could be said to lack, achieved by learning to see their world as otherwise, is as striking an example of acknowledgment as one finds in Shakespeare's comedy.

Conceiving of Benedick and Beatrice's situation in terms of acknowledgment and avoidance provides a frame in which to make sense of the scene of their mutual repudiation in Act 5, as well. As we have seen, Henze, among others, attempts to account for the action in this scene in terms of emerging into self-knowledge from the darkness of self-deception. Without wanting necessarily to object to such terminology, it is clear that this type of account is mistaken as to what constitutes self-deception and self-knowledge. Specifically, since Benedick and Beatrice have realized their love for one another in the middle Acts, even swearing love privately to one another in Act 4, it is unclear how or why we ought to conceive of the pair's mutual denials at the altar as another instance of lying to *themselves*, as opposed to lying to each other and everyone else.

The distinction is important, particularly with respect to the way that evidence functions to counter what can fairly be called the untrue claims of each character in this scene. Having already made the movements of acknowledgment, having already, in fact, spoken the words of love privately to one another, having sworn and acted upon them, the pair find themselves, as it were, hovering in the air. The exchange deserves to appear in full.

> BENEDICK: Soft and fair, friar. Which is Beatrice?
> BEATRICE: [Unmasking] I answer to that name. What is your will?
> BENEDICK: Do not you love me?
> BEATRICE: Why, no; no more than reason.
> BENEDICK: Why, then your uncle and the prince and Claudio
> Have been deceived; they swore you did.
> BEATRICE: Do not you love me?
> BENEDICK: Troth, no; no more than reason.
> BEATRICE: Why, then my cousin Margaret and Ursula
> Are much deceived; for they did swear you did.
> BENEDICK: They swore that you were almost sick for me.
> BEATRICE: They swore that you were well-nigh dead for me.
> BENEDICK: 'Tis no such matter. Then you do not love me?
> BEATRICE: No, truly, but in friendly recompense.
>
> (5.4.72–83)

Sarah Beckwith has earlier associated skepticism, the attitude of avoidance, with seeing our "words and expressions not as showing but as hiding us," and I have drawn out the way in which Beatrice and Benedick each wield their criteria in Act 1 as a way of keeping the world at a great cool remove. Having undergone a certain conversion once in the play already, the above claim of each protagonist *not* in fact to love the other can be imagined neither as a failed attempt to reflect a true belief nor as a successful attempt to instill a false belief in others. In short, the concept of *deception*, either of oneself or others, is inappropriate here; that is not what these rejections do, or amount to. Rather, what we in the audience and they on the stage witness is a *reversion* to skeptical distance through the movement of avoidance, the return to using words and criteria as a means of concealing rather than revealing oneself.

Each of the lovers is enormously conscious of the way their community views them. Benedick in particular expresses concern over the way any public proclamation of his love for Beatrice will be taken: he notes that "I may chance have some odd quirks and remnants of wit broken on me because I have railed so long against marriage" (2.3.223–225). Despite reasoning out that the appetite alters, and that such railing ought not to "awe a man from the career of his humour" (2.3.228–229), the mockery he stands to endure obviously occupies his mind. It is in this light noteworthy to see that the two places in which Benedick and Beatrice have so far expressed their love for one another have been in soliloquy (immediately after the gulling) and in private (immediately following Hero's shaming). While each, thanks to the gulling, thinks it a public fact that he or she is beloved of the other, each takes his or her *requiting* of that love to be as yet undisclosed. At the altar, then, in Act 5, they stand poised to make their mutual love public for the first time, or so it is possible for them to imagine.

It is important to hear the jarring strangeness of Benedick's question when he calls Beatrice forth, the strangeness of the very fact that he opens with a question: "Do not you love me?" One must imagine Benedick's demand as an attempt to re-create in public his own moment of elated surprise: "Love me! Why, it must be requited." Since he, at the moment of his demand, does not yet know that the rumored information of Act 2 was false, and since he was present for Beatrice's earlier and private declaration of love, he has no reason to expect Beatrice to deny it now. But that does not explain why he withholds his own declaration until he has received hers. In 4.1, in private, Benedick is the first of the pair to announce his love. His public demand for Beatrice's declaration of love is an attempt to ground or justify his own requiting of that love on the basis of a fact to which Beatrice is called to testify. But Beatrice wishes to requite his love in kind, as she both verbally purposed (after the gulling) and in fact demonstrated (after Hero's shaming). Her needs, then, also require that he speak first: her "no more than reason" is thus equally a withholding of acknowledgment, an attempt at avoidance.

The evidence that the lovers do and do not call upon brings this out more clearly: Beatrice and Benedick revert to treating love in the way that they had publicly handled it in Act 1: love once again becomes either a necessary consequence of, or a logical impossibility due to, certain conditions. In the repudiation scene, each therefore cites what they take to be *public* knowledge, on the basis of which each might then offer their requital: "Why, then your uncle and the prince and Claudio / Have been deceived. They swore you did [love me]," says Benedick (5.1.75–76), which Beatrice counters with the testimony of Margaret, Ursula, and Hero. Benedick and Beatrice thus withhold their love—the love of which neither can be said to be *ignorant*—from one another until that love can be made to *follow* from the fact of the other's love.

If it were *merely* the fact of the other's love that were required, each has ready evidence at his or her disposal, namely, the private avowals and protestations of love exchanged between them in Act 4. That neither lover raises this evidence suggests that it is not the fact itself, but an aspect of that fact's publicness, that is at issue. Each is ready to requite; neither is willing to confess. The fact of their love is not hidden from either lover; each, however, imagines that it is hidden from everyone else. Their mutual denials of love in this scene are therefore acts of avoiding what neither can fail to know: in declining to acknowledge publicly what has already been acknowledged privately, each lover is forced to repudiate love in the second person, which smacks of a singular kind of cruelty.

This is particularly disappointing inasmuch as it renounces or at least misunderstands the conversions, the creative discoveries, achieved in Acts 2 and 3.

What each lover wishes to *perform* publicly in 5.1 is the requiting of the other's love. But the creative discovery that each has made, I wish to reiterate, is a discovery of the logical necessity of the "must" that attends Benedick's determination to requite Beatrice. This "must" is visible, as I have said, in Benedick's finding his criteria animated in, or animating of, the person of Beatrice. The public acknowledgment of the world in which the logical "must" attaches to the notion of requiting Beatrice's love obviously would indeed be achieved by actually and publicly requiting that love, but it *need* not take this form alone. The acknowledgment that Beatrice is the home of Benedick's concept of one beloved would just as completely show the logical necessity of requiting her love, and *this* acknowledgment is achievable simply by declaring that he loves her. Requiting Beatrice's love is sufficient, but not necessary, to making public the creative discovery of a new world.

In erroneously taking the requital as necessary to the acknowledgment of their conversions, in waiting on the public declarations of the other, Benedick and Beatrice each find themselves forced to deny their conversions wholesale. Their creative discoveries are thereby not merely hidden but renounced. Indeed, to deny the publicness of such a conversion is to deny it privately as well. As Cavell says, "What I withhold myself from [when I withhold my acceptance of criteria] is my attunement with others—with all others, not merely the one I was to know" (Cavell, *The Claim of Reason* 84). Beatrice and Benedick show that it works the other way as well: when one withholds oneself from public attunement, one inevitably withholds oneself from private attunement, too. The repudiation of love at the altar is therefore a real repudiation, but this cannot be understood as the mere denial of a fact; it is a failure to acknowledge something already in plain view, a failure to acknowledge the world, let us say, under the condition of conversion.

The way in which the sonnets that Hero and Claudio produce serve to restore this converted world also supports such a reading. At issue in the task of reanimating or reengaging the logical necessity of the "must" that Beatrice and Benedick alike attach to the requital of the other's love will be whether such a reanimation is achieved in grasping that "a fact about the world is otherwise than [one] supposed" or in understanding that "the world is otherwise than [one[see[s]." In claiming, as in the previous paragraph, that the repudiation cannot be understood as a mere denial of fact, I do not mean to suggest that no facts are denied. Indeed, to the contrary, the repudiation we witness occurs by way of denying that either group of conspirators has given voice to any facts. For this reason, as I have suggested, Benedick and Beatrice do not and cannot raise the evidence of their private vows of love in order to refute each other's denials: characterizing her love for Benedick as "friendly recompense," for example, makes Beatrice's love and all previous expressions thereof dependent upon the *fact* of his love. When this is denied, all such expressions are emptied out of their significance—including, importantly, the expressions of love ossified in the sonnets. Benedick and Beatrice's denial of the facticity of their love also denies their poetry's ability to express it: the sonnets, under this denial, express only something like a fantasy or a lie or an error.

It is therefore significant that Hero and Claudio are the ones who produce these sonnets, significant because *this* action accomplishes the necessary proving, the overcoming of skeptical repudiation. That the sonnets function as proof in the hands of Hero and Claudio, that they *work* to this end in direct spite of the poems' logical inability to represent or express any facts contrary to the denials the audience has just heard, speaks to the sense in which others find themselves in a position to *teach* Benedick and Beatrice about themselves, and to the simultaneous sense in which Beatrice and Benedick find themselves in a position to *learn* or to be reminded of such knowledge at the hands of others.

When Cavell calls self-knowledge "the capacity for placing oneself in a world," he is referring to the practical adoption of the learner's stance in relation to others, to other inhabitants of one's world. While it can seem that the sonnets themselves are brought out to establish the fact that Beatrice and Benedick love one another, the sonnets themselves contain no facts that have not already been publicly denied. The sonnets can attest to nothing: they are red herrings.

Rather, following Beatrice's final denial of Benedick, Leonato steps in: "Come, cousin, I am sure you love the gentleman," which Claudio seconds with, "And I'll be sworn upon't that he loves her, / For here's a paper written in his hand" (5.4.83–85). The sonnets have been stripped of their testamentary power, and what thereby becomes clear is that the testimony with persuasive force appears in Leonato's surety and Claudio's oath. It is the acceptance of *this* testimony, the inheritance of *this* bequest, the taking on of *this* education that amount to the recovery of the lovers' engagement in the world.

I have used the scene of Beatrice and Benedick standing before one another at the altar as the very figure of skepticism, the quintessence of the capacity of teaching and learning to fail or to come up short. While a logical regress is often pictured vertically, as in talk of "groundlessness" or an "abyss," Benedick and Beatrice offer a different image of this regress, a horizontal one, as in two mirrors opposing each other, each reflecting the other's empty infinity. The horizontal figure of this regress is only disrupted in the play via the reorientation of each protagonist toward Hero, Claudio, and Leonato, as toward the vertex of a triangle. Such reorientation might also be characterized as the acceptance of this opposite vertex as *belonging* to the figure that Beatrice and Benedick also compose. Self-knowledge is hereby also expressed, as Heidegger says, in the discovery of "others among whom I am one too" (Heidegger, MacQuarrie, and Robinson 118); that Beatrice and Benedick accept their ability to learn of themselves from others exhibits Cavell's sense of self-knowledge as the "capacity" for "placing oneself in the world."

The previous attempts of each of the lovers, both in Act 1 and again in Act 5, to deny the ability of anything but abstractly conceived facts to educate them about their worlds amount to movements of isolation from others and the world, the isolation that results in the horizontal regress of Act 5. In turning toward or accepting the testamentary power of others with respect to the truth about themselves, Benedick and Beatrice find themselves able to forego the requirement of *requiting* love in virtue of the fact that they find themselves reminded by others of what they could not fail to know. In a movement directly counter to that of avoidance, they recover themselves, each other, and their community at a single stroke.

It will be worth noting at this point, and worth bearing in mind through the next chapter, that the way I have pictured Beatrice and Benedick recovering their love for one another—overcoming an impediment more internal to the relationship than external—has in fact been studied exhaustively by Cavell, despite the absence of any citations in this chapter. In *Cities of Words* and *Pursuits of Happiness*, especially, Cavell focuses on cinematic "comedies of remarriage," which he associates with the concerns of several American films of the 1930s and 1940s. In the two aforementioned works, Cavell contrasts these filmic comedies with what he calls "classical comedies," a generic designation in which he explicitly includes the works of Shakespeare. Unlike Shakespeare's comedies, he says,

> where the problem is to get a young pair past some the obstacle of an older figure, usually a father, and see them married (as, for example, in *A Midsummer Night's Dream*), these films concern getting a somewhat older pair who are already together past some inner obstacle between them and hence together *again, back* together.
> (Cavell, *Cities of Words* 10)

Elsewhere Cavell notes that the "fact of marriage in it [in remarriage comedy, that is] is subjected to the fact or the threat of divorce" (Cavell, *Pursuits of Happiness* 2). The study of Beatrice and Benedick in this chapter shows that the skeptical threat to already united couples is by no means a 20th-century invention. Even in the case of Claudio and Hero, as I have set it out here, one might conceive of the prompting that Claudio's thronging desires do in terms of Cavell's statement that "the achievement of human happiness requires not the perennial and fuller satisfaction of our needs as they stand but the examination and transformation of those needs" (Cavell, *Pursuits of Happiness* 5). This observation all goes doubly, of course, for Benedick's discovery of his ability to apply his criteria for loving to Beatrice in particular. I will wonder, in the next chapter, whether Cavell's characterization of *Midsummer Night's Dream* above is limited in its attention to skeptical threats that arise internally, rather than externally, to the loving pairs. Although Egeus certainly does explicitly forbid Lysander and Hermia's marriage this is by no means the only, or even the most difficult, bar to their happy union; and no such "senex figure" appears to complicate Helena and Demetrius's relationship at all.

3.3 CONCLUSION

I have struggled to make evident, and by multitudinous means, the limitations of conceiving of the action of *Much Ado About Nothing* in the overly cognitive or rational terminology that Henze, in particular but not alone, employs. Against such a view, I have gestured toward Wittgenstein's differentiation of a "disquietude" from a "problem" as a means of addressing the ordinary facts of our relations to the world. Treating disquietudes as problems to be solved requires that one access and articulate the inarticulable "background" that lies beneath and before our capacity for action, treating all action, meaning, or value as explicable in terms of causal conditions. As Wittgenstein shows, attempts to transform disquietudes into something we could address through rational means inevitably yield unsatisfying answers, whose inadequacy lies in the distortion of the disquietude in view.

Henze's article provides a foil to my own thinking precisely because it attempts to render a disquieting feature of *Much Ado About Nothing* in reasonable terms, in the form of a question: what causes the play to turn out well? The success and happiness of the play's ending, in Henze's reading, is a triumph of "intuitive trust" over a predilection to suspicion. He assumes in his argument that such trust, like such suspicion, ought to have a factual and knowable basis, such that one deserves lauding for the proper extension or withholding of trust and one deserves blame for the opposite. He likewise implies that the sheer prevalence of trust in the play renders the triumph over suspicion a foregone conclusion. But as my analysis makes clear, the distinctions Henze draws between suspicion and trust, and the cases he selects to illuminate his concepts, prove inadequate in accounting for the action of the play.

In taking *Much Ado*'s most disquieting aspect—the co-presence at the play's conclusion of the joy that is and the tragedy that might have been—as a point of departure, and thus treating it as real, I seek instead a way into the comedy without, in Wittgenstein's words, "wanting to explain" the necessity of the ending. Indeed, on my reading, the multiple marriages are in no way structurally assured, as the only factor that can bring about a happy ending—an atheoretical acknowledgment of the world, an acceptance of the world as given or converted—is a great hardship for the characters to maintain throughout the play and is in fact lost, repudiated, or renounced on multiple occasions over the course of the comedy. Further, the scene of Benedick and Beatrice's brush with skepticism in the final Act reminds one of the fragility of such acknowledgment: "join hands as we may, one hand is mine and the other is yours," as Cavell has said. The fact of our separateness, despite our joined hands, always entails the possibility of eventual renunciation, the withdrawal of ourselves from the world of our happiness. But giving rest to the disquieting aspects of the play is also achieved in the happy ending, and this, as in all learning, entails the assembly of reminders of what we have long been familiar with: intrinsically separate though our hands may be, they can yet be joined together.

From a methodological perspective, the way of reading Shakespeare's plays that appears in this study, the types of data employed in making my points evident, and even the findings expressed herein may appear markedly similar to the ways and means of New Criticism and, in places, earlier Romantic critics like A. C. Bradley. The apparent similarities here partly motivate the use of Henze's study as an object of comparison: if there are similarities in the evidence we wield and the disquietudes to which we attend, there remain marked differences as well. Henze's assumptions, already discussed, about the ways in which works of literature communicate something like universal human truths, which it is the job of a critic to decode and make public, differ substantially from those I inherit from Cavell.

Specifically, one need not assume the *communication* of any "truth" about human nature in the encounter with literature. When I aver, as in the previous paragraph, that *Much Ado* shows that however separate our hands may be, they can yet be joined together, this cannot be considered any type of "message," precisely because no member of the audience could be imagined to be simply *ignorant* of the news contained; and if one could imagine an audience that *were* ignorant of such news, it is impossible to conceive of that news being of any *use* or *interest* to such an audience, which is to say, it is impossible in another way to imagine such abstract information to be *comprehensible* to, to bear at all upon the form of life of, such an audience.

Contrasting the sense in which a work of literature has in previous generations been taken to communicate messages or truths with the way in which I suggest viewing works of literature as capable of assembling reminders of what we have long been familiar with, of which we cannot fail to know, allows one to see that the position(ing) of the audience matters. As Cavell says, "If an utterance is meant to tell someone something, then what you say to him must be something he is in a position to understand" (Cavell, *The Claim of Reason* 209). A first condition of literature's educative capacity lies in a scholarly acknowledgment that we are in a position to learn about ourselves and others, our lives and worlds, from it. This acknowledgment cannot be compelled by inference from facts about our own biology or psychology, or from facts about literary works themselves, say syntactical or semantic facts, or the type of truisms contained in an axiom like David Kastan's, that "a literary text must be read as a physical object" (Kastan 4). The fact that literary texts have materiality does not in itself necessitate any particular methodological process. Acknowledgment is something further: it bespeaks our capacity for placing ourselves in a world.

Among the things we might be reminded of in studying works of literature is precisely that we do occupy such a position or can be recalled to it. I wish to characterize works of literature, or say, literary artists themselves, in terms that Mulhall aligns with exemplarity. Mulhall describes such educative exemplarity as emerging in "a capacity to put the world of one's aesthetic responses to words—for if we are able to bring others to see what we see, we must be capable of identifying what it is that we see" (Mulhall, *Stanley Cavell* 29). The way in which the critical task, and the literary task, of which Mulhall speaks here are capable or reminding others of, or returning them to, the necessarily public conditions of literary art is also what Mulhall later characterizes as "redemptive reading" (Mulhall 185), a reading that is redemptive specifically in its active acknowledgment of both that publicness and its necessity. Simon Glendinning speaks to this same point in suggesting that the "'being with others' which belongs to communication in general and the use of a word language in particular is *structural*, not *epistemological*" (Glendinning 106), which merely reiterates Mulhall's contention that our fundamental relation to the world is not one of knowing.

For this reason literary scholarship need not wait—and has never waited—upon any universally correct or foundational theory that might ground our readings, our uses and varieties of evidence, our rules of inference, and so on. In taking literary works and the practice of critical reading in terms of exemplarity, on the other hand, one might see that we already have ways of using evidence, of making readings evident, and so on, in scholarly and ordinary reading practices alike. These need not, because they do not, stand on any secure theoretical ground. That they work as examples worthy of following is a function of acknowledgment rather than transcendentally logical compulsion.

This conclusion is mirrored in and by my reading of *Much Ado*. The love that Beatrice and Benedick *find* does not and cannot proceed from any abstract facts. Rather, it must be founded on the examples and testimony of others, and this founding requires that Beatrice and Benedick also *find or acknowledge themselves* to be in a position to accept or inherit—to go on in following—such examples, which is to discover themselves as being *with* others, including, obviously, each other. My reading of *Much Ado* is also meant to bring out the way that literary scholarship can, in like manner, proceed by means of acknowledging a certain pedagogical relation with the literary works it explores, by means of holding up scenes from such works—the characters and the words in which they express themselves—as reminders of knowledge that requires, in some sense, a return.

The distinction from Henze's assumptions, and indeed from earlier critics like Bradley, is that such a returning to that which we cannot fail to know is achieved not by reducing what is to be learned to propositional maxims, including maxims of the form "intrinsically separate though our hands may be, etc." Rather, the reminding and the returning are achieved through homing in upon and reanimating the particular moments of works in which exemplary characters confront exemplary disquietudes. Such a practice allows examples—and their exemplarity—simply to *show*. How to do things with miracles, how to inherit the miracle of the existence of the world, may defy *saying*; its learning requires that it nonetheless be made to stand out.

NOTES

1. All citations of Shakespeare's plays come from Wells's edition of *The Complete Works*.
2. Parenthetically, though he mentions Don John's attempt to convince Claudio that the Prince woos Hero for himself, he does not address the fact that the Prince pretends to be Claudio in the same scene, which would seem to be a deception of Hero. But it's not deception, on Henze's reading, but a mere convention of arranged marriage.
3. One could also argue that from the perspective of their eventual marriage it is somehow clear that Benedick and Beatrice have always loved one another, but that would still require that a Shakespearean marriage credibly indicate a long-standing love, which is hardly the case.
4. It could be argued that Don John isn't really Claudio's friend. But even if one concedes this point, none of Claudio's actual friends opposes his view; the Prince sees the same evidence that Claudio does, and he comes to the same conclusion. In this one case, trusting the evidence and trusting his friends amount to the same thing for Claudio.
5. I am aware that Don John has a villainous past, as well, and so it wouldn't necessarily be "in the absence of evidence" that one would suspect him. In fact, Claudio *does* suspect him when he brings his claim of Hero's infidelity, which is precisely why Don John insists in multiple places that Claudio and the Prince ought to trust "that you see" (3.3.109) and what he "now will manifest" (3.3.86) rather than his word. Doubting Don John, no less than intuitively trusting Hero, must be orthogonal to any evidentiary claim, and that is the point.
6. Of course, the device of the death and resurrection in this play is imported from Shakespeare's sources, including the narrative by Matteo Bandello and its various iterations in Aristo's *Orlando Furioso*, among others. But to explain its presence in Shakespeare by means of simply pointing to its presence in the sources is to dodge the question, for while it may be *one* way of accounting for *why* we find the death and resurrection in Shakespeare's play, it gives a *cause* where a *reason* was called for. Taking the cause to be a sufficient explanation overlooks the fact that Shakespeare amended the source material to include such momentous figures as Beatrice and Benedick (Greenblatt, "On the Edge of Slander"), and so it is hardly unreasonable to ask what reasons Shakespeare may have had—and why they might have been reasonable—for leaving the source material as it is in other cases.
7. Sarah Beckwith, in a personal communication, urges a deeper consideration of the movement from sin to redemption in Claudio's actions and in the resurrection scene, as well as to the relation of sin to self-knowledge in the English Reformation. This is a major feature of her scholarship, and she does much more with it than I can hope to do. I do not wish to simply exclude or gloss over it, but readers interested in this particular aspect would do well to consider her *Grammar of Forgiveness*.
8. Critics of my argument will doubtless point to 1.1.157, in which Claudio says to Benedick, "Is she not a modest young lady?" Modesty is a virtue and Claudio asks about it, and so it might appear that Claudio's evaluation of Hero depends upon her moral qualities after all. But Benedick's answer reveals that "modesty" here is supposed to indicate some *outward* feature of Hero's, not an inner virtue.

Benedick's response: "Why, i'faith, methinks she's too low for a high praise, too brown for a fair praise, and too little for a great praise. Only this commendation can I afford her, that were she other than she is she were unhandsome, and being no other but as she is, I do not like her." Benedick understands Claudio to have asked about her appearance; it is telling that Claudio does not attempt to redirect Benedick into a judgment of Hero's virtue, responding instead, "Thou thinkest I am in sport. I pray thee, tell me truly how thou likest her."
9. The difference between forgetting and forgiving is developed fully in Nietzsche's "Genealogy of Morals" (Nietzsche and Kauffmann).
10. Another wonderful Cavell-inflected note on skepticism, voiced by Stephen Mulhall: "Skeptics repudiate what we ordinarily count as knowledge because it appears anthropocentric, partial, and mediated. But it would make sense to think of the conditions of human knowledge as limitations only if we could conceive of another cognitive perspective upon the world that did not require them; and philosophers from Kant onward have variously striven to show that there is no such perspective—that the absence of the concepts in terms of which we individuate objects would not clear the way for an unmediated knowledge of the world, but would rather remove the possibility of anything that might count as knowledge" (Dauber, "Ordinary Language Criticism").
11. I like to think this is what Nietzsche has in mind when he talks about Hamlet's nausea—it is the skeptical abyss wherein no amount of knowledge will suffice, and Hamlet's nausea is the recognition of the ungrounded nature of involvement in the world: "In this sense, the Dionysian man resembles Hamlet: both have once looked truly into the essence of things, they have *gained knowledge*, and nausea inhibits action; for their action could not change anything in the eternal nature of things; they feel it ridiculous or humiliating that they should be asked to set right a world that is out of joint. Knowledge kills action; action requires the veils of illusion: that is the doctrine of Hamlet, not that cheap wisdom of Jack the Dreamer who reflects too much and, as it were, from an excess of possibilities, does not get around to action. Not reflection, no—true knowledge, an insight into the horrible truth, outweighs any motive for action, both in Hamlet and in the Dionysian man" (Nietzsche, *The Birth of Tragedy*).

REFERENCES

Cavell, Stanley. *Cities of Words: Pedagogical Letters on a Register of the Moral Life.* Cambridge, MA: Harvard University Press, 2005. Print.

———. *Conditions Handsome and Unhandsome.* Chicago: University of Chicago Press, 1990. Print.

———. *Pursuits of Happiness.* Cambridge, MA: Harvard University Press, 1981. Print.

———. *The Claim of Reason.* New York: Oxford University Press, 1979. Print.

Cook, Carol. "'The Sign and Semblance of Her Honor': Reading Gender Difference in *Much Ado About Nothing*." *PMLA* 101.2 (1986): 186–202.

Dauber, Kenneth. *Ordinary Language Criticism: Literary Thinking after Cavell after Wittgenstein.* Evanston, Il: Northwestern University Press, 2003. Print.

Dawson, Anthony B. "Much Ado about Signifying." *Studies in English Literature, 1500–1900* 22.2 (1982): 211–221.

Dennis, Carl. "Wit and Wisdom in *Much Ado About Nothing*." *Studies in English Literature, 1500–1900* 13.2 (1973): 223–237.

Dreyfus, Hubert L. "Overcoming the Myth of the Mental: How Philosophers Can Profit from the Phenomenology of Everyday Expertise." *Proceedings and Addresses of the American Philosophical Association* 79.2 (2005): 47–65.

———. *What Computers Still Can't Do: A Critique of Artificial Reason*. Cambridge, MA: MIT Press, 1992. Print.

Findlay, Alison. "Much Ado About Nothing." *A Companion to Shakespeare's Works, Volume 3*. Blackwell Publishing, 2007, pp. 393–410.

Friedman, Michael D. "'Hush'd on Purpose to Grace Harmony': Wives and Silence in 'Much Ado About Nothing.'" *Theatre Journal* 42.3 (1990): 350. Print.

Glendinning, Simon. *On Being with Others*. New York: Routledge, 1998. Print.

Greenblatt, Stephen. "On the Edge of Slander." *New York Review of Books* Sept. 2013. Web. 6 Oct. 2013.

Heidegger, Martin, John MacQuarrie, and Edward Robinson. *Being and Time*. New York: Harper & Row, 1962. Print.

Henze, Richard. "Deception in *Much Ado About Nothing*." *Studies in English Literature, 1500–1900* 11.2 (1971): 187–201.

Hunt, Maurice. "The Reclamation of Language in 'Much Ado About Nothing.'" *Studies in Philology* 97.2 (2000): 165–191. Print.

Kastan, David Scott. *Shakespeare and the Book*. New York: Cambridge University Press, 2001. Print.

Lewalski, B. K. "Love, Appearance and Reality: Much Ado about Something." *Studies in English Literature, 1500–1900* 8.2 (1968): 235–251.

Mulhall, Stephen. *Stanley Cavell: Philosophy's Recounting of the Ordinary*. New York: Oxford University Press, 1998. Print.

———. *The Cavell Reader*. Oxford, UK; Malden, MA: Blackwell, 1996. Print.

Nietzsche, Friedrich. "The Birth of Tragedy." *Basic Writings of Nietzsche*. Ed. Walter Kaufmann. New York: Random House, 2000. Print.

Nietzsche, Friedrich, and Walter Kauffmann. "Genealogy of Morals." *Basic Writings of Nietzsche*. Ed. Walter Kaufmann. New York: Modern Library, 2000. Print.

Scheff, Thomas J. "Gender Wars: Emotions in 'Much Ado About Nothing.'" *Sociological Perspectives* 36.2 (1993): 149–166.

Shakespeare, William. *The Complete Works*. Ed. Stanley Wells et al. 2nd ed. Oxford, UK: Oxford University Press, 1986. Print.

Williamson, Marilyn L. "Doubling, Women's Anger, and Genre." *Women's Studies* 9.2 (1982): 107.

Wittgenstein, Ludwig. *Remarks on the Foundations of Mathematics*. Cambridge, MA: MIT Press, 1983. Print.

4 A Midsummer Night's Dream

If one troubling aspect of Henze's approach to *Much Ado* involves taking Claudio's deception to be simple, that is, to be reducible to an ungracious or ignoble character trait—"suspicion"—that he has and that others lack, then a similar sort of lacuna characterizes critical work surrounding *A Midsummer Night's Dream*. The machinations of the play's primary romantic plot are understood to be so simple that this plot only rarely occasions sustained critical investigation at all. The critical responses to *Dream* evidence a number of other sites of disquietude, including a focus on the play's aesthetics and meta-aesthetics (Liebler; Grady); the complex structural relations among the societies and cultures of the fairies, the rude mechanicals, and the court (Grady; Moffatt), and the difficulties in staging the play itself, as in the long tradition of Charles Lamb and William Hazlitt, and later carried forward by New Critical practitioners as well (Marshall, "Exchanging Visions"). Keith Oatley, in his studies of character and emotion, does examine the relation of love to action in the plot and the play's ability to represent the same (Oatley, "Shakespeare's Invention of Theater as Simulation That Runs on Minds"; Oatley, "Simulation of Substance and Shadow"), which I will take up in some detail in this chapter. However, what is overlooked or at least shunted to the side in the above foci of examination is the *disquieting* nature of the resolution of the primary lovers' plot in Act 4.

The resolution—and the relative lack of critical attention to the ways in which it occurs—is surprising precisely because the issue had been a settled legal question to this point. Indeed, the satisfactory resolution of this plot requires Theseus to "overbear [Egeus's] will" (4.1.178) in direct contradiction of his own proclamation in Act 1 that the law of Athens is something that "by no means we may extenuate" (1.1.120). The absence of critical work on this extenuation is also surprising in light of the way a very similar question of adequate justice has drawn so much, and such steady, critical attention in the context of *The Merchant of Venice* (Willson; Lee; Benston; Waddington; MacKay).

Where scholars have made note of, and sought to account for, Theseus's simple overbearing of the law, an approach typified in Guilhamet's reading (Guilhamet), the law's circumvention tends to be understood in terms of achieving an Aristotelian "balance" through an appeal to a transcendental unity. In other words, the contradictions among Hermia's desire, Egeus's claim, and Theseus's ruling are not to be understood as conflicts among *human* positions, but are rather the raw materials of the dramatic representation of a certain cosmic structure or divine order. On this reading, Theseus's ruling is necessary to restoring harmony among something like opposing forces in the universe, as symbolized by the characters. Among the manifold problems with this way of reading the play is the rather glaring and unaccounted-for issue that the ruling more or less banishes Egeus from any resulting harmony. Rather than restoring order among competing powers, the romantic plot's resolution transforms existing power relations completely.

Taking these competing positions as human, rather than as metaphysical or symbolic—witnessing the transformation of "Athenian law" from a force of impersonal determination to something like the spirit animating the person of Theseus—opens the space for a critical account of the ways in which what is *given* has to be *accepted* in order to take its effect. *How* this acceptance occurs, or what constitutes accepting what is given, suddenly appears as a site of contestation.

To take the courtroom confrontation between Egeus and his daughter in *Dream*'s opening scene and its reiteration in Act 4 in light of the Beatrice-Benedick altar scene from *Much Ado* invites a scholarly treatment of the play that has to this point gone unappreciated. Rather than an (authorial) invocation or representation of divine scholastic balance through mechanistic characters, understanding Egeus and Hermia's opposing claims on each other in Cavellian terms may help one to see the resolution scene aright. Rather than the restoration or even the achievement of any transcendent balance, one might glimpse instead the difficult and painful work of "joining hands" in the face of human separateness. In this play, no less than in *Much Ado*, the great difficulty in going on with one's inheritance, in learning what another has to teach, and in accepting a particular given is made dramatically problematic. In this play, too, an early avoidance, a retreat into the security of ostensibly non-negotiable reason, requires a later reversal, an acknowledgment, and a recovery. This play, then, likewise makes itself exemplary of such movements.

4.1 LEGAL AND BIOLOGICAL DETERMINATION IN *DREAM*

The action of the play's opening scene—in which Egeus storms into Theseus's court "full of vexation" against his daughter—is readily understood to establish the many binary oppositions that crop up across the drama as a whole: not only between father and daughter, but also between Athens and the wood beyond its walls, between love and reason, and so on. But a central focus on the scene's production of certain shaping contradictions can lead one to gloss over the sense of the storminess of Egeus's entry, an unrest that intrudes upon the reveries around, and preparations for, Hippolyta and Theseus's wedding.

Egeus's "vexation" leads him to seek the remediation of a particular kind of problem, and he takes it that Theseus's court is the place where this remediation is to be found. This often overlooked issue—a jurisdictional issue, one might say—enables a critic to examine both the source of the problem and the fitness, so to speak, of the remedy that Theseus, in his role as supreme ruler of Athens, can provide. I will argue here, as in the previous chapter, that what makes itself apparent in Egeus's rage is something that I have associated with skeptical withdrawal, namely, a distorted and even Lear-like view of a father's relationship with his daughter, that, once effected, is irreparable by way of simple refutation of the skeptical doubt.

Egeus has, in point of fact, two separate complaints, although only one seems legally actionable here. He levels his primary accusation against Hermia's disobedience, and he begs the law's intervention: "As she is mine, I may dispose of her, / Which shall be either to this gentleman / Or to her death, according to our law" (1.1.42–44). Within the structure of Egeus's argument, Hermia is considered only in terms of her legal relation to her father; she is her father's chattel; her "obedience," as Egeus characterizes it at line 37, is the only appropriate response to any particular order of his. As Theseus questions Hermia on this matter, the abyss between Hermia's wish for her father's responsiveness and her legal constraints presents itself clearly:

> HERMIA: I would my father looked but with my eyes.
> THESEUS: Rather your eyes must with his judgment look.

As in the case of Benedick and Beatrice standing before the altar, each side demands a concession from the other, and no compromise position appears: the conflict is diametrical.

In Egeus's argument, then, Hermia's personhood and filial relation to her father manifest themselves solely in legal terms: under Athenian law, she is ascribed the status of mere property, infinitely subject to Egeus's will; a person, perhaps, but one to whom, as Theseus says, "her father should be as a god" (1.1.47). In other words, the duty she here refuses is the duty to respond appropriately to her father's command, which in this instance is only to marry Demetrius. Where this godhead proves insufficient to entreat, the law, Egeus claims, can step in to compel. But then what sort of godhead presents itself here? The rhetorical question is meant to suggest a sort of remainder in the conflict, an unaddressed space. According to Theseus's own words in the same excerpt, the god of his imagining is a creator god, one that "compose[s]" a person's "beauty," and "To whom [that person is] but as a form in wax, / By him imprinted, and within his power / To leave the figure or disfigure it" (1.1.46–51). This account of Egeus's divinity certainly accords with the interpretation of the law's own claim to absolute priority: the ground of correct action, on this view, is singular and knowable. The remainder appears, or the disquietude emerges, in the paradoxical figure of the god whose power is only enforceable by the laws of men, if I can put it that way.

In other words, Egeus, who ought to appear to Hermia (simply) as a god, appears in Theseus's court to call upon the law to bestow or restore his divine power. The very fact that such divine power would require any *other* foundation is somewhat self-contradictory: it is not immediately obvious that *this* is something the law is capable of accomplishing. The law becomes, in this construction, both the foundation of mutual intelligibility, in that Hermia and Egeus are who they are vis-à-vis one another in its light, and also the enforcer thereof. Egeus may (or may not), in this light, achieve the goal of compelling Hermia to marry Demetrius, but this will not necessarily be the same as achieving the restoration of his godlike patriarchal position with respect to Hermia; in fact, it seems to preclude or abandon such a hope.

In appealing to the law, in storming from his house with Hermia and the suitors in tow to barge into the court and demand Theseus's judgment, Egeus engages in a Cavellian form of avoidance or deflection. The very pursuit of his parental rights might indicate Egeus's evasion of his daughter's concerns. As the legal scholar Thomas Dumm has noted, "In focusing primarily on rights and agency, we are 'deflected,' in Stanley Cavell's terms … from a confrontation with what [Cora] Diamond calls 'the difficulty of reality'" (Dumm 278). Put simply, Egeus's godhead with respect to Hermia is supposed to be self-evident, a matter of course (*selbstverständlich*, in Wittgenstein's terms); but this *obvious* godhead is precisely what the law cannot restore to him. While it can condemn Hermia either to an unwished marriage or to her death, and while this unwanted marriage may be the outcome that Egeus desires, her obedience in this instance would not be to *him* but to the law. The difficulty avoided in seeking Theseus's ruling is precisely the difficulty in resolving the clash between Hermia's desire for Egeus to see with her eyes and Theseus's urging her to rather look with her father's judgment. In turning to a legal recourse, Egeus effectively makes wide and final the distance already opened between himself and his daughter: the impersonal intervention may provide, in a small sense, the outcome he desires, but this Pyrrhic victory comes at the price of his own divinity.

Egeus's pretensions to omnipotence fall apart in his second complaint as well, this one more deeply personal and slanderous, and aimed against Lysander. When Egeus turns his wrath directly upon the object of his daughter's affection, claiming that Lysander has "filched" Hermia's heart, "bewitched" her bosom, and "stol'n the impression of her fantasy"

(1.1.27–36), Egeus evidently recognizes that powers outside of himself are also capable—whatever their moral quality—of directing his daughter's actions. While the language game of the law fixes the relations among Hermia, Egeus, and Lysander in a particular and "robust" way, as Dumm acknowledges, the legal language game is neither the only nor the deepest source of intelligibility at work here.[1]

Dumm notes that "The problem, then, is … that the subject we are to understand as the agent and bearer of rights is not, despite its robustness, an accurate reflection of the complex reality of his or her human existence" (Dumm 278). The "complex reality" of his relation to Hermia, or, more accurately, her relation to him, is precisely what Egeus seeks to deflect or avoid. Like the statue of Hermione, which Cavell also associates with Othello's "stoning" of Desdemona, the invocation of the law's terms transforms Hermia into *nothing but* "a form in wax" (1.1.50). The "complex reality" here recalls Cavell's reading of Othello's motivations: Egeus's own godhead, his own power, is dependent and partial: it relies upon Hermia's acknowledgment, her appropriate responsiveness. Like Othello once more, Egeus would prefer to destroy the person he loves in the interest of protecting the divinity of his own self-image rather than to suffer the loss of that self-understanding in acknowledging, except as criminal actors, the presence of others in Hermia's firmament.

The parallel with Othello and Leontes is not perfect: it is not an act of murder, or of sacrifice, that Egeus performs—he does not, for instance, smother his daughter with a pillow—but there is equally a finality here. In resorting to the machinations of the law, in subsuming his familial strife under the legal auspices of the state, Egeus has already given up on what he had striven to protect: his own jealous divinity. In other words, the power that the law can restore is not the power over his daughter that he would wield. Theseus urges Hermia that her "father *should* be as a god" (1.1.47), but this urging comes before Theseus's ruling ("Upon that day either prepare to die / For disobedience to your father's will, / Or else to wed Demetrius" (1.1.86–88)), and it must be understood as an exhortation to acknowledge the proper place of her father's "judgment." The law can punish Hermia for disobedience, but it cannot compel her acknowledgment of her father's divine status. Egeus, in appealing to the law of Athens, forsakes the possibility of Hermia's acknowledgment, and in refusing to "look but with [Hermia's] eyes," he has already withdrawn or withheld his own acknowledgment of her "complex reality." In the place of an acknowledgment-based, harmonious obedience, Egeus consoles himself with the law's power to enforce his decision.

While the question that Egeus brings before Theseus is a straightforwardly legal question, as I suggested in introducing this chapter, Theseus's own counsel to Hermia—that her father *ought* to be as a god to her, that to him she is "but a form in wax"—reveals the limitations, one might say, of a person's *legal* intelligibility: his counsel acknowledges that there is something that the law cannot do alone. Theseus's advice ought to be heard as an attempt to remind Hermia of her proper relation to her father, that is, to recall her into that proper arrangement, to entreat her acknowledgment of her father. Theseus concludes his disquisition on her father's unadulterated power to "leave [her] figure or disfigure it" (1.1.51) simply by averring in the next line that "Demetrius is a worthy gentleman." The assertion of her father's boundless power over her is directly undercut by the attempt to convince her of, or point out to her, the worthiness of her father's choice of suitor: Theseus thus extends to Hermia with one hand the agency that he has just withdrawn with the other. In making this motion, Theseus owns up to the fact that his ruling, even if in Egeus's favor, will not achieve the larger end that Egeus seeks.

In other words, the legal question in this scene, as to which of the suitors Hermia ought to marry, might be settled by Theseus's ruling, but the questions that motivate the action here and throughout the play are not obviously reducible to the axis of the legal. Hermia expresses her determination not to accede to her father's will, whatever the penalty, and she expresses this determination in terms that fall outside the boundaries of the law: she will not "yield" her virginity "Unto his lordship whose unwished yoke / [Her] soul consents not to give sovereignty" (1.1.80–83). Sovereignty of the kind Egeus seeks to arrogate to himself by means of the law is accurately figured here as requiring Hermia's consent. The invocation of the law seems not only to render such consent unnecessary, but it further makes any acknowledgment impossible.

In this way, the daughter that Egeus would command goes dead for him: she is not stone exactly, but perhaps ink; *merely* a legal entity and certainly not flesh and blood. Hermia's citation of her soul's consent and Theseus's attempts to appeal to Hermia on the basis of Demetrius's merit, however, gesture in the direction of a broader kind of intelligibility in light of which legal personhood appears *as* a reduction, as reduced. While Egeus seems to win, the world he inherits is uninhabitable by human others. Moreover, his victory is at best partial, since the legal realm in and through which he triumphs is merely a module, one might say, that opens up on a larger world in which the laws that force Theseus's hand have meaning. The aid promised by Lysander's "dowager" aunt far beyond the city walls, in addition to the very fact that "the law of Athens" does not extend into the wood outside, figures this modularity more or less directly, as critics commonly, albeit not in these terms, note.

Scholars often miss the importance of the ungrounded nature of acknowledgment and avoidance, the way in which a skeptical stance is not overcome via a process of refutation. Having read Egeus's legal claim as deflecting the "complex reality" of his relation to Hermia, and having noted that even as Theseus appeals to Hermia's rationality in order to cajole her to accept her own proper relation to her father, the Duke sees no means of extenuating the law once his cajoling is refused, what remains—and is commonly taken up by critics—is a sense of the law's determinative power to individuate and specify. If Theseus's ruling in the first scene, condemning Hermia to death or single life, is understood as incorrect or unjust, as arriving at the wrong conclusion, then it is tempting in the critical world to imagine that the incorrectness of this conclusion is visible in virtue of some other formalizable position, which is to say that Theseus or Egeus must be guilty of a sort of a *technical* error. This is where Keith Oatley comes in.

Certain critics, and Keith Oatley in particular, take Theseus to be basically correct in imagining that Hermia's love, and love in general, is structurally determined or determinable, and that Theseus and Egeus alike are only in error as to its real source. The opening scene's injustice, on such a view, has to do with mistakenly identifying the *law*, or its valorizing of Egeus's will, as that which does the determining; we in the audience, Oatley claims, can be made to see the true source of such determination. Our sense that Theseus goes wrong in his judgment is afforded by the fact that we can see where Theseus ought to have looked for the determining structure, namely, on Oatley's view, to the core essence of emotion.

Taking up Oatley's claims with respect to *Dream*, I will show that this view is equally unsatisfying as a critical response to a central disquietude of the play, and that just as the invocation of the legal discourse deflects the "complex reality" of the characters and their relations, Oatley's appeal to a determinative force driving the experience of love is inadequate to understanding the complexities of *A Midsummer Night's Dream*. If the "robustness" of the law's view of the legal subject and bearer of rights deflects the complexity of reality, Oatley's essentialist appeal to a representational view of character will evince the same deflection.

For Oatley, the device of the Western flower in *A Midsummer Night's Dream*, the juice of which causes the recipient to love the next living thing he or she sees, provides an example of how the play's "simulation" "accomplishes a transformation that engenders in the audience a clarification (a good translation of Aristotle's *catharsis*) of the real" (Oatley, "Simulation of Substance and Shadow" 20). In Oatley, plays "simulate" for their audience by providing the audience with a model of the world and the internal, psychological natures of the people within it.

On Oatley's understanding, the emotions are central both to the characters' understanding of each other and to the audience's understanding of fictional characters, for emotions (as also in the "moral sentiment" picture taken from the English and Scottish Enlightenment, visible in the work of Locke, Shaftesbury, Smith, Mandeville, Hume, and Hutcheson) provide the motivations necessary to action, and hence can do explanatory work in terms of a given character's deeds. Emotion can therefore also be modeled literarily, as literature features characters who act upon motivations and whose purposes are emotional at heart. As Oatley says in an earlier article:

> Narrative is the computational language for expressing such purposes, and within it the structure of causation in both the interpersonal and

physical world. "She was so angry that she took all his stuff out into the garden and made a bonfire of it." The reader/listener infers, and mentally constructs, the causal sequence: purpose→action→outcome-with-the-aid-of the-physics-of-combustion. (Oatley, "Shakespeare's Invention of Theater as Simulation That Runs on Minds" 4)

The role, in *A Midsummer Night's Dream*, of the "western flower," which engenders love when applied to the eyes of someone unsuspecting, models or simulates for the audience the nature of emotion as a causal agent, the motivating force of resultant human action. As such, the flower device symbolizes or "simulates" what an emotion *is,* and what love is, in particular. Thus, the ways in which the flower can be invoked to explain the flightiness and changeability of characters' words and actions in the play reveals how we might appeal to an emotional essence itself in accounting for the words and actions of real others in the world.

But it will be important to bookmark the equivalency that Oatley draws or highlights between an emotion and a "structure of causation." I will not argue against Oatley's claim that *Dream* reveals something of the essence of love. Rather, I will argue that Oatley's picture of emotion as a "structure of causation" emerges not from within the concerns of the play but from without, and that his *a priori* commitment to this model causes him to ignore important aspects of the phenomenon of love as it appears in *Dream,* and to overlook difficulties for his model that the action of the play creates.

Once more, as in Chapter 2, it bears mentioning that it is the very nearness between Oatley's focus and Cavell's interests that makes Oatley a suitable candidate for comparison: both see characters and real others as existing on the same ontological plane, as Paul Guyer has noted,[2] which means that the ways in which we understand literary characters and their motivations has a direct bearing on our relations to ourselves and to others in the real world. In registering the shortcomings of Oatley's approach to this project, I wish to make evident the insufficiencies of the general model of structurally determinative accounts that Oatley spies in the play, shortcomings that efface entirely the necessity of acknowledgment and avoidance.

Specifically, Oatley has this to say regarding the function of the Western flower that drives the mistaken-identity tomfoolery in the romantic plot:

> One can see this as merely funny. Alternatively, one can consider whether thoughts and due consideration result in love, or whether it is the other way round, so that the emotion of love summons up thoughts appropriate to loving another person. And with this transformation—this dream as Shakespeare carefully explains to the audience—we can think about love in a way that has been made strange (as the Russian Formalists said), that has become defamiliarized, a revealing way, a way that is perhaps closer to the truth than many conventional ideas.

(Oatley, "Simulation of Substance and Shadow: Inner Emotions and Outer Behavior in Shakespeare's Psychology of Character")

I agree with Oatley's broad claim that this fictional device allows us "to think about love in a way that has been made strange." My criticism of Oatley's reading, however, has to do with the nature of his response to these defamiliarizing effects, which is simply to reverse the poles of causation. Against a view on which thoughts cause love, he suggests that love causes thoughts; in both instances, *thinking* and *loving* are two discrete phenomena, related to one another causally. Oatley's objection has only to do with the direction of the causal arrow. Such a starting point delimits what we might learn about love from the play and its characters: the *essence* of love is already known, it seems, and it is represented in Oatley's model; the play, therefore, contra the "revealing way" that Oatley takes the flower to operate, reveals nothing. It only confirms.

Examining the many and various instances of loving in the play, on the other hand, might serve to remind one of the many behaviors, feelings, and words that we associate with loving another person. The very point of enumerating cases is to bring out the conceptual breadth of loving as it appears in the play, to which one might contrast the restricted range of instances that Oatley, working with a very specific model, takes as typical. Oatley's unargued-for assertion of representativeness of the flower's figuration of loving, which omits, for example, Helena's experience of love, recalls the way in which he uses single lines from *Othello* in order to express the essence of characters. Such artificial standardization allows the flower's external and psychotropic power to more or less fully mythologize the concept of abrupt love, if one can call it that. But this may turn out to be nothing like a full picture of love, as it is figured in the play.

The flower in *A Midsummer Night's Dream* acts in two ways, as Oberon describes it to Puck: "The juice of it on sleeping eyelids laid / Will make or man or woman madly dote / Upon the next live creature that it sees" (2.1.171–173). The flower both has the power to *cause* one to "madly dote" and to specify the object thereof. In Oatley's interpretation, these two processes are run together in an imbalanced sort of way: that is, he emphasizes the biochemical inducement of love and pays little attention to the particularization of the object, or an object's ability to induce love.

Oatley's reading of the flower as symbolic of a "structure of causation" goes awry in a familiar, bifurcated way: he offers a causal explanation that fails in its explanatory task and that, moreover, ends up occluding a perspicuous view of the emotion he would study. Even beyond these complaints, however, his focus on his picture of the causal structure of the flower's operation causes him to misapprehend certain facts about the working of the flower itself. He overlooks, for example, the fact that in the actual cases in which Puck applies and misapplies the flower to various characters in the play, the primary dramatic effect of Puck's machinations is not to *engender* mad doting from nothing, but rather to *change* the specification of the love object. Titania already bears loving attachment to both the changeling boy and (romantically) to Oberon at the time of her interaction with the flower, and both Lysander and Demetrius already love Hermia.

The flower, then, in point of fact, stimulates no new *emotion* in any of the characters. When Lysander professes his artificially produced love to Helena, for example, he recognizes both his former attachment to Hermia and his new one to Helena as instances of the same phenomenon. What he feels the need to justify is the shift in the *object*: "Who would not change a raven for a dove?" he asks. "The will of man is by his reason swayed, / And reason says you are the worthier maid" (2.2.120–122). The fact *that* he loves at all does not seem to call for explanation.

Nor does it arise, it might be noted, in Egeus's initial accusations pertaining to Lysander's relation to Hermia, which was not, to the best of our knowledge, caused by the flower's magic: Egeus casts the "bewitching" that has occurred, the one that has forced Hermia to disobey him, as having been willfully perpetrated by Lysander, which makes possible Egeus's view that Lysander has "with cunning ... filched [his] daughter's heart" (1.1.36) and "stolen the impression of her fantasy" (1.1.31). But here, as in the case above, the ire has to do with a perceived *misdirection* of loving, not with Hermia's *having* of "fantasy" itself.

Whatever else it might mean to say that Lysander has "filched" Hermia's heart, and however misguided the notion that Egeus could postulate or command the object of Hermia's affection, the bewitching that Egeus names clearly refers to the directionality of something that already exists. Indeed, as Theseus questions Hermia on the matter in the same scene, the central issue concerns yet again what ought to determine the *proper object* of her love:

> THESEUS: Demetrius is a worthy gentleman.
> HERMIA: So is Lysander.
> THESEUS: In himself he is;
> But in this kind, wanting your father's voice,
> The other must be held the worthier.
>
> (1.1.51–55)

All these questions concern the relative merits of two potential love objects, which are identical, as Lysander argues, on objective indices of desirability, such as fortune and family name. The genesis of loving itself, one of the things the flower supposedly accounts for, remains unquestioned. What appears to require an accounting is the particular vector of loving.

Again, Oatley takes the flower to symbolize or "simulate" for the audience a neuropsychological view of the emotion of love in which biochemical processes in the physiological brain, stimulated by various features of a love object, generate "thoughts appropriate to loving another person."

Oatley's particular target is something like a Kantian sense of autonomy in which love is a matter of decision, in which "thoughts and due consideration" lead to the emotional or behavioral comportments of love. It is true that the absurdity of Lysander proclaiming Helena the "worthier maid" while under the spell of the flower serves to illustrate the problems with considering love to be a matter of applying reason to facts, but Oatley's neurocognitive view merely substitutes an *internal biochemical* response to external facts for the application or intervention of reason, and in doing so he maintains the basic structure of the view he criticizes, a world in which "thoughts" and "love" are clearly distinct from one another, and in which one must be the cause to the other's effect. Oatley merely displaces the activity of "reasoning" onto the neurological processing of brain circuitry. Love remains something like the result of deductive logic; only now the processes of deduction are preconscious or unconscious.

The problem with reading *Dream* through Oatley's model is twofold. In the first place, the plausibility of Oatley's linear view of love, as I wish to call it, falls apart in the examination of cases of loving in *Dream* that do not directly result from the flower, and so its explanatory accuracy comes in for questioning. In the second place, whatever the imagined nature of the determinative force imagined to produce love—whether it be the law of Athens or the flower's biochemical function—this determinative force cannot help in responding to the disquietude raised at the opening of this chapter, the impasse between Egeus's judgment and Hermia's soul. The law sides with Egeus; if that feels insufficient or incorrect, it is by no means immediately clear that appealing to biophysiological necessity, which one would imagine as justifying Hermia's love for Lysander, would prove any more satisfactory, at least to Egeus. At issue, once more, is a problem of mutual intelligibility, which requires something like receptivity or acceptance.

The disquietude involved, as I drew it out in the courtroom scene earlier, pertains to making something like the appropriateness or inappropriateness of love's directionality intelligible to another, or to a community. Discourses of structural necessity on either side deny that such directionality could ever be *unintelligible*, at least once the causal structure of love is made clear. But the nature of the argumentation in the play's opening scene, and even the language of Theseus and Egeus, reveals that there is something here with respect to these love relationships that structural determination cannot do. The facts alone are not enough to bring concept and world, or emotion and action, together. What makes something appropriate, and which facts will be relevant, remains an issue unresolvable by appeal to structural necessity.

But it is not even clear that Oatley's view of the Western flower as symbolizing a neurocognitive picture of loving *works*, even within the specific context of the play. For example, Hermia loves Lysander throughout the play and does not love Demetrius, though Lysander proclaims himself and

Demetrius relatively identical on matters of derivation and wealth. Only two features actually individuate these suitors, in Lysander's words: first, that Lysander is "beloved of beauteous Hermia," and second, that Demetrius is a "spotted and inconstant man," having already "made love to" Helena and "won her soul" (1.1.99–110). In the former instance, Lysander refers to precisely the factor that seems to require explanation, so that is of no help in terms of causal accounting. But in the latter instance, an evocritical perspective might really seize upon something: Lysander's fidelity makes him the preferable mate, which would cause Hermia to love him and scorn Demetrius. But then Helena's continued devotion to Demetrius makes no sense, as it represents awful mate-selection strategy. Moreover, since the mortals remain entirely unaware of the fairy realm and the flower, Hermia's *persistence* in loving Lysander both during and after he abruptly scorns her for Helena in Act 2 fails to fit this account as well.

In other words, if Demetrius and Lysander are distinguishable in the way that Lysander enumerates in the first scene, they do not *remain* so distinguishable throughout, and yet throughout the play each female protagonist loves one man and neither one loves the other. Maurice Hunt has also noted this issue, calling it the play's "problem of individuation" (Hunt). Certain features surely distinguish Demetrius and Lysander in fact—they are two different people. But those that Lysander takes to matter to Egeus and Theseus, at any rate, such as fortune and family, do not adequately particularize either suitor throughout the play, and features one might take as biologically or evolutionarily advantageous prove likewise insufficient to mark one as meaningfully different from the other. It seems that the upward-looking causal account cannot reach all the way to the particular features of particular differences between potential love objects, and that the downward-looking justifications according to reasons stop short of solid ground. There is something that facts and reasons alone cannot do.

As Hubert Dreyfus has pointed out, moving from any general account to a particular situation in matters of emotion or intelligence requires a determination of relevance, in terms of which certain among the unreckonably multitudinous features of a given situation will stand out as meaningful. Attempting to account for love in purely general or objective terms means accounting for love regardless of situational specificity, which prevents the general from gaining any traction in the particular. Mattering and relevance, on Dreyfus's view, are inconstant over time, varying according to differing particular concerns within a presupposed whole. For this reason, they are unspecifiable *outside* of a particular situation. Indeed, Cavell takes the attempt at causal explanation, that is, an explanation offered *in general*, as a refusal of the demands of the particular situation, the context in which a particular account is called for.

Dreyfus's language, in his discussion of attempting to skillfully or intelligently navigate the world by means of disengaging with it in order to assume an objective viewpoint, recalls in another register Cavell's discussion of the movement of skepticism. As Dreyfus says,

> Only if we stand back from our engaged situation in the world and represent things from a detached theoretical perspective do we confront the ... problem. That is, if you strip away relevance and start with context-free facts, you can't get relevance back. Happily, however, we are, as Martin Heidegger and Maurice Merleau-Ponty put it, always already in a world that is organized in terms of our bodies and interests and thus permeated by relevance.
> (Dreyfus, "Overcoming the Myth of the Mental" 49)

Cavell's insight—his addition to the above formulation—is precisely that this world, while ordinarily "organized in terms of bodies and interests and thus permeated by relevance" can be, and indeed regularly is, refused or denied. We can come to lose touch with it; "we have the power to undermine ourselves in the name of an, as it were, unachievable or rather illusory rationality" (Cavell, *Little Did I Know* 376).

In claiming that Oatley's picture of the emotional basis of love does not meaningfully improve upon any error in Theseus's judgment, I seek to make evident the way in which each of the aforementioned views seeks to treat the problem that storms into the court in disengaged terms, which prevents any question of relevance or appropriateness from arising at all. Instead of such a question being settled, which I take it is what Oatley imagines his cognitive or psychological model to achieve, it is simply avoided. Theseus's ruling in favor of Egeus and Oatley's implicit support of Hermia are, for this reason, equally dogmatic: as skeptical withdrawals from the world, they are incapable of restoring the engagement they would effect.

In seizing upon the manifest or phenomenological falsity of a view of love wherein, thanks to the radical freedom of the will, a person simply *decides* to fall in love and then freely chooses the object of one's affection, Oatley's model takes up an opposite extreme, where love is fully determined without any subjective intervention at all. But this turns out not to work in practice: the role of Oatley's "emotion" would be the mirror image, and thus would retain the basic flaws, of Egeus's role. Where Egeus specifies an appropriate object, Hermia's soul does not respond in kind. Oatley's emotion, meanwhile, may well lead to thoughts of love, but, as it were, without sufficient *direction*; affixing those thoughts to a particular person remains unaccounted for.

Oberon's description of the flower, once more, accomplishes both genesis and directionality at once, causing the afflicted to "madly dote," in the first place, and second, in particular, "Upon the next live thing it sees." Oatley's interpretation of the flower's function mistakes the nature of the issue as one of explaining the causality of the emergence of love. The disquietude, however, and the way in which the flower engenders confusion in the play speak more directly to issues in accepting or rejecting the *effects* of shifts in love's directionality. In this, it again raises issues of attunement, acknowledgment, agreement, and avoidance.

The bipolarity involved in framing either thoughts or emotions as masters of the other in this case again raises Fogelin's paradox of interpretation: if thoughts directed at another particular person cannot of themselves engender an inner emotion, then the internal sparking of emotion cannot in and of itself specify the object of one's love. It appears that something more is necessary to bring the two together, but the paradox of interpretation implies that these two things, the emotion and the object, only ever come *apart* when one examines them from a detached perspective.[3] One never experiences the emotion of love intransitively, as it were, without an object. A thorough reading of the flower's working—which, following Oatley's lead, might genuinely reveal something important about the nature of love—must account for this aspect of the matter.

4.2 A HANDSOME, ENCHANTED VIEW OF THE WORLD

The disquietude with which I opened this chapter—the way in which Theseus comes at length to rule against Egeus on a matter in which the Duke previously declared himself compelled to uphold Egeus's claim—might be helpfully explored alongside a fuller view of the flower's function than the one we find in Oatley's reading. Where Theseus, in the first scene, holds the law to be something that "by no means we may extenuate," his view alters entirely by the arrival of the fourth Act. There, Theseus arrives at the position from which, upon hearing the lovers' tale, he simply asserts that he will "overbear [Egeus's] will" (4.1.178) in the matter. Having examined the way in which the emotion of love cannot be adequately symbolized by the Western flower as long as that emotion is imagined to be simply produced, biophysiologically, from an assemblage of various facts about another person, it might be helpful to think of Theseus's relation to the law along similar lines.

The initial disquietude emerges, once more, from noticing that as far as the law is concerned, nothing has changed; there are no new legally relevant facts for Theseus to have learned. Hermia remains her father's daughter. Egeus retains the legal right to "dispose of her" as he wishes. But if no new *legally* relevant facts have emerged by Act 4, then legal relevance no longer possesses the monocular claim that it did in the opening scene. This will be another instance of a view shifting not by noticing that a fact about the world was otherwise than anyone supposed, but that the world is otherwise than one has heretofore seen.

Oatley's understanding of the flower does not and cannot account for this sort of shift. Not only does Oatley's reading of the flower's symbolism fail to bear up under any critical weight, inasmuch as no internal arising of emotion could by itself specify an external object or vice versa, but such an interpretation also ignores many other contextual features of the play. Where Oatley takes human agency, including emotional attachment, either to be completely determined by the will or completely determined by the physiological-psychological workings of emotion, *Dream* presents the audience with a particular kind of enchanted world, one in which the working of magic acts on something like Dreyfus's "order of significance" rather than on any particular, isolated facts. On such a view, agency or proper action is neither dictated by the law one gives to oneself, as in Kant, nor entirely circumscribed by internal physiological processes. Rather, a sort of responsiveness or attunement with a situation of which one is a part becomes necessary.

If the Athenian law requires and produces strictly defined legal subjects, the bearers of rights and duties, and if this law can be wielded as Egeus does—in order to determine a particular outcome in a particular situation—*Dream* highlights and dramatizes other, responsive modes of determining human action. From out of the "forgeries of jealousy" that Oberon and Titania enumerate in the opening scene of Act 2 emerges a new vision of divine power and the way in which it relates to questions of intelligibility and appropriate response. Titania accuses Oberon of infidelity to her, referencing not only a Zeus-like dalliance with Phillida, but also his romantic history with Theseus's bride-to-be, Hippolyta. Oberon's reply, however, merits exploration:

> How canst thou for shame, Titania,
> Glance at my credit with Hippolyta,
> Knowing I know thy love to Theseus?
> Didst not thou lead him through the glimmering night
> From Perigouna whom he ravished,
> And make him with fair Aegles break his faith,
> With Ariadne and Antiopa?
>
> (2.1.74–80)

Oberon provides a vision of human activity that contravenes or at least supplements the version that Theseus himself has cited to Hermia. Oberon's description of Titania's "leading" Theseus away from the various women that populate his mythology offers a version of an external source of power that is not solely creative and prescriptive, as in the godhead that Theseus ascribes to Egeus as Hermia's father, but rather is attractive in the sense of gravitation, drawing one's activity toward attunement with a divine situation.

In the world as Theseus and Egeus perceive it, correct action proceeds from and indeed requires knowledge of a god's will and the subjective decision to submit to it, both aspects of which are highly cognitive in character. But the portrait Oberon paints of the god-human relation is altogether different. Titania does not *order* Theseus from the arms of Perigouna or anyone else; rather, she "leads" him and thus "makes him with fair Aegles [et al.] break his faith." On this view, there is no mention at all of Theseus's obedience to any order or wish on Titania's part, which would require explicit knowledge thereof; rather, Theseus's response to Titania's lead constitutes something of an attunement to her. Theseus's action in this light is not an act of autonomous will at all but is rather demonstrative of responding to being drawn by something external to him.

Dreyfus and Kelly locate precisely this sort of phenomenon in the practices of the Homeric gods; it is noteworthy, of course, that Theseus and Hippolyta are mythological figures. As Dreyfus and Kelly have it, "For Homer moods were important because they illuminated a shared situation; that is, they manifested what currently mattered and they thereby drew people to perform heroic and passionate deeds" (Dreyfus and Kelly 83). Reading the working of the purple flower in a receptive or responsive light, as opposed to a mechanistic or deterministic one, will prove fruitful.

With Oberon's words on one side and Theseus and Egeus's on the other, the play's primary plot explores the struggle between these two broadly sketched understandings of the bases of proper human action in the world. On the one hand, detached reason enables (certain) knowledge of the divine will and the (willed) acceptance of that divinity's authority, and such knowledge provides the basis upon which one individually wills correct action in the world. On the other hand, one arrives at correct action not by reasoning one's way to knowledge or certainty, but rather by experiencing the correctness as given, in a manner of speaking, but as a givenness that must be accepted and hence one that can also be refused.

Cavell, in lectures on the writings of Emerson, reads this sort of responsiveness in terms of the "handsome" and "unhandsome" aspects of the human form of life. On Cavell's view, "handsome" ought to be understood in terms of Heidegger's *Zuhandensein*, that is, as expressing a mutuality of fitness, a compatibility, between a holistic world or an aspect thereof and human intentionality. Cavell reads Emerson as contrasting such a view with a position from which we attempt to get ahold of the world more firmly, as it were, to clutch at it, which Cavell takes also to be the motivating force of the skeptical impulse I have spent considerable time drawing out—the experience of skeptical estrangement motivates the need to "get [the world] nearer."

In a passage from "Experience," Emerson notes that objects "slip through our fingers when we clutch the hardest," and he calls this "the most unhandsome part of our condition" (Emerson 85). In the same passage, Emerson notes that "Nature does not like to be observed. ... Direct strokes she [nature] never gave us power to make; all our blows glance, all our hits are accidents." Cavell associates this passage with Emerson's attempt at "transforming or replacing founding with finding": instead of approaching the world from an objective standpoint directly, Cavell notes that "indirection ... is precisely the direction of reception, of being approached, the attractive, handsome part of our condition"

(Cavell, *This New Yet Unapproachable America* 109). Approaching the world through indirection, understanding the world as drawing upon one, as attractive, puts one in the position to *find* oneself in the world.

One way in which Oatley misinterprets the role of the Western flower in *Dream* is by taking it to reveal something primarily pertaining to the genesis of love and its directionality. That is, the disquietude that he perceives is imagined to be settled by getting clear about how the emotion of love *really* emerges and affixes itself to an object. This sort of reading, however, renders the conflict at the play's heart, and its ultimate solution, in far too pat a manner: it overstates the ability of new facts to enlighten the misguided characters and thereby to bring about a universal accord. If Lysander and Hermia's mutual love in Act 1 were understood in terms of the structural determination symbolized later in the working of the flower, then the antiquated view on which Egeus's judgment has anything at all to do with directing Hermia's soul will simply lose its explanatory power, on Oatley's understanding.

This is a misinterpretation of the flower's function or symbolism precisely because it risks treating Egeus's objections to Hermia's choice of husband as *merely* benighted, as expressing ignorance, as proceeding from misunderstanding the facts. One might point out that even if that model were correct, even if the emotion of love were completely structurally circumscribed, and even if Lysander was unassailably and absolutely the correct object of Hermia's love, the question of what to *do* about that, the decision of marriage, would remain a further issue. Egeus's objections express something of the difficulty in receiving or accepting something given; in other words, his objections also express a certain kind of denial or refusal, the same sorts of denials or refusals that show up in Othello's tragedy. These objections would remain untouched by even the most perfect theoretical account of the way in which Hermia's emotions function. The flower's symbolic work in the play—the way in which it dramatizes the effects of love—has far more to do with the problem presented in Hermia's inability to bring her father to see Lysander through her eyes than it does with any problems related to her ability to pick out Lysander as the one to whom her love attaches.

Hermia, one might say, is given to know Lysander's appropriateness for her in a way that Egeus is not; perhaps this is always the way with the objects of one's children's affections. At any rate, Lysander's appropriateness is not given to either Hermia or her father in any way that Egeus can acknowledge. Egeus's invocation of the law as a corrective is, in this respect, "unhandsome": in trying to clutch at Hermia in just this way, she (and Lysander) slip more or less literally through the law's fingers and out into the Athenian wood. If the flower can be taken to symbolize something along the lines of the truth in Hero's proclamation that "loving goes by haps," then the action surrounding the flower's spell reveals the struggle to accept or receive—to learn—that the world is otherwise than one has seen. The four romantic protagonists themselves best reflect Titania and Oberon's understanding of the world and its inhabitants as responding to the external pull of others. Strangely, it is Helena and Hermia, the characters who are *not* dosed with the flower's juice, who prove most capable of revealing this sense of things.

Helena bootlessly and helplessly loves Demetrius from the beginning of the play to its end. Lysander sums up the matter in the play's opening scene, claiming that Demetrius has wooed Helena "And won her soul, and she, sweet lady, dotes, / Devoutly dotes, dotes in idolatry, / Upon this spotted and inconstant man" (1.1.108–110). The depiction of Helena's love here as involving "her soul" first of all mirrors Hermia's protestations to Theseus about her own soul's consent; but further, Lysander invokes the language of devotion and idolatry to express the godlike power with which Demetrius has drawn, and is thus responsible for, Helena's quasi-religious fixation upon him.

Helena herself reiterates this sense of things directly to Demetrius in the next act:

> You draw me, you hard-hearted adamant,
> But yet you draw not iron; for my heart
> Is true as steel. Leave you your power to draw,
> And I shall have no power to follow you.
>
> (2.1.195–98)

She figures herself as subject to an external, gravitational force. She likewise, in recognizing that Demetrius loves Hermia, characterizes Hermia's beauty in equally gravitational terms: "Happy is Hermia, wheresoe'er she lies; for she hath blessèd and attractive eyes" (2.2.96–97). Much more straightforwardly, Helena says to Hermia, reiterating the above yet more clearly in lamenting the fact that Demetrius loves Hermia rather than herself, "Your eyes are lodestars" (1.1.183). Helena's understanding of the phenomenon of love bespeaks the sense in which one experiences the object of one's affection as attractive in a literal sense, as drawing the lover in. On this view, it might be noted, the emergence of the emotion of love and its directionality are not separate at all: there is no gap to be accounted for between the inward emotional experience and the outward projection toward an object.

Once the lover has found him- or herself in the position of being drawn by another, this relation (re)frames the facts of the world. This reframing of facts is an aspect of the phenomenon that the flower's role in the drama accurately captures, and one that also makes Oatley's reading superficially plausible, at least insofar as the flower indeed undercuts the role of conscious deliberation in the lived experience of love. Lysander awakens under the spell of the Western flower, and he proclaims his love for Helena: "Who will not change a raven for a dove? / The will of man is by his reason swayed, / And reason says you are the worthier maid" (2.2.120–122). Neither Helena nor Hermia is in either fact or feature changed upon Lysander's awakening:

the facts from which Lysander's "reason" reads remain the same. That he now takes one to be a raven and one to be a dove, and mistakenly calls this the operation of (disinterested, as it were) reason, merely indicates that the former facts now show up under a new light. Dreyfus's earlier depiction of the "creative discovery" reflects this as well: Lysander suddenly "must view himself as having lacked and needed this relationship all along. In such a creative discovery the world reveals a new order of significance which is neither simply discovered nor arbitrarily chosen" (Dreyfus, *What Computers Still Can't Do* 276).

Oatley's misinterpretation of the flower's revelatory power limits his investigation to the flower's causal force—a force that acts upon an individual consciousness or the brain's emotional centers—which leads him to his inadequate conclusions. But Hermia's eyes, after all, have the power of lodestars without the help of the flower; Demetrius possesses the "power to draw" Helena unaided by psychotropic magic. When the Western flower spontaneously reassigns or relocates this attractive power, the difficulties the device reveals are, I wish to say, the same difficulties the characters faced in the play's opening courtroom scene: with whose eyes, or with whose judgment, ought this new order of significance to be seen? This is not a disquietude to which a causal account of the emergence of love can adequately respond. This is a difficulty in making one's world intelligible to another or to others generally.

Helena herself reveals the level of difficulty present here, a difficulty not itself solved or solvable through the intervention of either magic or neuroscience. From the moment of Lysander's accusation of Demetrius as a "spotted and inconstant man" to the scenes in the wood beyond Athens, Helena expresses only one desire, and that is for Demetrius to return her love in kind. All facts about herself appear to her in the light of Demetrius's estimation: he is the only extant order of significance for Helena. On this ground, she refuses Hermia's compliments: "Call you me fair? That 'fair' again unsay. / Demetrius loves your fair" (1.1.181). "Through Athens," Helena says in soliloquy later on, "I am thought as fair as she. / But what of that? Demetrius thinks not so" (1.1.227–228). Having been spurned again by Demetrius after telling him of the lovers' flight, she says to herself, "No, no; I am as ugly as a bear, / For beasts that meet me run away for fear" (2.2.100–101). Demetrius's power lies not only in attracting Helena; his opinion is the only frame of relevance in which the facts about herself have their particular value. Others—Hermia, the rest of the Athenian populace—think her fair. But without Demetrius sharing this view, whatever features lead others to call her "fair" have no bearing upon her own sense of her beauty. Demetrius rejects her; for this reason, she is "as ugly as a bear."

Helena thus ascribes a sort of sovereignty to Demetrius with respect to her own value, her own beauty. She, along with all others save Demetrius, appears powerless to validate the facts around her worth or her beauty; Demetrius seems *solely* capable of this feat. It is well worth noting that the divine power she ascribes to Demetrius with respect to herself—the power to draw—is more akin to the godhead Oberon describes than to the one Theseus figures: the power of attraction is not the power of command.

Indeed, Demetrius's words come up painfully short for Helena throughout. He can neither convince her to drop her claim on him, though he tells her many times, plainly and cruelly, that he does not requite her love; nor can his words, uttered under the spell of the flower, move Helena to accept his sincere declarations of love. She can learn one type of fact about herself from him, but she evinces an extreme difficulty in taking on another kind of education from him. Helena, in the midnight Athenian wood, refuses to learn of her beauty or her value *even from* Demetrius, the only one to whom she has bequeathed this power.

The level of difficulty depicted here—the difficulty in taking on one's education—stands out starkly when one attempts to imagine what Helena would want for Demetrius to say to her, the (magic) words that would indicate to her that all of her pleas, her declarations that she is his "spaniel," have taken their intended effect; and that now, just as she desires, he finally pledges her his love. That is to say, the level of difficulty involved becomes apparent when one examines the words that Demetrius actually does speak to Helena in Act 3, under the spell of the flower: "O Helen, goddess, nymph, perfect, divine! / To what, my love, shall I compare thy eyne?" (3.2.138–139). Helena's response to this is revealing: "O spite! O hell! I see you all are bent / To set upon me for your merriment" (3.2.146–147). Her reaction is telling in two ways.

First, Demetrius's words alone suddenly prove insufficient to give Helena what she has heretofore wanted. It is difficult to envision what words Helena would have desired instead—if *these* vows of Demetrius's do not have the power to make his love for her known, then none will. His power to establish her own sense of her value requires her acceptance, which she here withholds: if he is the only one who has such power, it nevertheless here meets its limit. Second, her reaction is also telling insofar as it reveals her newfound, and certainly understandable, skepticism. Having already taken Lysander, whose love's translocation has occurred with credulity-defying speed, to be mocking her (2.2.129; 3.2.122–130), she interprets Demetrius's vows in the same light. Her rejection of Demetrius's ability to tell her of her beauty or value amounts to the refusal to learn about herself from anyone else, period. Hearing Demetrius profess his love had been specifically what she desired. To refuse such professions of love is not the seizing of an autonomous agency or any movement of empowerment; it is much more negative than that.

While both suitors are, at this point, under the influence of the flower, and while one might remain agnostic for the time being as far as the *truth* of this psychotropic love goes, I merely point out that Demetrius—and Lysander, for that matter—have no means of expressing *any* inner truth, any true love, other than the ones they employ here in Act 3. They swear in pretty rhymes;

they challenge each other to a trial by combat; they take turns spurning Hermia before Helena's eyes. For Helena to maintain a skeptical stance at this point is to defeat the possibility of discovering or learning anything at all about Demetrius's true feelings, including the fact that he loves her. Sarah Beckwith once more notes the power of skepticism in this respect: "Once we see those words and expressions not as showing but as hiding us, we lose touch with our only means of self-knowledge and contact with others" (Beckwith, *Shakespeare and the Grammar of Forgiveness* 9).

Helena's skepticism is understandable at this point in Act 3, as I have noted. Lysander has never before professed to love her; up to this point, he has been entirely committed to Hermia. Hermia, too, has difficulty accepting this transformed world, and for just this reason: she responds to Lysander's statement that he no longer loves her, and loves Helena instead, by saying, "You speak not as you think. It cannot be" (3.2.192). But Hermia, by line 272 of this scene, has come to accept the truth of what Lysander says, and she turns her resultant wrath on Helena: "O me, you juggler, you canker blossom, / You thief of love—What, have you come by night / And stolen my love's heart from him?" (3.2.283–285). I raise Hermia's converted view of the matter mainly as a means of evidencing the fact that, however unlikely such sudden transformation in Lysander and Demetrius is, it is not *simply* or structurally beyond Helena's ability to accept.[4]

The difficulty in this scene, as in the courtroom scene that opens the play and the resolution scene in Act 4, is misconstrued if it is taken to be resolvable by a "correct" account of love's genesis, whether this depends on biochemical brain processes or upon magic. The most difficult issue here is one of making the world's "new order of significance" public, shareable, intelligible to others; and another's acceptance of one's converted view of the world is not, as we have seen, achievable via theoretical proof. Demetrius and Lysander are doing everything in their power, quite literally, to make themselves, their converted selves, understandable to Helena and to Hermia. This presents a congruent difficulty, for others, of accepting or learning that the "new order of significance" that Lysander and Demetrius express is also theirs as well. The emergence of such difficulties threatens insanity, isolation, irreparable separateness. In the stakes thus revealed, *Dream*, too, features the types of concerns that Cavell has already explored in Shakespeare's tragedies.

In this scene, Helena is presented with precisely the words and actions from Demetrius that she has desired throughout the play, and yet she here refuses them. Demetrius, under the spell of the flower, really does mean what his words say, but he finds these words, these actions, powerless to achieve their effect; in this way, Helena and Demetrius discover themselves tragically isolated from each other. The play's opening scene likewise features the consequences of a similar isolation: Hermia wishes that her father looked with her eyes; Eegus (in Theseus's voice) wishes that she looked with his judgment. Hermia and Egeus each find their words incapable of moving the other.

Egeus's recourse to the power of the law in order to compel the outcome he desires is not at all the same as making the world that he envisions intelligible and thus habitable for Hermia. Such intelligibility would require her acceptance, and that is what his invocation of the law precludes. In the light of the law, she is, once more, "as a form in wax," a figurine, no longer flesh and blood. This, too, is a movement of tragedy. Yet in this play, as in *Much Ado*, all ends in happy resolution and tragedy is held at bay. Examining the nature of the resolution involved will return our attention once more to the play's opening scene, to the legal arguments presented there, and to Theseus's dramatic reversal of his view of the law's constraining power.

4.3 MINE OWN AND NOT MINE OWN

Helena's skepticism, with respect to Lysander's and Demetrius's professions of love alike, manifests what I have been calling the substantial difficulty of accepting something like a converted world, a "new order of significance." That such skepticism takes hold in Helena, in particular, is at least mildly surprising, given her consistent recognition of the way in which she experiences her love for Demetrius and indeed the facts about her beauty, and so on, as given from without. The way in which she finds herself in Demetrius's thrall mirrors and recalls Titania's flower-imposed words to Bottom: "Mine ear is much enamoured of thy note; / So is mine eye enthrallèd to thy shape" (3.1.131–132). Helena experiences her thralldom, as my earlier reading has shown, as drawing particular responses out of her.

For Helena to reject Demetrius's words, to refuse their power to speak truth, is thus to momentarily deny the possibility that he—or anyone—could experience love in the way that she does, or has. If she has felt herself isolated up to this point by his insistent rejections, left out of the merry company of lovers in virtue of being the object of no one's devotion, then the world's sudden conversion forces her to find herself in a new relation to these others. She is hardly alone in experiencing the difficulty of mutual intelligibility, of finding one's feet in a converted world. The contingent, optative possibility of *Dream*'s tragedy stalks the action of the play in the constant threat of finding oneself to be isolated from all others and thus from oneself. Breakdowns in mutual intelligibility in the play start with asserting one's position with respect to others, as it were dogmatically, and simply demanding that others recognize the relation thus posited. These scenes and strategies of discord preview the means of their resolution. This is the case with both Helena's acceptance of Demetrius's love and Theseus's overbearing of Egeus's will.

I have already described how Egeus's legal complaint amounts to establishing or asserting a narrow sense of the relation between himself and Hermia, one in which he is a god and she a waxen form, and thus a relation in which Egeus might impose his forming or deforming will upon Hermia without regard or responsiveness to her protestations. His invocation of the law in this case is therefore a means of isolating or insulating himself from any responsibility to her, though he might cast himself as carrying out the burdensome responsibility for finding her an adequate match. But any resulting intelligibility is solely one-way. The law demands that Hermia recognize her father's position or else forswear all human company and live a fruitless, barren life; it demands no such recognition of Hermia from her father. Despite the fact that Hermia herself voices the desire for her father to look with her eyes, that desire is immediately ruled invalid by Theseus, and Egeus remains simply unmoved.

Other schisms in the comedy also manifest this type of demand, with equally disorienting and disappointing results. Titania and Oberon, for example, on the cusp of "chid[ing] downright," face each other across such a divide in Act 2. Oberon attempts to compel Titania's acknowledgment by citing his position or role with respect to her, much in the same way that Egeus's suit relies upon his own (legal) position with respect to Hermia. As Titania turns to storm off, Oberon commands her to stay:

> OBERON: Tarry, rash wanton. Am not I thy lord?
> TITANIA: Then I must be thy lady; but I know
>   When thou hast stol'n away from fairyland
>   And in the shape of Corin sat all day,
>   Playing on pipes of corn, and versing love
>   To amorous Phillida.
>
>   (2.1.63–68)

Titania's response acknowledges two important features of the relationality on which basis Oberon demands that his command ("Tarry, rash wanton") be obeyed. In the first place, she recognizes herself or finds herself "interpellated," in Althusserian terms, by this particular hailing; she takes on her relation to him, just as he demands. But she simultaneously, in the second place, troubles the security of this relation by reminding Oberon that his lordship entails not only the privileges of command but also the duties of fidelity. Titania's immediate citation of Oberon's dalliance with Phillida is thus meant to assert that his failures to perform his duties with respect to her vacate his right to assert the privileges that he would. The failure Titania points to is a failure of mutuality, in spite of which Oberon yet wishes to issue commands. Like Oberon, Egeus voices no sense of the necessity of fulfilling any duty with respect to Hermia; Hermia's dutiful obedience to him is, in his eyes, the only issue in the first scene of the play.

Indeed, characters' attempts to *find* themselves correctly in the world by reminding and being reminded of their relations to others is directly implicated in struggling to adjust to what I would like to call the conversions of the world—and this is so in both successful and unsuccessful resolutions. Hermia and Helena each take turns reminding the other of their girlhood closeness in situations in which the security of their relationship is threatened in one way or another. Hermia, for example, confides in Helena that she and Lysander will meet "in the wood where often you and I / Upon faint primrose beds were wont to lie / ... / And thence from Athens turn away our eyes" (1.1.215–218). In recounting the lovers' plan to elope, Hermia in fact indicates the schism between herself and Helena engendered by the fact of their growing up: Lysander, in Hermia's locution, takes Helena's place in this wood. Helena, for her part, and under the misconception that Hermia, Lysander, and Demetrius are all in "a confederacy" set to mocking her, seeks to remind Hermia, on the basis of their erstwhile friendship, that Hermia ought not to "rend our ancient love asunder" (3.2.216). Helena cites their closeness in terms of a former unity: "So we grew together / Like to a double cherry: seeming parted, / But yet an union in partition" (3.2.209–211). She calls upon Hermia to remember their friendship, even in the face of the fact that she, out of love to Demetrius, has betrayed Hermia and Lysander to him.

Both of these particular reminders, Hermia's and Helena's alike, bespeak failures of mutuality: they are attempts to assert or call upon the duties of friendship and allegiance despite each friend failing in turn to fulfill her duty with respect to the other. Hermia replaces Helena with Lysander and asks Helena on the basis of her now-usurped role to keep their secret; Helena betrays Hermia and Lysander to Demetrius, and then demands, on the basis of their former "union in partition," that Hermia not mistreat her as she perceives Hermia to do. Each demands a particular response from the other, a response on the basis of which each believes that order will be restored and all will be well. But the moments of successful resolution, where these occur, involve the opposite sort of movement, an assertion of belonging rather than or prior to any demand for recognition from the other.

Oberon lays bare, as we have seen, one such troubling schism by demanding this sort of recognition from Titania with the line, "Am not I thy lord?" But much later, when Oberon removes the charm from Titania's eyes, he does not ask, as he did before, for her confirmation of their relationship. Rather, he claims her in the genetive, without the necessity on her part of any prior recognition of his lordship: "Now, my Titania, wake you, my sweet queen" (4.1.74). Her response makes the same claim upon him: "My Oberon," she begins, "what visions have I seen!" (4.1.75). Similarly, Helena, who could not accept Demetrius's vows of love to her in the moonlight madness of the previous night, has, in the morning, "found Demetrius like a jewel, / Mine own and not mine own" (4.1.190–191). Helena's discovery here—the figuration of Demetrius as both and at once belonging and not belonging to her—merits particular attention with respect to its implications for coming to accept, or to learn of, a world's conversion.

I was saying earlier that part of the difficulty that Helena undergoes in responding to Lysander and Demetrius's professions of love, but particularly Demetrius's, involves the fact that she finds herself forced to reject, albeit on comprehensible contextual grounds, the very words, the only words, that she wishes to hear from Demetrius—indeed, the very words for which she has followed him into this wood, endangering her virtue, as he threatens (2.1.214–219), in order to hear. In 2.1, she pitiably says, "I am your spaniel, and, Demetrius, / The more you beat me I will fawn on you" (2.1.203–204). Having positioned herself as one who invites his abuse, and indeed relishes it; having in fact vowed, at the end of this scene, on the conditions of this abuse, to "follow [him], and make a heaven out of hell, / To die upon the hand I love so well" (2.1.243–244), Helena at length finds herself disoriented or lost, and at last driven away, by Demetrius's sudden conversion to loving her, of all things.

Her rejection of Demetrius, I once more argue, amounts to an inability to see the world become otherwise, a failure to undergo or to take on the world's conversion. After having been attacked once by Hermia, who evidently has come to take Lysander's love-pleas in 3.2 for the truth, Helena calls herself "simple" and "fond," for having continued to follow Demetrius, and she pledges to "bear [her] folly back" to Athens. Not Demetrius's threats, nor his spurning and chiding, but his professions of love have brought Helena to see the hopelessness of her love for him. And Helena does persist in this love: Hermia's response to Helena's resolution is, "Why get you gone. Who is't that hinders you?" To which Helena replies, "A foolish heart that I leave here behind / … / With Demetrius" (3.2.319–321). Helena's hopelessness here must be understood not as the result of any failure to fulfill her desires. Rather, and starkly differently, her hopelessness must be seen to emerge from her failure to *accept* the very fulfillment of her desires, to hear the words she longed to hear as expressing the love that she so "fondly" pursued.

In Demetrius's vows of love, Helena has gotten exactly what she wanted, and *this* is what proves disastrous for her. She thinks he mocks her; she hears his vows as false. But as these are the only words with which he might express his love, and his the only voice capable of expressing his own soul, the sense of hopelessness that she expresses in pleading with Hermia to let her go stems from her own repudiation of the only words she longs to hear, her own inability to learn of Demetrius's changed heart from his own tongue. This is, I contend, the emergence of Helena's own tragic possibility. Like Othello, she finds that she cannot yield to the knowledge Demetrius attempts to impart. Having figured herself as Demetrius's spaniel; having offered her virtue to his "privilege"; having presented herself for spurning, kicking, and the rest, she will not, at this crucial juncture, make herself vulnerable to his professions of love for the skeptical reason that these might be false; but this means also that she is entirely unable to learn what she wishes to know, or to hear that he loves her, even though, in virtue of the same uncertainty, such vows *might* be true. She finds—discovers—that it is impossible for her to *receive* what she desires.

Demetrius calling her "goddess, nymph, perfect, divine!" is a best-case scenario for Helena; where this fails, she must face the fact that nothing else could count as Demetrius expressing his return to her. She finds that it does indeed fail, and she turns homeward from the wood, leaving behind "with Demetrius" a "foolish heart." Her self-abnegation at this point evinces her recognition of this fact; it is meaningfully different from her previous claims that she is "ugly as a bear" or that she lacks Hermia's attractive eyes. When she speaks ill of herself in this scene, it is not because Demetrius finds anyone else more fair than she, as was the case in Act 1; it is no longer a question of her fairness or features. She has come to understand her fondness not in terms of a misdirection of her love, or in terms of loving where that love is in fact unrequited; rather, she understands herself to have been unable to bear the actual requiting of her love. While she does see her foolishness in terms of her love's impossibility, she recognizes that it is *she* who is unable to bear the possibility of her love's fruition. The fault, she realizes, lies not with Demetrius or with Hermia, but with herself: this is the torturous sense in which, at the end of the Act, weary and lost, she pleads for sleep to "Steal me a while from mine own company" (3.3.24).

Like the tragic heroes in *Lear* and *Othello*, and like Egeus as well, Helena has become the obstruction to her own happiness. This is one way in which *Dream*, contrary to Cavell's commentary on it, features the same sort of "internal obstruction" to a relationship that he reads as typical of "remarriage comedies."[5] In an important and prescient sense, Helena has denied her soul the possibility of consenting to Demetrius's love. She turns against herself, in other words, the same humanity-denying power that Othello turns upon Desdemona and that, I argue, Egeus turns against Hermia. Cavell reads Othello as wishing to deny the conditions of his own existence "as dependent, as partial"; Egeus wishes to deny the same conditions, to elevate himself to the status of a god, which also has the effect of denying Hermia's humanity, of "stoning" her, in Cavell's terminology. Helena's disappointment in herself, the loathing she feels as she lies down to sleep, stems from having made a similar denial of her own humanity, from having protected herself from what she takes to be mockery by means of denying the very possibility, the only conditions, of her own happiness. Helena's repudiation is reversible and is indeed eventually reversed, while Egeus's is not; for this reason, contrasting their situations will help this comedy's exemplarity stand out. Such a contrast will require revisiting once again the opening scene of the play.

In Act 1, scene 1, Hermia's soul forbids her to bear Demetrius's "unwishèd yoke"; Hermia's love somehow invests Lysander with a "right" to pursue her, a right that he may "prosecute." Although these claims lie outside the law as it is strictly conceived, the audience easily grasps their sense, the truth they reveal. But Egeus in a very important sense is deaf to the sense of these words, and it is this, and his mistaken view of Lysander as usurping agent, that merits, discussion here.

Egeus evidently believes that the "bewitching" that has occurred, the one that has forced Hermia to disobey him, has been willfully perpetrated by Lysander, which makes possible Egeus's view that Lysander has "with cunning ... filched [his] daughter's heart" (1.1.36). Caught up in the discourse of titles, rights, and will, Egeus sees the world in binary terms—if Hermia does not bend her will to him, she must bend her will to someone, and that someone, Egeus believes, is Lysander. That is the sense in which he can claim that Lysander has "filched" and "stol'n." Once to have filched and stolen is now to have.

But this is a confusion of the issue, a confusion stemming from Egeus's aforementioned deafness. Hermia's primary allegiance appears in her protestation that she cannot wed Demetrius because *her soul* "consents not." Lysander does not have Hermia's obedience at all in the sense that Egeus believes; rather, Lysander's love has the consent of Hermia's soul.

Hermia's appeal to her soul's consent gestures toward something that she recognizes as simultaneously her own and not her own; we might call this Hermia's discovery in Act 1, a discovery that Helena must likewise make in Act 4. It is *her* soul, on the one hand, but it is also something from which she requires *consent* in order to take appropriate action in the world. As her refusal to wed Demetrius indicates, neither the law of Athens nor her father's sovereign will can displace her soul's consent in navigating the terrain of the decision before her. In this sense—that her soul's consent lies beyond the province of her father's will and the law's command, to say nothing of her *own* will—it is not hers. In the sense that it watches over and guides *her*, however, that *she alone* requires its consent, it belongs to Hermia.

The phenomenon thus documented speaks once again to the sense in which reason, will, and obedience must operate in the light of or on the basis of something like an "order of significance"; that something must first be given (and accepted) in order for reason and will to function as they do; that people are not most basically self-sufficient, isolated agents, willfully seeking the maximization of their individual interests.

Contra Oatley, as well, the limitations of reason and the will, which require a more primordial basis upon which for reason and the will to operate, do not therefore lead us to any "unleashed conclusion" (Cavell, "Knowing and Acknowledging" 63) about the fitness of structural determination and thus the appropriateness of causal accounts of human activity that would attend them. Hermia faces a real choice, one option of which is to ignore her soul's protestations and simply marry Demetrius. It is certainly possible for her to exercise that option, and in that sense, the phenomenon holds open some possibility for autonomous action, if it still indicates that the appropriateness of action lies outside autonomy's power. That which is given is not *determinative* of action in a way that would require or benefit from a causal account. The power of the given, it would seem, does not require the total acquiescence of a personal choice.

In this way, our human activity in the world is at once both our own and not our own. The distinction might be formulated this way: while Hermia can *take* whatever action she wills, she cannot *choose* which action is most appropriate for her to take. Cavell, as I have already quoted, puts it best: "I cannot *decide* what I take as a matter of course, any more than I can decide what interests me; I have to find out" (Cavell, *The Claim of Reason* 123). Egeus's attempts to simply impose his will upon Hermia in the first scene of the play is precisely an attempt to deny or deflect any responsibility for responding to Hermia as a full person, that is, as someone who is both and at once guided by her duty to him and someone who claims the right of his responsiveness to her. Egeus's denial of this responsibility has the simultaneous effects of reducing his daughter to a waxen creation and elevating himself to the status of a god, as Theseus's words proclaim. Egeus thus seeks to escape the human condition "from above," as Cavell has it, and finds himself tortured after Othello's wont, by the intimation—the threat—of the dependency or partiality of his own existence.

By seeking to exercise her own choice, Hermia primarily asks that her father recognize her as his daughter, and yet not entirely *his*. This is what Egeus refuses—the difference between his daughter being his own and his daughter being also her own. Terry Eagleton has characterized the tragic action of *Macbeth* in similar terms, as the process of "becoming nothing in the act of seeking to be all" (Eagleton 118), and Egeus's appeal to the law in response to his daughter's plea certainly comports with this tragic impulse. He compels the law to deliver his daughter back to him, as though what the law could restore were the relationship that he imagines. But what Egeus attempts to compel—indeed, what the law is capable of compelling here—is not a full daughter. The daughter he here demands is monstrous, inhuman, a legal artifact—one devoid of smiles, of charity, of blood, of warmth, of insight and compassion. He wants his daughter to respond to him as a father, but in attempting to coerce a particular response in a particular context, he forecloses on the very possibility of *her* responsiveness. He would have his daughter, then, at the very expense of his daughter.

In exchange, though, he would also have *himself* precisely according to his most grandiose imaginings—"as a god" according to Theseus's understanding, as a creator and disfigurer, a giver of commandments, a voice that requires obedience and circumscribes the wills of others. In attempting to simply declare Hermia's answer for her, he not only precludes the possibility of anything that would count as her actually "responding" to him, but he simultaneously absolves himself of the responsibility of responding to *her*, to the claim that she makes upon him. In depriving Hermia of her responsiveness, Egeus strips her of her humanity; at the same time, however, he seems to shed his own humanity as well, but for a place *beyond* the human. His success would be apotheosis. Through Egeus's attempt to insulate or absolve himself from the onerous requirement of human responsiveness, he refuses the very conditions upon which fellowship with others depends.

At the resolution of the play's primary love plot in Act 4, Egeus is among the company that stumbles upon the sleeping lovers. Again, for the second time in the play, Egeus demands that the law remediate what he takes to be a grievous wrong against him. But two factors render this second invocation of the law markedly different from the first. In the first place, the explicit target of the law is now Lysander: "Enough, enough, my lord, you have enough. / I beg the law, the law upon *his* head" (4.1.153–154, emphasis added). Where in the play's opening scene, Egeus comes "full of vexation … with complaint / Against my child, against my daughter, Hermia" (1.1.22–23), Egeus now seeks to prosecute his daughter's paramour. The legal question that Theseus considered in the play's opening scene pertained to the status of Hermia's duty and obedience to her father. It is her duty, as Theseus reads the law, to obey her father and to reconcile herself to his choice of husband. But it is not at all clear that the law considers it a criminal offense for Lysander to leave Athens in the company of Hermia.

In 4.1, then, Egeus repeats and reinforces the repudiation of that opening scene. Having once refused the claim of his daughter to recognize or respond to her as also her own person, Egeus now entirely denies Hermia's personhood: Lysander's apparent crime is to have stolen something, something like a right or property, from Egeus and, by extension, from Demetrius. Despite the fact that Theseus explicitly reminds Egeus that this is "the day / That Hermia should give answer of her choice" (4.1.124–125), Egeus interrupts Lysander's recounting of the night's events and demands revenge without ever posing a question to Hermia at all; Hermia's "answer of her choice" proves entirely immaterial to Egeus.

In the opening scene, Egeus spoke of Lysander having filched Hermia's heart, having won her obedience away from Egeus, but it remained Hermia who was criminally liable for violating her filial obligations. In this scene, Egeus frames himself as the immediate victim of Lysander's thievery, and he paints Demetrius as equally wronged in this, claiming that the elopement amounts to an attempt "Thereby to have defeated you [Demetrius] and me—/ You of your wife, and me of my consent, / Of my consent that she should be your wife" (4.1.156–158). Hermia is not "Hermia" in this accusation, nor even "my daughter," as she was in the first scene of the play. Lysander and Hermia, in Egeus's complaint, have conspired simply to steal from him that which he mentions not once but twice: his *consent*, which is the only manifestation of the godlike power to figure and disfigure that he prizes.

The second and most obvious difference between the two scenes in which Egeus begs the law's aid is that Demetrius never asks, implicitly or otherwise, for Egeus's consent in Act 4. If anyone might be said to have "defeated" Egeus "of [his] consent," then, it is Demetrius. Where Egeus has aspired to godlike power with respect to Hermia, he here runs up against its limits: he cannot "bestow" his daughter in marriage upon a suitor who is not requesting her hand of him; the very specter of his attempt brings out starkly the humiliating limitation of Egeus's attempts to wield his patriarchal prerogative. In this scene, Egeus reveals—by omitting Hermia from his complaint entirely, by charging Lysander with a sort of theft, and by positioning himself as the wronged party—the full depth and scale of his denial of Hermia's personhood.

The overreach involved here, tragic in its nature, once again recalls Cavell's treatment of Othello: Egeus's power, his godhead, is entirely staked upon Hermia, but it extends no farther than "its confirmation in her" (Cavell, *The Claim of Reason* 485). By passing over the necessity of Hermia's coming to look with his judgment, and in seeking instead simply to shape events, Egeus has cut himself off from the only possible source of his godlike potency. By failing to acknowledge Hermia, he precludes the possibility of her words or actions acknowledging him.

If Egeus errs in the play's opening scene by imagining that the law can compel her confirmation of his power, as opposed to, at best, her grudging obedience to an order, then he here faces the double humiliation of almost clumsily calling upon the law to impose his will on all of the unwilling lovers together: Hermia, Lysander, and Demetrius alike. Two items are noteworthy here: Egeus never speaks another line in this scene, or in the final Act of the play,[6] but Theseus's "overbearing" of Egeus's will also goes beyond simply negating Egeus's insistence that Hermia marry Demetrius—it strips Egeus of all power of consent, period. In declaring that "by and by with us / These couples shall eternally be knit" (4.1.179–180), Theseus entirely obviates the applicability of Egeus's consent to Hermia's choice of husband. Egeus's repudiation of Hermia as her own person as well as his own daughter deprives him in one and the same movement of both, simultaneously.

In direct contrast to Egeus's personal tragedy, the very next line that Helena speaks in the play, following, that is, her plea for sleep to provide her with respite from herself, declares in a kind of wonderment that she has "found Demetrius like a jewel, / Mine own and not mine own" (4.1.190–191). Where Egeus's repudiation of Hermia's being also her *own* person costs him any sense of Hermia's belonging to him, Helena's acknowledgment that Demetrius is *not*—could not be—entirely her own allows her to accept their togetherness as mutually dependent, as partial. In relaxing her grip, forgoing her attempts to clutch at him, she allows him to return; she allows his words to have their effect.

Helena's skepticism of Demetrius's vows, given in the wood beyond Athens, is obviously, as I have said, warranted. In addition to the contextual factors that would encourage doubt—primarily, for example, Lysander's sudden conversion to Helena from Hermia—there remains the stubborn fact that Demetrius himself had converted so finally to Hermia that Egeus has been called upon for his consent in the matter of their marriage. If Lysander's accusation against Demetrius in the first scene is meant to demonstrate the latter's unfitness to become Hermia's husband, in virtue of his being a "spotted and inconstant man," Helena also has ample cause to suspect his constancy. Her refusal to accept his love's pronouncements in the wood is best understood as denying that he is really, truly converted.

In light of this, I note the particular language that Demetrius uses in describing to Theseus and the general party his return to his "natural state." Demetrius recounts how it came to pass that he was in the wood at all—in pursuit, that is, of Hermia and Lysander, with Helena in pursuit of him. He thus does not gloss over the fact or the profundity of his conversion: "I wot not by what power—/ But by some power it is—my love to Hermia, / Melted as the snow" (4.1.163–165). Now his eye finds his melted love for Hermia akin to "the remembrance of an idle gaud, / Which in childhood I did dote upon" (4.1.166–167). He further acknowledges that his love for Helena predates his fixation upon Hermia: "To her, my lord, / Was I betrothed ere I saw Hermia" (4.1.170–171). And the trope in Demetrius's final quatrain will bear particular exploration:

> But like in sickness did I loathe this food;
> But, as in health come to my natural taste,
> Now I do wish it, love it, long for it,
> And will for evermore be true to it.
>
> (4.1.172–175)

At this speech's conclusion, one is tempted to ask whether Helena believes him when he pledges fidelity to this state of affairs "for evermore." But such a question would be misconceived: it would make Helena's acceptance of Demetrius's vows hang upon whether she takes her previous doubts, the ones that got the better of her in the Athenian wood, to have been vanquished by these words. But her *finding* him, and discovering him to be both hers and not hers, speaks against such an interpretation.

The skeptical distance that Helena staked out in the wood the night before ought not to be understood as the result of being suspended in *doubt* of Demetrius's sincerity, as though she hung in the balance between accepting his words of love and rejecting them. Quite to the contrary, she *immediately* takes Demetrius's protestations of love to be mockery; she demonstrates no doubt at all. In the wood, the fact of the matter is that Demetrius loves Hermia; any proclamations to the contrary are mere deceptions. This is the sense in which Demetrius's true testaments of love are as powerless as any false ones could be. His words are the only tools at his disposal with which to reveal himself, and Helena finds, in the wood, that she will not permit a certain variety of revelation, or that she cannot bear it.

Meanwhile, before Theseus and his company, Demetrius owns up to his inconstancy: he acknowledges that he came to "loathe" Helena's sustenance, that in so loathing he turned toward Hermia, and even that this new love at length, and by some power, has "melted as the snow." It cannot be the case that Helena believes that he has *become* constant now. Such a speech cannot be imagined to defeat her skeptical doubts about the constancy or the truth of his love.

Helena does, however, come to share the sense of Demetrius's conversion; the speech must be construed as making himself intelligible to her and to all present. Her declaration that she has found him "mine own and not mine own" bespeaks her understanding of this conversion, or in other words, her understanding of Demetrius, and of the world, as (perpetually) convertible. The certainty of his constancy—or her faith in it—is precisely not at issue. Her skepticism is not refuted but has rather become inapplicable, or has gone cold. His speech casts his former loathing of Helena's metaphorical food as a sickness, and he has found himself recovered to his "natural taste," which figure does not pledge to Helena any imperviousness to all future illness. But it does cast Helena as the gratification of his "natural taste," the object of a desire and an affection to which Demetrius finds himself "returned." Being true for evermore might only mean taking his love for Helena as his natural state, and Helena as the emblem of his health, the health in which he understands himself to be returned from illness. If there is in Demetrius's metaphor a pledge, it is simply the grammatical promise that I cited in Chapter 2: if one can fall ill, then one can also recover.

The drama of Helena's acceptance of Demetrius's love in 4.1 is precisely its countermovement to her rejection thereof on the previous night. Her disappointment with herself, evident both in her plaintive request to Hermia to allow her to "bear [her] folly back," and in her recognition and revelation to Hermia of "how simple and how fond [she is]," arrives after she has already spurned Demetrius's words as mockery. Cavell is particularly attuned to this sense of disappointment and the myriad ways in which it might be overcome. He takes refusals such as Helena's as amounting to failures in the futile (skeptical) attempt to get the world nearer than it is or could be, which is perhaps the most traditional strategy for overcoming skeptical disappointment.

Helena initially rejects Demetrius's vows, on this view, because these vows cannot overcome her skepticism; his words do not do enough, despite their being all that he has and therefore all that he could give her. Cavell frames this problem as one of "there is no nearer for [her] to get since [she] is already there; somehow that itself is what is disappointing, that this is what there is" (Cavell, *This New Yet Unapproachable America* 108). Helena's finding of Demetrius as her own and not her own, and nevertheless "like a jewel," leaves the facts exactly as they are: "this is what there is." Only now, it does not disappoint. When she has desired Demetrius's love, *this* and nothing else is what she has desired. To have *learned* this is to have come to "understand something already in plain view," not to have taken in "new facts." The world has simply become otherwise than she had seen.

As in the presentation of the sonnets at the end of *Much Ado*, Demetrius's *public* pronouncement of his love for Helena—offered in the presence of Hermia, Lysander, and Theseus's hunting party—has the seeming effect of allowing Helena to *find* him "like a jewel." The impossibility that Helena faced, the content of her own torture, was one that the later Wittgenstein characterizes in terms of not knowing how to go on, not knowing how to continue a series: Demetrius had given her precisely the words and precisely the gestures for which she had long been pining, and she had discovered that she could do nothing with them, that she could not put them to use, could not take them into her heart. In Demetrius's words to Theseus, spoken aloud and in public, one must imagine that Helena finds her way, that she discovers how to inherit or accept Demetrius, in his now appearing as simultaneously her own and not her own, as belonging to a public, finally, that includes her, too.

4.4 CONCLUSION

At various points in this chapter, I have said that Oatley's interpretation of the device of the Western flower is both plausible and misguided, or misleading. My objection to Oatley's way of reading the play, and the flower's role within it, lies in the way that it fails to do justice to the public contestability of love, as it were, or to the way in which love's social consequences are in fact negotiated or negotiable. Obviously, attention to such matters does not require a primarily political reading, or indeed any theory of the ways in which sociopolitical forces shape the play's eventual outcome. Rather, one must simply see love's proffer and acceptance as both a public and a private phenomenon. If falling in love has the character of something like an internal or private conversion, then *being* in love, or getting around in the world once in love, requires making public *sense*, one might say, of one's nonsensical love.

Oatley's reading treats the transformation of the world—the new order of significance given to a lover from without, an order simultaneously emergent with the discovery of one's loving attachment to another—as something like the end of the story, or at least the decisive move. Oatley reads the flower's function as undermining views, such as those of Lysander, that take love to be a matter of will, guided by reason, imagined on a model of applying logic to facts; and as far as this goes, Oatley is perfectly correct in lodging his objection. But as I have shown, inverting the above model retains the erroneous assumption that the causal determination of love is that which the working of the flower most fundamentally illuminates. While Oatley attends to the way in which one's own world changes under the influence of love, or the way in which a new order of significance comes over a person, he omits a consideration of the ways in which other characters must be brought into or repulsed from a world thus converted.

Taking comedy as a kind of countermovement of tragedy, however, and exploring the work on Cavell's model of reading allow one to see the comic foibles of the human lovers as bearing genuine import. If an initial conversion of the world is accomplished simply by the flower, the strife in the play is not, on those grounds alone, simply reducible to something like mistaken identity or misplaced love. Rather, these multiple conversions of the world compel the characters to find their feet in a foreign realm, and this demands not only significant effort, but also significant courage. Failures to make the effort, which are failures of heart—manifested in retreats into the safety of skeptical distance—renounce at once citizenship and belonging in such converted orders. Helena's abject sadness in 3.3, her disappointment in herself and in the world, allows one to see that even where the stakes are so elevated, that even when there is so much to gain by revealing oneself, that where remaining safe and protected means losing the very object of one's heart's desire, even there, enacting such a self-revelation is no easy step. Indeed, the tragic heroes, with all the advantages of their "powerful, ranging minds," their nobility, their wealth, and so on, find themselves incapable of overcoming this threat of exposure, incapable of bearing others' knowledge of them.

Theseus's "overbearing" of Egeus's will in Act 4 is thus best understood as an example of a third party coming to find his feet in a converted world, moving from a refusal to respond to any but narrow, legal mandates to a position from which his responsiveness takes a broader set of claims into account. This is not to say that the legal question in the play's opening scene is or was equally and narrowly conceived by all parties involved. Although Theseus initially presents himself as helpless in enforcing the law, and although the law sides with Egeus's claim, it is worth recalling that Lysander believes that Hermia's soul has invested him with a "right" that he may "prosecute." Demetrius's history with Helena is raised in the earlier scene in order to cast doubt on Egeus's judgment, or at least his particular interests in this case. Both of these facts are offered in the hopes of troubling precisely the narrow view of the matter into which Theseus initially retreats.

When Theseus declares the lovers "fortunately met" in Act 4 and ultimately renounces his earlier ruling, he comes to acknowledge the world's converted position, an acknowledgment he had earlier withheld. From a legal standpoint, in this scene, Egeus has no claim against Lysander, at least not according to the particular laws cited in the play's opening scene. Egeus has likewise, just a moment before, been "defeated" of his consent by Demetrius's withdrawal of his suit. When Theseus overbears his will, then, this is not simply a reversal of the Duke's earlier position with respect to the law, which would free Hermia from her previous constraint either to marry with Demetrius or to foreswear the company of men, through death or convent. Indeed, Theseus's pronouncement that "in the temple by and by with us / These couples shall eternally be knit" (4.1.179–180) goes well beyond any such legal reversal. Theseus here in fact steps into Egeus's position, or arrogates Egeus's patriarchal prerogative to himself, and the Duke thus supplants Egeus entirely. What Theseus overbears when he overbears Egeus's will is effectively the latter's legal standing in the community as such, altogether: Egeus is stripped simultaneously of his power to draw upon the law's privileges, to give or to refuse his consent to Lysander, and to compel Hermia's obedience.

As there is, after all, a consent given to Lysander in this scene, and Hermia will indeed have to obey a command, Theseus has left the law intact. It has not, in fact, been "extenuated"; Theseus merely assumes the status of Hermia's father. But Egeus thereby finds himself marooned or cast out of the new world. Theseus's overbearing of Egeus's will makes the latter's repudiation of his daughter, Egeus's failure to acknowledge her personhood, legal, final, and literal. His avoidance of Hermia's claim upon him has thus *actually* severed the father-daughter relationship that the law recognizes. By denying Hermia *as* a daughter, he denies himself the status of anyone's father. As I have already noted, Egeus never speaks again in this play. But this is not surprising: having forsaken through skeptical avoidance his bonds with his daughter and the community, to whom does one imagine that he would he speak?

"The failure to acknowledge a best case of the other is a denial of that other, presaging the death of that other," as Cavell has said (*Disowning Knowledge in Seven Plays of Shakespeare* 138), and Hermia's initial sentence bears out just this presaging. But Cavell also notes that a failure to acknowledge a best case of the other presages equally "the death of our capacity to acknowledge as such, the turning of our hearts to stone, or their bursting" (ibid.), and in Egeus's overthrow, in his reduction to nothing, we witness the self-inflicted aspect of the tragic avoidance: Egeus has made himself a stranger in a converted world, which remains the only world there is.

The emotion of love and its potent figuration in the Western flower certainly merit critical attention of the type Oatley bestows upon it; and the phenomenology of its world-altering effects certainly do, as Oatley points out, undermine any notion that reason and the will could direct one's heart. But the alterations of the world, the events of falling in and out of love depicted in the play, do not account either for the lovers' successes or for Egeus's failure. Indeed, Helena's struggle with herself, the difficulty she faces in hearing the words she yearns to hear as expressing Demetrius's soul, renders clearly the sense in which the emotion of love, even mutual love, is a necessary but not sufficient condition for such happiness. Taking on one's education, taking one's life upon oneself, is something further.

With regard to Shakespeare's comedies, critics have sometimes complained that the marriages, the happy endings, are somehow lacking; that the wrongs that characters have done to one another over the course of the play are not so easily forgotten or dismissed.[7] The obstacles to accepting the happiness at the end of *A Midsummer Night's Dream*, including the spectacle of Egeus's ignominious and emasculating defeat and the scornful, murderous words the characters have spoken to one another earlier, both under the flower's influence and sober, as it were, are also, for some critics, difficult to overlook. The happiness we witness, such complaints suggest, is not *real* happiness; we in the audience cannot *believe* in the bright future that promises to stretch before these characters.

In closing this chapter and anticipating the next, I note once more Cavell's thinking on Emerson and the way in which it responds to the genre of complaints lodged above.

> What seems to me evident is that Emerson's finding of founding as finding, say the transfiguration of philosophical grounding as lasting, could not have presented itself as a stable philosophical proposal before the configuration of philosophy established by the work of the later Heidegger and the later Wittgenstein, call this the establishment of thinking as knowing how to go on, being on the way, onward and onward. At each step, or level, explanation comes to an end; there is no level to which all explanations come, at which all end.
> (Cavell, *This New Yet Unapproachable America* 116)

Worries that the comedies do not show forth genuine happiness, I would contend, stem from a certain chimerical view of happiness. The lovers at the end of *Dream* have found themselves in a position to go on from and with the very words that they have earlier spoken.

Helena, for example, has heard Demetrius declare that he is returned to her, that she is the one to whom he returns. Not, "O Helen, goddess, nymph," and the like, but just *these* words she finds herself capable of going on with, capable of bearing onward. Helena's acceptance of Demetrius as "mine own and not mine own" speaks both to the sense in which she finds and founds their mutual love in receiving these words, and also to the sense in which it will have to be found and founded again in the days and years to come.

The happiness, the love, that we witness in the resolution of comedies in marriage is happiness at the moment of a finding or a founding—in other words, a beginning. There is no level toward which all happiness proceeds, as I would like to paraphrase the matter, or at which all ends. If comedy is, as I am consistently arguing, the drama of acknowledgment, then what we witness is simply what happiness amounts to. No moment of acknowledgment precludes the possibility of future skepticism, or obviates the need for future revelation, future responsiveness. We find—found—our happiness together, and we bear it onward as we may.

NOTES

1. My interpretation of a "deeper" sense of intelligibility than the Athenian legal code is, I find, somewhat similar to Savigny's understanding of the law as being, in Mitra Sharafi's words, "a cultural artifact, a unique product of the *Volksgeist* of a community, its history, and its belief systems." On this view, Egeus's mania for the letter of the law, a particular code, is "reckless and culturally inappropriate" (Sharafi, *Law and Identity in Colonial South Asia Parsi Legal Culture, 1772–1947.* 163).

2. In a discussion of Cavell and literature at a symposium on 6–7 September 2013 in Stockholm called "Perfectionism and Education: Kant and Cavell on Ethics and Aesthetics."
3. Simon Glendinning refers to this as "phenomenon-splitting."
4. Hermia employs the same metaphors as her father in this speech: Helena stands accused of *stealing* Lysander's heart from the one to whom it rightfully belongs. In Hermia's case, she focuses on Helena's features—such as her height—that might "draw" her Lysander, while when Egeus accuses Lysander of filching his daughter's heart, this is done willfully, by trickery—feigned rhymes, and so on.
5. Helena and Demetrius were, in fact, together at some point before the action of the play begins, and therefore, just as in the comedies of remarriage, the challenge here is not to get them together but to get them "*back* together, together *again*," as Cavell says of a different genre. It also ought to be mentioned in light of earlier commentary on this relationship that Helena's failure to hear Demetrius's words as true might be a justifiable or understandable position, but it is only reasonable on the basis of her having learned to mistrust him, given that she had *earlier* taken his words as true when they *turned out* to be false, a lie on whose basis Lysander labels Demetrius a "spotted and inconstant man." So it is not *simply* a refusal to believe Demetrius when he speaks the words Helena longs to hear; the issue for her is not believing Demetrius's words, but believing them *again*, and after the specter of their potential insincerity is already manifest. At issue is her ability to return to a position from which she can accept his words of love as true; and if she initially took them as true out of a naïve faith in their absolute sincerity, she will undertake their truth a second time in full knowledge of their potential insincerity. Going on in the face of imperfect vehicles of love is dramatized in this play—to no less a degree than in any remarriage comedy.
6. This claim depends upon the edition that one is reading. My own copy of the complete works (see Chapter 3 references, pg. 86) notes that "an unusual quantity and kind of mislineation in the first edition has persuaded most scholars that the text at the beginning of 5.1 was revised, with new material written in the margins" (423). In this case, Egeus is assigned the lines that, in other versions, are spoken by Philostrate. But the effect is much the same: if Egeus has these lines, he is reduced from a would-be god to a buffoonish emcee.
7. While I leave these to the side for now, I will address several such complaints in the following chapter.

REFERENCES

Beckwith, Sarah. *Shakespeare and the Grammar of Forgiveness*. Ithaca, NY: Cornell University Press, 2011. Print.
Benston, Alice N. "Portia, the Law, and the Tripartite Structure of the Merchant of Venice." *Shakespeare Quarterly* 30.3 (1979): 367–385. Print.
Cavell, Stanley. *Disowning Knowledge in Seven Plays of Shakespeare*. London; New York: Cambridge University Press, 2003. Print.
———. "Knowing and Acknowledging." *The Cavell Reader*. Ed. Stephen Mulhall. Malden, MA: Wiley-Blackwell, 1996. Print.
———. *Little Did I Know: Excerpts from Memory*. Stanford, CA: Stanford University Press, 2010. Print.

———. *The Claim of Reason*. New York: Oxford University Press, 1979. Print.

———. *This New Yet Unapproachable America: Lectures After Emerson After Wittgenstein*. Chicago: University of Chicago Press, 2013. Print.

Dreyfus, Hubert L. "Overcoming the Myth of the Mental: How Philosophers Can Profit from the Phenomenology of Everyday Expertise." *Proceedings and Addresses of the American Philosophical Association* 79.2 (2005): 47–65.

———. *What Computers Still Can't Do: A Critique of Artificial Reason*. Cambridge, MA: MIT Press, 1992. Print.

Dreyfus, Hubert, and Sean Dorrance Kelly. *All Things Shining: Reading the Western Classics to Find Meaning in a Secular Age*. New York: Free Press, 2011. Print.

Dumm, Thomas L. "The Dead, the Human Animal, and the Executable Subject." *Who Deserves to Die? Constructing the Executable Subject*. Ed. Austin Sarat and Karl Shoemaker. Amherst: University of Massachussetts Press, 2011. Print.

Eagleton, Terry. *After Theory*. London; New York: Penguin Books, 2004. Print.

Emerson, Ralph Waldo. *Self-Reliance, and Other Essays*. Mineola, NY.: Courier Dover Publications, 1993. Print.

Grady, Hugh. "Shakespeare and Impure Aesthetics: The Case of *A Midsummer Night's Dream*." *Shakespeare Quarterly* 59.3 (2008): 274–302.

Guilhamet, Leon. "A Midsummer-Night's Dream as the Imitation of an Action." *Studies in English Literature, 1500–1900* 15.2 (1975): 257–271.

Hunt, Maurice. "Individuation in 'A Midsummer Night's Dream.'" *South Central Review* 3.2 (1986): 1–13. Print.

Lee, Randy. "Who's Afraid of William Shakespeare: Confronting Our Concepts of Justice and Mercy in *The Merchant of Venice*." *University of Dayton Law Review* 32 (2006): 1. Print.

Liebler, Naomi Conn. *Shakespeare's Festive Tragedy: The Ritual Foundations of Genre*. London: Routledge, 1995. Print.

MacKay, Maxine. "*The Merchant of Venice*: A Reflection of the Early Conflict Between Courts of Law and Courts of Equity." *Shakespeare Quarterly* 15.4 (1964): 371–375. Print.

Marshall, David. "Exchanging Visions: Reading A Midsummer Night's Dream." *ELH* 49.3 (1982): 543–575.

Moffatt, Laurel. "The Woods as Heterotopia in a Midsummer Night's Dream." *Studia Neophilologica* 76.2 (2004): 182–187. Print.

Oatley, Keith. "Shakespeare's Invention of Theater as Simulation That Runs on Minds." *Empirical Studies of the Arts* 19 (2001): 27–46. Print.

———. "Simulation of Substance and Shadow: Inner Emotions and Outer Behavior in Shakespeare's Psychology of Character." *College Literature* 33.1 (2006): 15–33.

Sharafi, Mitra. *Law and Identity in Colonial South Asia Parsi Legal Culture, 1772–1947*. New York: Cambridge University Press, 2014. Print.

Waddington, Raymond B. "Blind Gods: Fortune, Justice, and Cupid in *The Merchant of Venice*." *ELH* 44.3 (1977): 458–477. Print.

Willson, Michael Jay. "View of Justice in Shakespeare's *The Merchant of Venice* and *Measure for Measure*." *Notre Dame Law Review* 70 (1994): 695. Print.

5   As You Like It

The way in which Cavell relates Emerson's finding as founding to Wittgenstein's and Heidegger's conceptualization of thinking as being on one's way or knowing how to go on strikes me as crucial to reappraising *As You Like It* as well, and not mainly because of the ways in which the many banishments, exiles, and escapes enacted or referenced in the play's opening Acts might be taken as figurations of such existential sojourning. Rather, bearing in mind the notion of finding as founding in attending to the ways in which knowledge of oneself and others, the ways in which characters seek to remind or teach others of one or another's place in the world—even to the point of violent insistence—and the ways in which such knowledge and placings come about over the course of the play's action, significantly disrupts several standard readings of *As You Like It* and reanimates live and fruitful tensions that emerge in the play.

When I speak of disrupting standard ways of approaching the play and comedy in general, I have in mind the sort of claims I referenced at the end of the previous chapter, claims that what we witness in the reconciliations of comedies cannot be *real* happiness. In addressing this issue more directly, it will be necessary to refer to the ways in which Northrop Frye's "green world" interpretation of Shakespearean comedy (Frye, "The Argument of Comedy") became an influential touchstone for the criticism and theory of the comedies generally, including C. L. Barber's location of a similar "saturnalian pattern" therein (Barber, *Shakespeare's Festive Comedy;* Frye, Grande, and Sherbert, *Northrop Frye's Writings on Shakespeare and the Renaissance,* xxix). Both of these patterns center on comedic resolutions as consisting in the "social integration" achieved in a retreat from and a return to what Frye called a "normal world." This will provide some context in which to consider the ways in which this particular way of examining the comedies came under fire from later critics, who were scrupulously careful to point out that the "social integration" of the comedies was often predicated upon various problematic exclusions.

I note below one particular iteration of this latter critical thread in citing examinations of the gendered power dynamics whose effects are effaced in such utopian readings as Frye's (Stirm, "'For Solace a Twinne-like Sister'"; Erickson, "Sexual Politics and the Social Structure in 'As You like

It.'"; Tvordi, "Female Alliance and the Construction of Homoeroticism in *As You Like It* and *Twelfth Night*"; Montrose, "'Shaping Fantasies'"). The point asserted in such critical responses is precisely that "social integration" comes with, and indeed depends upon, ignoring certain collateral damage, so to speak: if it is the context of happiness, then that happiness must be understood as profoundly mixed. By juxtaposing views pertaining to the relative success of the "social integration" that seems to resolve the comedies, I point out merely that the *height* of the standard for such happiness or integration is a height that Frye and his critics seem to share alike.

The complaints against Frye from later critics—which are hardly limited to scholars interested particularly in issues of gender—seize upon the places in which Frye describes the formation of a "new social unit," a formation that, first, is simultaneous and coextensive with "the moment of the comic resolution," and that, second, is constituted in "all the right-thinking people in the play com[ing] over to" the romantic hero's side (Frye, Grande, and Sherbert 103). Frye contrasts such "right-thinking" people to the "humorous" characters in the plays—humorous in the sense of imbalanced volatility rather than being funny. "These are always people," Frye says, "who are in some kind of mental bondage, who are helplessly driven by ruling passions, neurotic compulsions, social rituals, and selfishness" (Frye, Grande, and Sherbert 5). The happiness of the play's conclusions, Frye points out, is ascribable to the inculcation of a "moral norm," which he says "is not morality but deliverance from moral bondage," a type of bondage that Frye also refers to as "a lack of self-knowledge" (Frye, Grande, and Sherbert 176).[1] In gesturing to the sweeping influence of Frye's approach to Shakespeare, one might note echoes of the above approach in Henze's references to "social peace" and "social harmony" afforded by freeing Claudio in *Much Ado* from his own form of moral bondage, that is, his ignoble suspicion. One might also, though differently, hear these echoes in Alpers's critique of *Lear's* "sight pattern," which is imagined to underscore the tragic hero's arrival at "moral insight."

Critics of Frye's middle-distance understanding of the patterns at work in the comedies generally point to the inherent fragility of, or exclusions occasioned by, the formation of this "new social unit," as well to the clean divide presupposed between "right-thinking" and "humorous" characters, particularly where this divide is couched in the diametrically opposed terms of a freedom found in "self-knowledge" and the "mental bondage" suffered by those whose "ruling passions, neurotic compulsions," etc. confine them to "a predictable self-imposed pattern of behavior." Louis Montrose, writing on *A Midsummer Night's Dream*, points to the problems with both aspects of Frye's position at once, noting, against Romantic notions of a "harmonious" social situation resolving the play, that

> the harmonious marital unions of *A Midsummer Night's Dream* are in harmony with doctrines of Tudor apologists for the patriarchal

family: marital union implies a domestic hierarchy; marital harmony is predicated upon the wife's obedience to her husband.

(Montrose 61)

Montrose makes clear that Frye's "new social unit" can hardly be thought as a utopian or egalitarian paradise, since differential inflections of power filter or determine one's belonging to this unit. Montrose also observes that, therefore, no freedom/bondage dichotomy can hold: the "right-thinking" and therefore "free" characters are equally enslaved, if not to their "neurotic compulsions," then to what Montrose aptly calls "a socio-historical construction of sexual identity, difference and relationship; [and] an appropriation of human anatomical and physiological features by an ideological discourse" (Montrose 62).

Succinctly, then, and in a single source, Montrose represents two muscular responses to Frye's interpretive approach: the happiness at the end of the comedies can only appear as happiness from a patriarchal point of view, and to the extent that the end *does* appear happy, this very fact troubles the relations linking happiness, freedom, and self-knowledge. On Montrose's view (as on the view of Žižek, Marx, and Althusser), self-knowledge is imagined as a corrective to the false consciousness of ideology: it is knowledge of one's chains.

In raising these criticisms of Frye, I note once more a certain resemblance to the ways in which evocritics such as Oatley respond to post-structuralists, namely, by retaining or conserving the *terms* of those to whom they object while simultaneously inverting those terms. Without questioning the centrality of the relations among freedom, happiness, and self-knowledge, Montrose simply asserts that Frye has gotten them backwards, as it were. In contrast to Frye's view that the happiness attending the "social integration" is caused or afforded by the (individual, internal) freedom that follows from true self-knowledge, Montrose points out that any happiness enjoyed in "social integration" requires one's public enslavement to a governing ideology. If the resulting bondage looks like happiness to the characters or to the audience, this is precisely due to a *lack* of self-knowledge. But, as with the Oatley case, it is not clear that merely reversing the relations among the key terms of another approach will adequately address the disquietudes that arise and resolve in any particular play, the disquietudes that seem to compel precisely these terms.

Both Frye's and Montrose's views might be said to make use of the same chimerical standard of happiness that I noted in the case of *Dream*; that is to say, if the plausibility of Frye's sense of the happiness at the conclusions of the comedies requires omitting or ignoring any and all forms of structural (as opposed to personal or moral) inequality, then the plausibility of Montrose's standard of happiness requires the denial that anyone has ever known or experienced happiness, or indeed, that anyone knows what happiness is. It may even be possible to argue that the genuine "happiness" Montrose has in mind is (therefore) an incoherent notion, seeming to require conditions that human beings have never yet experienced.

My (counter)argument with respect to *Dream* presented in the conclusion of Chapter 4 simply amounts to asserting that (a) we do know what happiness is, (b) the play's conclusion provides an example thereof, and (c) the happiness or resolution we witness on the stage *need* not be understood as either unclouded by denials and exclusions or, at the other extreme, necessarily *unhappy* because of such imperfections. Quite the contrary: Hermia's happiness is one that includes a complete severance from her father—"includes" a severance, that is, rather than either occurring "despite" or "because of" this rupture. Helena's joy lies in Demetrius's returning to her, which need not be imagined as achieving happiness *in spite of* having, for a time, lost him.

Being held captive by an ideal of *perfect*, otherworldly social harmony, it is easy to see Frye's work unwarrantedly or hastily celebrating the consummation of that ideal, whereas Montrose's work seems to rain, as it were, on all possible parades. If a play's end satisfies, however—that is, if it is found to be gratifying or apt, a fit ending for this chapter of our characters' lives—then imagining some *other* sort of happiness with which to compare it, a more perfect one, whatever that might mean, becomes neither merely gratuitous nor merely ungracious (though it is both of these, also), but in fact counterproductive, harmful. It, too, is a moment of repudiation, and it critically incapacitates us. (*PI* §107: "We have got onto slippery ice where there is no friction, and so, in a certain sense, conditions are ideal; but also, just because of that, we are unable to walk. We want to walk: so we need *friction*. Back to the rough ground!")

In approaching the reading of *As You Like It* from the opening movements of this discussion, I circle back to Cavell's use of Emerson's finding as founding. In the foreword to a recent edition of Frye's *A Natural Perspective*, Cavell both acknowledges Frye's proclivity for thinking of literary works in terms of patterns or systems and credits Frye with the agility to avoid rigidity in this regard, contrary to the direction in which Frye's own words sometimes point. What Cavell attempts to draw out in Frye is the point of affinity between them: Cavell says of Frye "that you do not know a priori which terms are to do the theoretical work in his prose, as if nothing short of the powers of each word in the language is sufficient to understand the powers of language" (Cavell and Frye, xiv). Far from being *merely* a middle-distance student of patterns, then, Frye appears in Cavell's depiction as someone responsive to the "handsome" elements of a given work, and someone whose critical interpretations must also be approached in a similar, handsome manner. Where Frye's work is theoretical, on Cavell's account, the theoretical elements are discovered along the way of reading a work; they are found rather than provided at the outset, from the outside or, as it were, transcendentally.[2]

Whether this is an accurate characterization of Frye is beside the point; it is certainly an accurate and succinct statement of a Cavellian mode of reading, and that is what I am concerned to bring out. On the same page, Cavell might as well be describing his own critical endeavor in speaking of "Frye's way"

> of facing theory and practice with each other, letting the work under theoretical questioning provide the terms of its questioning, as if confessing from the beginning that the theory or science of the literary that he wants—which turns out to be as inclusive of a science of whatever may be called writing as such ... is a further work within the world of writing, a contribution that may modify the gravitational field it occupies, but which claims no perspective on that world that depends on a fantasy of freedom from its force.
> (Cavell and Frye xiv)

Contrary to Cavell's sense of things, in fairness, Frye's contributions to a general theory of comedy, in which "right-thinking" characters are free while the "humorous" characters suffer a "kind of mental bondage," certainly *do* seem to depend on what Cavell calls "a fantasy of freedom" from the particular conditions of any particular play. That is, these contributions do seem to posit and require that such things as self-knowledge, freedom, and happiness are terms available externally, or are transcendent ideals that characters might be judged to instantiate or to fail to embody. Montrose's criticism of Frye is similarly reliant on this fantasy of freedom from our words and expressions, but from the opposite direction: because we do have an (as yet historically unrealized) ideal of freedom, self-knowledge, and happiness, we can say definitively that Shakespearean characters fail to measure up to or embody it.

In his commentary on Frye, Cavell makes note of Frye's resistance to viewing Shakespeare as the conveyor of a moral message, of any truth about life. Frye contrasts his own "middle-distance" view to a moralistic one when speaking of Falstaff: "The word coward implies a moral judgment, and whether we apply it to Falstaff or not depends on whether we accept the heroic code as a value, instead of simply a dramatic postulate" (Frye, *A Natural Perspective* 41). For Frye it is beside the point whether or not Shakespeare desired his art to communicate anything about cowardice: "It is an offense against his privacy much deeper than any digging up of his bones to reduce him from a poet writing plays to an ego with something to 'say'" (Frye, *A Natural Perspective* 43). Cavell's reading of Frye's comment agrees with the basic tenet of Frye's claim, namely, that no play can be simply considered an occult medium interposed between the minds of playwright and audience.

For Cavell, however, it is a misreading, or a misunderstanding, of Frye to take his injunction to mean that learning anything from the plays or their characters is off limits. Cavell equates such a "mistaking" of Frye in terms of having "forgotten how to listen"; he takes Frye's reference to Shakespeare's bones as recalling Antony's famous lines in *Julius Caesar*, "thus remarking on our ingratitude as well as our tendency to magic thinking, identifying what is good or bad for us with relics. But whom do we appoint to teach us differences?" (Cavell and Frye xiii). Cavell's commentary on ingratitude and magic thinking further recalls his characterization of another kind of structuralist thinking as failing in the task of acknowledgment, as failing specifically to see education "not only [as] an acquirement but a bequest," which makes us "stingy in what we attempt to inherit." One need not deny Frye's claim about the intentional fallacy in order to argue that one's gratitude toward Shakespeare's comedies, inheriting them as a bequest, is expressed in learning, say by arriving at self-knowledge, a means of placing ourselves in a world, discovering how to go on with what we are given.

In a passage that Cavell allows to go by without comment, Frye continues on from his above discussion about "whether we accept the heroic code [with respect to Falstaff] as a value, instead of as a dramatic postulate," an argument that is clearly arrayed against the intentional fallacy:

> Naturally we prefer to say it is not we but Shakespeare who accepts or rejects the value. A tough-minded critic will insist that Shakespeare did accept it and that Falstaff is a coward; a tender-minded one will insist that he did not accept it and that he made Falstaff into an ironic hero. One approach turns Shakespeare into a stupid snob; the other turns him into a dishonest snob. When we reach a conclusion like that it is clearly time to retrace our steps.
>
> (Frye, *A Natural Perspective* 41)

The displacement of our learning onto Shakespeare's authorial intention, as Frye figures it above, wherein whether or not Falstaff is a coward is imagined to depend upon whether or not Shakespeare accepted "the heroic code," is a repudiation of *our* learning, as I would like to emphasize it—or in other words, a deflection of the difficulties *we* face in going on with or from "the heroic code" as it appears in *Henry IV, Part 1*. But the notion that cowardice as Falstaff embodies it, whether earnestly or ironically, is not an available subject for literary scholars or critical attention is another sort of repudiation, a rejection of our *learning*, a rejection of the capacity of the words and actions of others to be exemplary at all, to be capable of showing what kind of a thing *cowardice* is (for, in a Wittgensteinian phrase, even if one claims that Falstaff's antics are not cowardice, it is still "cowardice" that they are *not*).

This is a useless dichotomy. One side seems to deny that *we* are implicated in declarations of values or codes—it denies that the plays bear upon *us*—and the other side seems to deny that we can be said to learn anything *from*, as opposed to *about*, the plays. But the major purpose of this book is to demonstrate that there remains available a critical practice that amounts to taking on *our learning*, that is, one that simultaneously acknowledges that it is ourselves upon whom literary art bears and that this bearing-upon can be characterized in educative terms, which I have elsewhere cast under the heading of exemplarity.

All of this brings me to the point of being able to say clearly what I want to say with respect to a Cavell-inflected undertaking of *As You Like It* and its disruptions. Although this play would seem to be the very paragon of Frye's "green world" comedy, rigorous critical attention to the drama will show that no clear moral distinction between "right-thinking" or "humorous" characters is immediately available to the characters *in* the play, especially in the opening Acts. While there are numerous references to the previous "golden age" from which *As You Like It*'s world is apparently fallen, it is hardly simply given that such a golden world is recoverable or achievable. On the contrary, in the action of the play itself, it is not even entered as a possibility. Orlando's natural virtue, as Oliver describes it, is a pure liability; so much so that it takes Adam's interventions to convince Orlando to flee rather than simply to surrender to his brother's murderous plot. Orlando's total alienation, his otherness or nonbelonging in the world, is expressed in this unappetizing choice, and nowhere is any transvaluation of the world's values expressed as an option. However "right-thinking" he may turn out to be, Orlando is plainly ready to die at his brother's hand in the first scene of the play.

Similarly, when the Duke Frederick banishes Rosalind, his justifications to Celia take the form of attempts to teach her specifically that Rosalind's own virtues outshine hers and that, as a result, Celia is "misprized." When Celia protests that such things are unimportant to her, Duke Frederick twice declares her a "fool." It is a fallen world on which the curtain rises, and whether to internalize the fallen values to which it adheres or whether to disassociate oneself entirely from that world are the only two paths that present themselves to the characters. Frederick attempts to instruct his daughter in the ways of the world; it is by no means the case that these attempts at teaching her, at making the world as he sees it intelligible to her, come from anything more nefarious than feelings of legitimate fatherly concern. What "right-thinking" means within the context of the play, and whatever the "humorousness" with which it can be contrasted, is therefore precisely the bone of contention throughout the progress of the comedy. Therefore, it is something to be discovered along the way rather than simply known at the outset. Ingratitude and magic thinking also arise in *As You Like It*, but the central struggle in the comedy, a struggle whose conclusion is by no means foregone, is voiced in Cavell's allusion to *King Lear:* "Whom do we appoint to teach us differences?" With whom do we recognize ourselves to belong? From whom do we find ourselves willing to learn?

5.1 TEACHING DIFFERENCES AND THE STAKES OF *AS YOU LIKE IT*

Contrary to how Frye reads the comedies in general, then, and also to how Bloom, highly conventionally, sees *As You Like It* as a play in which "no authentic harm can come to anyone" (Bloom 206), it is important to bring out the sense of groundlessness that opens this play, the open and unsettled possibilities that stretch out before the characters. Charles the wrestler notes that the exiled Duke and his followers are fled to the forest of Ardenne,[3] "where they live like the old Robin Hood of England. They say many young gentlemen flock to him every day, and fleet the time carelessly, as they did in the golden world" (1.1.112–114). While Charles's location of the "golden world" in a time and space remote from the action of the play fits with Frye's "green world" pattern, we hardly need to wait for the wrestler's explicit reference in order to see both the fact and the consequences of the "normal world's" corruption. Orlando and Adam's first encounter with Oliver is perfectly sufficient to that task.

The fallenness of the world, as I will continue to call it, makes itself visible in two particular ways in the play's opening scene, namely, the failures of citations to (what are imagined to be) foundational elements of social belonging to effect the world's intelligibility, and the resulting violent attempts to impose a particular sort of intelligibility upon another character. The several references to knowledge and self-knowledge are particularly striking in this regard.

Orlando's "sadness," which he voices to Adam in the play's initial lines, proceeds from the fact that Oliver is reprehensibly depriving him of "the place of a brother" (1.1.18) by "keep[ing him] rustically at home" (1.1.5–6). In his complaint, Orlando contrasts his state with a more appropriate "keeping for a gentleman of my birth" (1.1.7–8). Within the play's first 20 lines, Orlando references traditional expectations afforded on the basis of brotherhood and birth, conventions that he believes ought to be *selbstverständlich*, a matter of course. That he must thus complain, and that his own state appears out of joint with these conventions, indicates well before Charles the wrestler enters the scene that the backgrounds undergirding the world's intelligibility have lost their use or are now impotent to render their proper effects.

In Orlando's confrontation with Oliver in the same scene, the sense of groundlessness, the emptiness of appeal—or the absence quite generally of anything meaningful to which to appeal—is only heightened. Orlando calls upon Oliver to recognize Orlando's own deserving in light of "the courtesy of nations," the "tradition" (1.1.43–45) that entitles, or ought to entitle, Orlando to better "keeping" than Oliver has heretofore provided his younger brother. Oliver, too, recognizes and appeals to precisely the same "tradition" in demanding Orlando's unquestioning obedience: "Know you where you are, sir?" Oliver asks Orlando; "Know you before whom?" (1.1.38–40). Adam, as well, in two later lines, attempts to quell the discord that arises between the brothers by summoning similar powers accorded to recollections: "Sweet masters, be patient. For your father's remembrance, be at accord" (1.1.59–60). Speaking once more of this departed father, Sir Rowland, and this time in an effort at comparison intended to make Oliver feel the appropriate guilt over Oliver's spurning of his servant, Adam says, "God be with my old master, he would not have spoke such a word" (1.1.80).

Each of the three characters in this scene recognizes the foundational importance that a certain codified tradition of primogeniture and bloodline is meant to provide; each of the characters in the dispute presented in this scene appeals specifically to the memory of the paterfamilias, Sir Rowland, in demanding others' *recognition* of proper place and action; and each of these appeals fails to effect the recognition it is imagined to ensure. It is on the basis of Sir Rowland's lineage that Orlando mounts his complaint against Oliver; it is on the basis of his status as the eldest that Oliver claims complete discretionary authority over both Orlando and Adam. Orlando's initial raising of his complaint is meant as a reminder for Oliver, an attempt to recall Oliver to the observation of his duties. Oliver's catechisms in response—"Know you where you are, sir?"—are equally offered in the spirit of reminding Orlando that it is not for him to raise such complaints at all. That it shares the form of Oberon's initial catechizing of Titania—"Am not I thy lord?"—ought to be lost on no one. In this case, as in *Dream*, the rhetorical question is entered as a refusal of Orlando's (legal) standing, a refusal of the sort of relation in which Orlando might offer to remind or teach Oliver at all.

Having found the traditional machinery of birthright incapable of the sorts of behavioral or attitudinal output that such machinery is called upon to produce in this instance, Orlando and Oliver each attempt to compel the other's recognition by means of violence. Oliver responds to Orlando's assertion that although "the courtesy of nations allows you my better ... the same tradition takes not away my blood. ... I have as much of my father in me as you" (1.1.43–146) by, in the words of the stage directions, "assailing" him. When Orlando fights back, seizing Oliver by the throat, Oliver interprets Orlando's use of violence as insurrection, saying, "Wilt thou lay hands on me, villain?" Orlando once more endeavors to make their equality in blood clear to Oliver, the sense in which, by slandering Orlando verbally and by failing to provide properly for his education, Oliver, in the second person, "hast railed on thyself" (1.1.58). When this attempt meets with no more success than any previous one, Orlando maintains his hold upon Oliver's throat, and, in refusing to release him, says, "I will not [release you] till I please. You shall hear me" (1.1.62). For the third time in the scene, Orlando then recounts to Oliver the ways in which Oliver has failed in his duties as an older brother with respect to Orlando, repeats his own sense of himself as his father's son, and demands the rectification of Oliver's wrongs. Under duress, at this point, Oliver seems to concede, saying, "You shall have some part of your will" (1.1.73), after which, of course, with Orlando gone from the room, Oliver begins plotting his murder.

I recite the dynamics of the opening scene in detail mainly to bring out the strategies for mutual intelligibility that the characters enact, the ways in which these strategies fail, and the sort of helplessness that attends this type of failure. Understanding Oliver and Orlando, with Adam's voice also in the background, as holding two radically different visions of Oliver's position with respect to Orlando; and understanding each as attempting to articulate this vision to the other, such that the other will act or comport himself properly in light of the vision that each means the other to share, underscores the bottomlessness of the abyss when mutual intelligibility is in fact denied.

I have said much earlier that when agreement in form of life gives out or is found wanting, nothing *else* can reengage one with the world or link one meaningfully with others. As *You Like It*'s opening scene provides as full a presentation of this problem as might any tragedy: first, the refusal or denial of the articulation of a given vision via the assembly of reminders (of lineage and custom, in this case); then an attempt at circumventing the necessity of another's willing acceptance through violence (or through the invocation of the law, as in *Dream*, or with a bribe, as in *Lear*). The result of this twofold movement is nothing like mutual intelligibility; it is actually the opposite, precluding the possibility of mutuality, period. Oliver's refusal of his brother's claim upon him will lead, as is the case with other, similar failures in this and other plays, to attempted murder, banishment, and exile.

A failed attempt at mutual intelligibility, one that takes the specific form of one family member somehow denying the claims made upon them by another, also opens the tragedy of *King Lear*, as has already been discussed. Indeed, the movement of repudiation, and the various methods of attempting to circumvent it not only open *Lear* and *As You Like It*, but also *A Midsummer Night's Dream*. While Cavell locates *King Lear*'s driving force in the protagonist's attempts to avoid detection or the shame of exposure, and while Frye's "Argument of Comedy" finds the successes of the comedies in the "right-thinking characters'" ability to shake off or recover from the "mental bondage" that attends the more "humorous" characters' "lack of self-knowledge," neither of these dynamics adequately describes the way in which the familial confrontation in *As You Like It*'s opening scene—a confrontation doubled, re-doubled, and repeated in other contexts and families over the course of the next Act as well—establishes the conditions of its own resolution later in the play. In particular, because my analysis hews more to the subject matter of Frye's and requires little of the sort of pathology-analysis in which terms Cavell takes up *Lear*'s action, I wish to distinguish once more, or at least in a new key, the notion of education, or teaching and learning, that I see at work in the comedies from that which is implied in Frye's vocabulary of freedom and arrival at "self-knowledge."

The danger aroused in Frye's vocabulary is precisely of the variety that later critics of structuralism would seize upon; indeed, it is a danger that has arisen several times over the course of this investigation. Putting it simply, the vocabulary of freedom and the arrival at self-knowledge presuppose a highly problematic (metaphysical) notion of the true, the right, and the good from which characters are to one degree or another alienated throughout most of the action of the play, but to which they eventually return or with which they eventually align themselves. Montrose's critique of this view's inherent conservatism represents one line of attack on Frye's basic tenets. And as we have seen, this type of critique successfully challenges the certainty or solidity of the metaphysical foundation, the notion of the *inherent* goodness or rightness, say the naturalness, of the patriarchal social relations valorized in the wedding scenes at the conclusions of comedies, which Montrose rightly casts instead as "Tudor ... ideological discourses": Montrose's point is well-made, as far as it goes.

But because such a line of attack shares a general metaphysical picture with Frye—that is, one on which any actual joy at the play's conclusion requires a chronically absent or recalcitrant *true* foundation—it follows that any apparent happiness in the closing scenes is but *mere* appearance, a sham happiness. This mode of taking issue with Frye's account rightly denies that characters can be imagined to have accessed some sort of natural axis of truth and value, but in making the denial, it wrongly denies the reality of the endings' happiness.

With Frye and Montrose reestablished in the background, it will be helpful to return to the microcosmic case of Orlando and Oliver's confrontation in the opening scene of *As You Like It* as a means of raising a defactoist middle-way means of understanding the matter. Each character—and Adam as well—attempts to appeal to a shared ground or foundation in order to compel the other character(s) to see matters properly. It cannot be the case that there *is* no foundation, or that the foundation to which they appeal turns out to be illusory or merely ideological, as critics of Montrose's bent would suggest: Sir Rowland du Bois haunts the scene from start to finish as foundational progenitor and legacy-leaver, and, moreover, as the foundational progenitor acknowledged as such by all disputants. The "custom of nations," this "tradition" of primogeniture, also provides an agreed-upon source of authority for them. That these customs, embodied in the ghostly presence of Sir Rowland, are just the kind of things that dictate the terms of the fraternal relation between Orlando and Oliver is taken for granted by the pair of brothers.

The problem that the pair confronts is precisely an instance of Fogelin's paradox of interpretation: that which is supposed to ensure or guarantee a particular action in a particular circumstance turns out to require some sort of further disambiguation—a judgment, an interpretation. The tradition of primogeniture, as Orlando appeals to it, requires morally of Oliver that the elder provide for the education of the younger; but the same tradition entitles Oliver to complete autonomy in the disposal of Sir Rowland's estate, including the handling and raising of any younger siblings. Orlando in fact allows that the tradition plainly values Oliver as his "better." Having assumed the head-of-household role in his father's stead, Oliver may, like Egeus as discussed in Chapter 4, dispose of Orlando howsoever he wishes; that is his power. Orlando might point to the proper duties attending such a position, but whether Orlando is ready for gentlemanly education would be a matter for Oliver, not Orlando, to judge.

Whether or not the foundational grounds of patrilineal traditions of property are themselves either natural or ideological is thus not the issue at hand: the problem that Orlando and Oliver encounter in the opening scene is that the ground that they both acknowledge *as* a ground seems incapable of *performing* the sort of determination that each character expects of such a foundation. Put more directly, Oliver is capable in principle of appealing to precisely the same tradition as Orlando, but with the opposite effect of denying his younger brother his education, just as he has been doing all along.

Laid out in this fashion, it is plain to see that whatever "self-knowledge" Oliver will have to achieve, in Frye's terms—assuming that he is the one operating under conditions of "mental bondage" at the play's opening—cannot be imagined as information about himself that he *lacks* at the play's opening. He will need to come to occupy the correct position of an eldest brother and take up the appropriate relation to his younger sibling; but it is precisely his status as eldest brother and inheritor of Sir Rowland's position that allows him dominion over Orlando, and it is in light of precisely this status that Orlando's claims upon him can take the form of a rebellion against nature. "Self-knowledge" cannot, therefore, take the form of uncovering new facts about patrilineal descent, the mutual obligations between brothers, or anything of the kind. Oliver knows all of this already. The problem is that this public foundation of the "custom of nations" proves insufficient to remove doubts with respect to the proper treatment of a brother by each; the problem is that this foundation fails to *found*.

For just this reason, Montrose's brand of critique also misses the mark. If the "doctrines" that establish hierarchies in the manner of "the custom of nations" are false, sociohistorically contingent, or the like, it is not in virtue of their *falsity* or *contingency* that they fail to effect the results they are imagined to entail: any *true* or simply *different* doctrines that Montrose might want to substitute would run into the same problem. Because Orlando and Oliver essentially interpret the tradition differently—Orlando justifying his rebellion and eventual violence on the basis of his brother's failure to honor his traditional obligations as the eldest, and Oliver taking Orlando's claims upon him as an insurrection against the social hierarchy imposed by the same tradition—it is not the specific tradition that is to blame, and so any eventual happiness that the characters find cannot be conceived as an endorsement of such a tradition, as opposed to a victory for the characters. The difficulty in the first scene, once more, is that the foundation upon which each of the principals relies fails to *found*.

In this way, the metaphysical verificationism presumed in Frye's view—where characters can be divided into the "right-thinking" and the "humorous," and where the action of the play traces a path from the "mental bondage" or "lack of self-knowledge" that manifests itself in rigid or dogmatic tradition—proves misleading insofar as it requires a specific and correct idea of "rightness" or "self" to precede and transcend the action of the play. While Montrose and similar critics successfully attack the notion that anything metaphysically "correct" or "right," not to say "natural," is revealed in a comedy's resolution, demonstrating instead that any such correctness or naturalness is merely the effect of re-inscribing contingent hierarchies of gendered power-relations, this line of criticism is equally misleading, as it remains focused on the relative correctness of a certain foundational ideology, thereby taking up the assumption that the *correctness* of said ideology is primarily at issue. If this is not the case, if the foremost issue revealed in the opening scene of *As You Like It* has to do with the inability of *any* foundational ideology or discourse to straightforwardly entail specific responses to particular facts, then what arriving at "self-knowledge" *means* will be altogether different from the discovery of facts about oneself or about a foundational social arrangement. In order to parse this issue, a defactoist practice that emphasizes the importance of attending to the words that characters speak will be required.

In addressing the "self-knowledge" at issue in *As You Like It,* the opening scene once again sets the tone. Orlando confronts Oliver with the facts that (1) Oliver is the eldest son of Sir Rowland, (2) Orlando is also Sir Rowland's son, (3) the "tradition" dictates that Oliver is Orlando's "better," in that his "coming before [Orlando] is nearer to [Sir Rowland's] reverence" (1.1.48), and (4) Sir Rowland's will has bound Oliver "to give [Orlando] good education" (1.1.63). None of this is imaginable as news to Oliver, as a factual discovery. In particular, Oliver's poor treatment of Orlando is precisely afforded by all of these facts, especially those pertaining to the order of succession.

So what can Orlando mean in responding to Oliver's "Know you before whom, sir?" with his "Ay, better than him I am before knows me" (1.1.41)? To what extent does he take himself to be *unknown* to Oliver, and what knowledge of *himself* does he thereby express in the comparison? Again, this cannot refer to the sort of self-knowledge or knowledge of others implied in Frye's vocabulary. What is it about Orlando, then, that Oliver does not know, or does not know well enough? What sort of claim does Orlando enter here, and to what does it pertain?

Within the play's first 70 lines, Orlando contrasts the way in which Oliver provides for him and his "keeping" with what he calls an "education" befitting a "gentleman." In fact, Orlando insists upon his status as a "gentleman" on no fewer than three occasions within this confined space (1.1.8; 1.1.65; 1.1.68). He likewise insists three separate times that he finds his own education in this regard lacking, particularly when compared with that of his other brother, Jacques (1.1.5; 1.1.19; 1.1.64); and as the cause of his rebellion or "mutiny," he twice names the "spirit of [his] father," which he feels growing strong within him (1.1.21; 1.1.66). Orlando evidently means to reveal something of himself to Oliver as a corrective to what he feels is Oliver's insufficient knowledge of him, an insufficiency embodied in Oliver's failure to treat him properly.

But Oliver is ignorant of none of these facts, as his soliloquy at the end of the scene demonstrates:

> I hope I shall see an end of him, for my soul—yet I know not why—
> hates nothing more than he. Yet he is gentle; never schooled, and yet
> learned; full of noble device; of all sorts enchantingly beloved; and,

indeed, so much in the heart of the world, and especially of my own people, who best know him, that I am altogether misprized.

(1.1.155–161)

In light of this soliloquy, Oliver's knowledge of the very facts upon which Orlando insists may be seen as also justifying (to Oliver) Orlando's mistreatment: Oliver's withholding of "all gentleman-like qualities" from Orlando (1.1.65) is meant to effect a reversal of his own misprizing. The respect he takes himself to be owed is imagined as an effect of his own status as the first-born son: this is what he feels to be under threat from Orlando's unschooled "noble device." Oliver's mistreatment of Orlando is not due to the elder's ignorance about Orlando, and it therefore cannot be converted through supplying heretofore undiscovered facts.

For that very reason, it is important to see that the fraternal confrontation in the opening scene concerns most basically the collision of what I have called frames of relevance: the facts themselves are not in dispute. The collision manifests itself in competing claims levied by each to occupy a certain position with respect to the other, namely, a position from which each may teach the other, via reminders, of a knowledge that is idle rather than absent, an idleness that is apparent in the offending behavior or attitude of each. In this light, the confrontation pertains primarily to the "order of significance" in which these facts are to be understood. Oliver's "Know you where you are, sir?" is an expression of the primacy or absoluteness of his own power, bestowed by the inheritance of Sir Rowland's position. Orlando's counterclaim, that Oliver's expression evinces an ignorance about his brother, coupled with Orlando's insistence that "You shall hear me" (1.1.62), expresses in turn the primacy and potency of the obligations that attend Oliver's position, and it includes the (violent) attempt to compel Oliver's acknowledgment of this fact.

These claims must be understood as what Cavell calls "claims to community," which is "always a search for the basis upon which it can or has been established" (Cavell, *The Claim of Reason* 19), and which he further, in the same paragraph, equates with the "wish and search for reason." It is important, in this sense, that the play opens on Orlando's pleading his case to Adam, that is, publicly: his recounting his mistreatment first to Adam and then to Oliver is the attempt at finding a shared sense of the unreasonableness of Oliver's withholdings. When Oliver meets these attempts by demanding through his rhetorical questioning that Orlando share *his* sense of the unreasonableness of Orlando's "mutiny" against the tradition and order of birthright, what emerges is a straightforward dispute not over facts, but over the frame of relevance that will light up the facts.

Richard Eldridge notes that "such claims of reason are lodged as reminders and vehicles of reorientation—to and on the behalf of both others and oneself—when the applications of the concepts expressed by these words are somehow both dimly available and yet attenuated or disputed" (Eldridge, *Stanley Cavell* 6)

The notion of such claims as both "reminders and vehicles of reorientation" recalls the discussions in previous chapters of the places of teaching and learning in the finding or founding of something like "social integration." The futility of the face-to-face encounter, a construction of the situation in which each demands that the other expose himself as bound by a tradition in a particular way as a prerequisite to (re)establishing social harmony, recalls nothing so strongly as the disappointing fruitlessness of Beatrice and Benedick's colloquy at the altar. The form of the demand is unbearable to each, and the violence with which each brother in *As You Like It* attempts to foist a reorientation upon the other amounts, in these terms, to a denial of the other's "search for community," and thereby of community itself. Each brother attempts to teach the other through such claims of reason—to teach not facts about himself or the other, but about the nature of the world—and when these claims are denied, the proffered world goes dead.

That is, indeed, the sense of the fallenness of the world with which the play opens. But it would be a mistake to think of this fallen world as *simply* dead. While the failures of each brother in turn to win acknowledgment from the other do indeed show forth an inanimate or unanimated world, the attempts themselves reveal that the world's dormancy is both exceptional and reparable. Neither brother *expects* his reminder to fail; each offers a reminder in precisely the hope that it will succeed. This once more shows that the world, imagined in these terms, is perpetually findable (foundable), and indeed the many attempts in the first two Acts to compel or entice characters through various "vehicles of reorientation" to share a world or acknowledge a community speak to this fact. The many repudiations that occur in these very opening Acts, of which the strife between Oliver and Orlando is merely the first example, speak also to the difficulty of *acknowledging* anyone's capacity to "teach us differences."

Positioning *As You Like It*'s stakes, as they are exposed in the play's opening scene, within a larger context—wherein the life of the world is bound up with assertions and acceptances of reason and community—only underscores the centrality of the notion that *education* best characterizes the claims that one character makes on another in the interest of establishing a certain relation in terms of which the conversion or "reorientation" of the world becomes possible. In explicit and obvious contrast to the brothers' strife in the first scene, in which reason or the community is made to depend upon one or the other brother acquiescing to the superiority of the other's claim, Celia rebuts Rosalind's initial withdrawal or repudiation by asserting their sisterly relation as a first and unconditional fact.

Celia opens Act 1, scene 2, by pleading with Rosalind to "be merry." Rosalind, to be sure, has ample cause to be otherwise, due to the banishment of her father, the Duke Senior. She cites this very fact in refusing Celia's claim, or at least in making it conditional: protesting that she "already show[s] more mirth than [she] is mistress of," Rosalind rejects Celia's encouragement by saying, "Unless you could teach me to forget a banished father you must not learn me how to remember any extraordinary pleasure" (1.2. 2–6).

Celia begs Rosalind to join her in merriness; Rosalind's deflection of this plea points specifically to the dramatic difference between their states, a difference upon which Rosalind draws for the express purpose of maintaining the felt distance between them. Rosalind's "unless" clause points to the impossibility of overcoming this very distance: that Celia should "teach" Rosalind "to forget a banished father" is out of the question, and therefore so is any hope of "learn[ing] her to remember any extraordinary pleasure." Yet 14 lines later, in the same scene, Rosalind has rejoined Celia's company after all, saying "From henceforth I will [be merry], coz, and devise sports" (1.2.22). Celia's refusal to accept Rosalind's rejection of their closeness, of her attempt to effect a permanent distinction between them, seems miraculously to have achieved the impossible. Rosalind has established the conditions upon which it would be possible for Celia to "learn [her] how to remember any extraordinary pleasure." Celia does indeed teach her to remember such pleasures, and it is not at all obvious or clear that Rosalind's conditions have anything to do with the successful outcome of this exchange.

The magic of Celia's spell works by other means. Celia's immediate response to Rosalind's refusal avoids the issue of the banished Duke Senior entirely, and thus the reply does not pertain to any forgetting that Rosalind must yet undergo. Rather, it seems to gesture in an accusatory posture toward forgetting that Rosalind has already done: "Herein I see," Celia says, "thou lovest me not with the full weight that I love thee.

> If my uncle, thy banished father, had banished thy uncle, the Duke my father, so thou hadst been still with me I could have taught my love to take thy father for mine. So wouldst thou, if the truth of thy love to me were so righteously tempered as mine is to thee.
>
> (1.2.7–13)

Celia repudiates most directly Rosalind's attempt to drive a wedge between them—Rosalind has a banished father that she cannot forget, and Celia has her own father fully available to her—by reorienting the conversation to the fact of their mutual, sisterly love. In exposing herself as loving Rosalind with a "full weight" sufficient to "have taught [her] love to take [Rosalind's] father for [her own]," were their circumstances reversed, Celia omits the issue of the Duke Senior entirely: the issue at hand has only to do with the two of them, and the love they bear one another. What is learned in this scene, or what is found, is their own relationship *as* a sufficient ground for happiness. It does not require, as Rosalind initially posits, that any negative fact be effaced; it only requires the "vehicle of reorientation" visible in Celia's explicit claim on Rosalind's love, a claim voiced by extending her own love, unconditionally, in the ungrounded expectation of its reciprocation.

I have said that these lines offer a contrast with the brotherly exchange in the first scene. They also offer certain grounds of comparison, available mainly in Rosalind's appeal to a mediating factor or condition upon which the mutual merriment Celia requests is made to depend. Orlando and Oliver's claims upon one another are each entered in virtue of a more or less codified tradition, the "custom of nations," and in virtue of the particular patriarch from which their own bloodline flows, the specter of Sir Rowland that haunts the scene. The inability of this mediating component or condition to settle the dispute that arises, resulting in the resort to violence, demonstrates again one axis of the "paradox of interpretation," namely, that it is impossible for an inert (or literally, in this case, dead) foundation to determine the conditions of a live relationship in the way that both Orlando and Oliver seem to expect it to do.

The way in which Celia meets Rosalind's attempt at interposing such a condition by entering a claim merely on the basis of the "full weight" of her own love, thus circumventing Rosalind's third-man factor entirely, demonstrates the other axis of the "paradox of interpretation," namely, that no such satisfaction of mediating conditions is *necessary* to going on with appropriate and mutually fulfilling brotherly or sisterly relations. Celia's direct appeal, made on the basis of her own self-exposure as one whose love for Rosalind is "righteously tempered," simply reorients Rosalind's view of her state and the condition of her own happiness. Celia has indeed taught Rosalind something, and Rosalind has indeed adopted the position of the learner with respect to Celia, but it was not to "forget a banished father"; it was rather to remember the "full weight" of their mutual affection.

Stirm's analysis of the course of the play's action (Stirm, "'For Solace a Twinne-like Sister'") notes roughly the same contrast between scenes 1 and 2 of the first Act—the difference in the quality of the relationship that Celia and Rosalind evince from that of Orlando and Oliver—but she reads this contrast in terms of gendered socialization. On such a reading, the comic resolution at the end of the play occurs via, or is caused by, the men's sibling relationships becoming more "sisterly."[4] The key difference, for Stirm, is the gender of the sibling or sibling-like pairs.

> The play tests differing modes of brotherhood, proposing alternatives through the women's relationship, and juxtaposing these alternatives with the antagonistic fraternal relationships set up in Act 1 and maintained in Act 2. In these middle acts the women's sisterly relationship becomes most clearly a model for the men's.
>
> (Stirm 383)

I have no objection to the basic shape of this interpretation, mostly because the relationships and reconciliations between the pairs of brothers in the latter Acts of the play not only bear a striking resemblance to what passes between Rosalind and Celia in the opening Acts, but also because, thanks to Rosalind's disguised interventions over the course of the play, it is by no means difficult to attribute the transformations in fraternal relations ultimately to Rosalind. I do, however, wish to resist either naturalizing or socializing the relative harmony in sibling relationships along gendered lines, and I simply wish to leave the matter there to rest.

In the first place, as my own analysis of Rosalind and Celia's interaction at the opening of scene 2 makes clear, the "sisterliness" of their relationship does not initially preclude Rosalind from raising an obstruction to the pair's shared merriment, an obstruction that bears a remarkable resemblance, structurally speaking, to the obstacles on which Orlando's and Oliver's fraternity founders. It is therefore not the case that their relationship *just is* different from the men's in virtue of the gendered dynamics of their faux-sibling bond. That Celia can call Rosalind back into alignment with the "righteous temper" of her own love in the way that she does, and that Rosalind can be so called back, is theoretically available to the masculine characters as well, though neither Orlando nor Oliver attempts such a recalling.

In the second place, the evidence of the uniquely sisterly relationship that Stirm cites includes Celia's protestations to her father that

> We still have slept together,
> Rose at an instant, learned, played, eat together,
> And wheresoe'er we went, like Juno's swans
> Still we went coupled and inseparable.
>
> (1.3.72–75)

Stirm highlights the allusion to Juno's swans, which, for her, "emphasizes the importance of the women's similarities, which enable them to move forward effectively together" (Stirm 382). Celia's protestation, though, is strikingly close in both form and content to the plea that Helena makes to Hermia in *A Midsummer Night's Dream*:

> We, Hermia, like two artificial gods
> Have with our needles created both one flower,
> Both on one sampler, sitting on one cushion,
> Both warbling of one song, both in one key,
> As if our hands, our sides, voices, and minds
> Had been incorporate. So we grew together,
> Like to a double cherry: seeming parted,
> But yet an union in partition,
> Two lovely berries moulded on one stem.
>
> (3.2.204–212)

Helena offers this vignette in an effort to mend a (perceived) rupture in their sisterly relationship, just as Celia appeals to this sisterly bond in an attempt to preclude a pending and enforced rupture. However, none of the sisterliness that Helena cites in her speech has prevented their fierce competition, first for Demetrius and then (erroneously) for Lysander.

Given that Helena has in fact betrayed Hermia and Lysander to Demetrius already, in addition to suffering the distance from Hermia entailed in envying her "lodestar" eyes, the sisterly unity that she calls upon in Act 3 cannot be imagined as any sort of foundation from which proper action or proper duty logically follows. In point of fact, the hours the two have spent twinned in needlework, song, and other activities have already failed to effect the sort of loyalty or "moving forward effectively together" that Stirm imagines such sisterliness to involve by the time Helena calls upon Hermia to recall their sisterhood. Celia may describe to her father the tenor of her relation to Rosalind, and this description may be accurate, but it cannot be imagined to cause or *ensure* that the two will "move forward effectively together."

In addition to acknowledging the work that others have done in areas at least roughly similar to my own, I wish to cite Stirm's example here to once more highlight and pivot back to my own point: attempting to posit a theoretical or ideological framework according to which one might understand the play, of which Stirm's use of gender differences among sibling pairs in order to account for the movement from strife to concord in *As You Like It* is but one example, will fail to bear up under scrutiny. The sisterliness that Rosalind and Celia evince does not prevent Rosalind from attempting a skeptical sort of removal from the dyad, withholding her merriment from Celia until and unless Celia can achieve an impossible feat; and the twinned nature of a sisterly upbringing does not preclude the betrayals, rivalry, and jealousy that arise in *Dream*.

Once more, no such foundation is either capable of or necessary to any particular version of carrying on together, like cherries on a stem or Juno's swans. Celia and Helena, in their respective plays, give voice to nearly identical experiences of sisterly upbringing, but the degree of sisterly fealty that we encounter in each play is markedly different. This suggests again that such histories, like reminders thereof, like all inheritances, must be accepted or taken up in order to generate the effects they are thought simply to entail; and it is once more to suggest that this acceptance itself is always groundless.

In the early scenes of *As You Like It*, the same sorts of skeptical difficulties that plague the other comedies I have studied here arise to confound what Stirm calls the principal sibling pairs of the drama. Where the skeptical assumption is reified in the Orlando-Oliver interaction, and reconciliation or mutual satisfaction is made to depend upon a mediating fact or framework, the characters find themselves at an unbridgeable impasse. Where the skeptical assumption is deflated, where the demand for a mediating guarantor of felicity is simply sidestepped, and where a relational belonging is asserted as a first fact, Rosalind and Celia find themselves capable of going on together in mirth and good humor. Acknowledging one's belonging to another is a moment in *As You Like It*, as in the other plays, of a finding and a founding; a finding, say, of common ground.

5.2 THE MADNESS IN LOVE

Rosalind has long been acknowledged as the center of this play: Harold Bloom has noted that *As You Like It* belongs to her as *Hamlet* belongs to its titular hero and *Henry IV, Part 1* belongs to Falstaff (Bloom 200–204). The ways in which, under the disguise of Ganymede, she puts Orlando though his exercises, chastises Silvius and Phoebe for the character of their romantic relationship, and crosses wits with Touchstone and Jaques have likewise been much remarked upon. I wish in this space to underscore Bloom's observation that "Rosalind herself is joyously in love and criticizes love from within its realm" (Bloom 211) and to relate this observation to the broader notions of teaching and learning, acknowledgment and avoidance, skepticism and its overcoming that have been the focus of this book from the outset.

The picture of teaching and learning that I take from Wittgenstein and Cavell is substantially different from a transmission model of education, that is, a model on which "teaching and learning" consists of the successful transfer of theoretically isolable bits of information from one consciousness, say, to another. This reminder is particularly important to the discussion of *As You Like It* insofar as certain traditional readings of the action (Bloom; Priest, "Oratio and Negotium: Manipulative Modes in *As You like It*"; Beckman, "The Figure of Rosalind in *As You Like It*")—and even more recent, nontraditional efforts aimed at the play's gender and sexual politics (Tvordi; Stirm; Erickson)—share the feature of taking Rosalind to be engaged in the process of *educating* the other characters in the play, especially Orlando.

As I will show, it is all too common for such scholarship to tacitly assume that the play's teaching and learning follows a transmission model. This view leads critics into problems similar to those Henze encountered with respect to *Much Ado*: drawing strained distinctions among characters on the basis of the *spirit* in which manipulations are undertaken, for example. It also leads Bloom, for instance, to bemoan the seeming fact that Rosalind is marrying well beneath her wit and intellect when she weds Orlando. This conclusion is more or less necessitated by thinking of the couple's woodland wooing as an extended and perhaps playful process of Rosalind informing Orlando of various truths that she possesses and that he lacks.

When Bloom describes Rosalind as "criticiz[ing] love from within its realm," this ought not to be understood as an exceptional accomplishment, an exceptional state of affairs. It is instead a quotidian feature of all (Cavellian-Wittgensteinian) education as such. When Cavell speaks of education, as I quoted in Chapter 2, in terms of *initiating* beginners "into the relevant forms of life held in language and gathered around the objects and persons of our world" (Cavell, *The Claim of Reason* 178), the one doing the initiating must already *belong* to the "relevant forms of life" embodied in the language game involved, and any resulting initiation into these forms of life will involve showing the initiate how to carry these into new contexts. In this way, such education-as-initiation requires the one doing the initiation to *go back over* the way in which such going-on might be modeled.

For this reason, as I have also said in Chapter 2, such education is always a *critical* education: if it teaches another how to go on in a particular practice (how to read, how to continue a series, how to follow a rule), it also inevitably forces the teacher to go back over how he or she has gone on with this practice, and how he or she came to learn to go on in the first place—a learning that is, in principle, never complete. Such education is therefore always "simultaneously turned toward oneself and toward one's contribution to the communal" (Saito and Standish 213). Richard Eldridge describes the dynamic of going back and going on in terms of having "an ability both to imitate and to redirect gaze and interest" (Eldridge, *Literature, Life, and Modernity* 15), something akin to what post-structuralists might call repetition with a difference. For Cavell, however, once again, this dynamic is by no means an abstract issue: "The anxiety in teaching, in serious communication, is that I myself require education" (Cavell, "The Normal and the Natural" 45). Going back, in the process of initiating a beginner in going on, is not precisely to retrace one's own steps; it is to go down the path again, with new and maybe wider eyes.

In *As You Like It,* one does find discussions of attempts to effect positive change, if I can call it that, from an *external* or abstract position rather than from "within" any particular "realm," but it is *this* type of attempt that ought to be conceived as the exception and not the rule. I point specifically to Rosalind's offer—as Ganymede, once more[5]—to cure Orlando of his love, and I note particularly her description of her cure: "I drave my suitor," she says, "from his mad humour of love to a living humour of madness, which was to forswear the full stream of the world and to live in a nook merely monastic" (3.2.402–405): I want to highlight the contrast between her two madnesses, the monk's forswearing against the lover's humour.

The madness of love is here opposed to a madness of monastic withdrawal from the "full stream of the world": the price of avoiding or rejecting love appears in her formulation as the denial of the world.[6] But the mad humour of love, as Rosalind understands it—as it is opposed, in other words, to a withdrawal from the world's stream—is not to be taken as an equal, or an equally negative, form of madness. The madness of love is counterpoised against a monastic madness precisely in virtue of its being a nonlogical, nonrational *engagement* with the world. Rosalind's mad humour of love, I want to say, refers to something like the groundless extension of acknowledgment.

Her exchange with Jaques on the subject of his melancholy in Act 4 also buttresses this sense of the matter, especially as Jaques bears unmistakable affinities to the picture of monastic forswearing. Jaques is concerned, in 4.1.10–19, to emphasize the unique character of his melancholy, to distinguish it from all standard categories of melancholy, which he proceeds to enumerate (the scholar's, the musician's, the courtier's, etc.). Instead, as he says, he has "a melancholy of mine own, compounded of many simples, extracted from many objects, and indeed the sundry contemplation of my travels" (4.1.15–17). Rosalind criticizes this traveler's melancholy in terms reminiscent of criticisms of skeptical withdrawal in general: "By my faith, you have great reason to be sad. I fear you have sold your own lands to see other men's" (4.1.21–22). She understands Jaques's measuring of his wisdom according to his many travels as a failure or refusal to take his own life upon himself.

While Jaques cites his melancholy as a badge of his worldliness and experience, Rosalind underscores merely the homelessness and isolation that his vision implies. As she says some lines later, bidding him farewell, "Look you lisp, and wear strange suits; disable all the benefits of your own country; be out of love with your nativity, and almost chide God for making you that countenance you are" (4.1.31–35). Jaques's melancholy does in fact single him out, just as he wishes, but this singling out is also the manifestation of his isolation from the ordinary world. Rosalind's words present Jaques's melancholy appropriately in terms of refusal or denial: in addition to "disabling" certain "benefits" that attend one's "nativity," she makes adopting this melancholic stance a form of "chiding God."

Jaques, then, best figures Rosalind's "living humour of madness," as he, too, forswears the full stream of the world and seeks out more monastic "matter." In criticizing Jaques, Rosalind poses the "mad humour of love" as the very opposite of his forswearing. Indeed, she frames the "mad humour of love" as a binding agent, something that links people not only to one another, but also to the ordinary or everyday world. It is therefore important to italicize the sense in which undertaking this melancholy disposition requires that Jaques fall "*out of love* with his nativity," which includes disarming the benefits of belonging and railing against God for one's countenance. Being in love with one's nativity, on this picture, is precisely the default condition under which the "benefits of your own country" are enabled, under which the background practices of a culture simply do their work and light up one's "order of significance." For Rosalind, the "mad humour of love" is indeed a madness; but it is also her name for the state of engagement with one's world, an engagement on the basis of which reason, logic, and sense have the powers that they do; it is Rosalind's name for the common, public sense manifest in ordinary and regular practical dealings in the world.

Jaques's melancholy, both as it appears in his own words and in Rosalind's mockery, is a form of skeptical withdrawal, a certain kind of failure to take seriously the claims that the world makes upon him. The negative terms in which he characterizes the world, his responses of raillery and critique, are deflections, just as Rosalind avers. Jaques's delight in railing at "our mistress the world" (3.2.272)—as well as his aim, once invested in his motley, to use his wit to "Cleanse the foul body of th'infected world" (2.7.60)—evidently takes third-person critique to be the appropriate response to a foul and diseased world. But Rosalind's chastisement targets his initial step, his very urge to disengage with the world in the first place. As she says, such a move disables all the practical power at one's disposal to achieve precisely the cleansing that Jaques desires. To undertake the rejection of, or withdrawal from, the world is to prevent the possibility of any "order of significance" whatsoever; it is to rob one's words of their power.[7] Withdrawal from the world is not, as Jaques imagines it, the first step toward cleansing the world. Once that movement of rejection has been made, as we have already seen, there is, in an important sense, no longer any world to cleanse.

Jaques's melancholy is a useful foil for considering Rosalind's relation to her own "mad humour of love" precisely because he couches it in terms of the skeptical repudiation of the ordinary world, however badly he may wish to cleanse it. Rosalind's own engaged experience in love—and the way in which her imagination bodies forth a world fit for this love's inhabitation—provides a worthwhile counterpoint to Jaques, particularly insofar as the kind of loving that she and Orlando embody is often misconceived as depending upon either Rosalind's active *deception* of Orlando or Orlando's profound, imbecilic naïveté, each of which takes Rosalind's interactions with Orlando as attempts to *tell* him something, transmit some sort of intelligence.

Once such an assumption—of what I have been calling the transmission model of education—is made, interpretations of the play inevitably turn upon erroneously posed epistemological questions of *belief*, problems whose solutions are meant to alleviate the nagging impression that Rosalind's education of Orlando while in disguise cannot be anything like the actuality of love, given the way in which Rosalind deliberately conceals herself and Orlando's gullible acceptance of this fraud. As with *Much Ado*, I want to say that asking whether or not Orlando *believes* that Ganymede is Ganymede rather than Rosalind is a way of misaddressing the central disquietudes in their courtship, construing such disquietudes as problems to be solved. And solving these problems, under the guiding assumption that Rosalind *knows* something of which Orlando is ignorant, will problematically invoke the transmission model of teaching and learning.

For one instance of a principal disquietude in this play that persistently goes misaddressed, the *reason* for which Rosalind adopts her counselor role with respect to Orlando under the disguise of Ganymede, in contrast to most standard readings, remains an open and unsettled matter. Several interpretations, including that of Dale Priest, have Rosalind assuming this role at least partly in the hope of cultivating something in Orlando that her paramour lacks, as though she planned such a cultivation from the outset, as though her initial attraction to Orlando was an investment, as it were, in some later, more perfect version of him. This is a highly conventional type of reading, one on which Rosalind undertakes to educate Orlando by means of supplying his ignorance and thus eradicating it. In Priest's work, what Orlando lacks is "the element of detachment that gives Rosalind a happier and more clear-eyed understanding of her own emotions" (Priest 279). Rosalind possesses something that Orlando does not, on this picture; her instruction of him is meant to fill out his abilities, to make him into a fit partner in this specific respect. Given the discussion of Rosalind's exchange with Jaques above, it is especially curious to note Priest's association of Rosalind's superior wisdom with a "detachment" from herself.

In another example of this type of exploration, the spirit in which Orlando acquiesces to this education often raises the question of how fully, if at all, he believes that Ganymede is Ganymede rather than Rosalind. In addition to his own wariness—evidenced in his questioning of Rosalind's nativity to the woods: "Your accent is something finer than you could purchase in so removed a dwelling" (3.2.331)—the abrupt about-face he makes with respect to Rosalind's offer to cure him of his love seems to call for an explanation. Orlando pivots from declining her proposal—"I would not be cured, youth" (3.2.409)—to full acceptance—"Now by the faith of my love, I will" (3.2.412)—in the space of just three lines, and on no great persuasion; the implication for many scholars is that his sudden change of heart only makes sense if we understand him to be able to see through Rosalind's disguise. Lastly, to raise one final disquietude that emerges in the play and upon which some critics seize, it is a matter of some debate whether or not Orlando's love for Rosalind is genuine. Indeed, this is also a matter of debate within the play. Celia, in particular, vocalizes such doubts I will address this concern specifically later in this chapter.

All of these questions hang together, and large-scale readings of the play as a whole coalesce around particular answers to these. For example, once one accepts Priest's response to the first question as a starting point—once one accepts a view upon which Rosalind's reason for adopting her counselor relation to Orlando results from a desire to provide Orlando with something that he currently lacks, that is—the other two issues settle neatly into place. If Priest's reading is correct, Orlando must surely believe that Ganymede is Ganymede: one consequence of his inability to detach himself and see things from a clear-eyed perspective is precisely the inability to distinguish mere appearance from underlying reality. This ability is something he must learn from Rosalind.

Similarly, whether or not Orlando's love for Rosalind is genuine receives a congruent, if ambivalent, answer once one accepts Priest's version of things. If "genuine" means "earnest," then he certainly does love Rosalind; analytic to lacking a skill for detachment is lacking the skill to dissemble, or indeed to *perform* himself at all. He is not therefore *lying* when he swears that he loves her. But if "genuine" means that the love he expresses is "true" in the sense of entailing the full maturity, behavior, and commitment associated with love, then the answer must be negative. On such a reading, Orlando is serious about his love for her, but in his guileless immaturity, he does not understand what it is that he is serious *about*. These are likewise things he must learn under Rosalind's tutelage.

In this way, settling any one of the disquietudes I present above also addresses the other two and indeed entails a fuller view of these characters and their relationship. Taking Priest's response to the first disquietude as an example, we are invited to see Orlando, not uncommonly, as something of an earnest and well-meaning dolt, a fixer-upper of a project for Rosalind; while Rosalind, thanks to her capacity for clear-eyed detachment, has a panoptic view of herself and her heart, the nature of love, and Orlando, all at once. She thus lords over and benevolently dominates the play. Such a view allows both Tvordi and Calvo, as well as Priest, to describe Rosalind's interventions in the lives of other characters as well-meaning or playful "manipulations" (Calvo, "Pronouns of Address and Social Negotiation in *As You Like It*"; Tvordi).

My strategy, by this point, will be predictable: the three examples of disquietudes pertaining to Rosalind and Orlando's love for one another that I offered are not in themselves mere distractions—quite the opposite, in fact— but the *assumption* that properly addressing such disquietudes requires treating them as problems to be solved along the lines of the conventional explanations highlighted above does indeed prove distracting. Indeed, in a manner highly reminiscent of Henze's reading of "deception" in *Much Ado*, Priest finds himself forced to distinguish among *types* of manipulation, or rather the various "spirits" in which characters' manipulations are undertaken (Priest 273). This form of explanation leaves perfectly intact what I have called Rosalind's panoptic view of things and what Priest labels her "clear-eyed" "detachment." With Rosalind thus equated with Jaques in terms of "detachment," then, Priest moves to differentiate her "manipulations" from those of Jaques on the basis that hers are offered in "a spirit of inclusiveness," while Jaques's manipulations come from a spirit of "scornful aloofness" or "cynicism" (Priest 273–274).

But Rosalind's "detachment" from herself, her community, and her emotions is precisely what I wish to question: Bloom's remark that Rosalind criticizes love from within its realm is insightfully accurate but requires some following-out, on my view. The evidence for her detachment and clear-eyed view of herself lies in her performance of "Ganymede" and the way in which she flouts at love, despite being in love herself. Postulating her "detachment" is a solution to the problem of how and why she can occupy another subjectivity, as it were, and thus disguised, seems to drive her "suitor from his mad humour of love." Making Rosalind's performance—fictional flouting, juxtaposed with her own true experience of loving—into a problem is very much what Wittgenstein has characterized as the "decisive move in the conjuring trick": once such disquietudes are rendered as problems, it becomes simply impossible to see the integrity or the accuracy of Rosalind's own characterization of the "mad humour of love."

That is to say, if one understands Rosalind's disguised performance before Orlando as most basically *a lie* (and thus opposed to a way of inhabiting the truth of her love), one will put entirely out of play the possibility that Rosalind is in earnest when she describes love, including her own love, as a "mad humour," madness without remainder—not a "mad humour" in service of a higher ideal (according to which its madness is only apparent), and not a temporary or put-on madness either, but rather actual madness, madness itself. Treating such disquietudes as problems thus renders it impossible to take Rosalind at her word: "Love is merely"—*merely*—"a madness" (3.2.386).

The other element of very traditional readings of this relationship, as I have said, is the notion that Rosalind has something specific to impart to Orlando. The degree of her success in this educative endeavor, the degree of Orlando's doltishness, and the degree of his love for her each depend upon (a) determinations of the other degrees, mutually, but also (b) this very assumption that Rosalind *knows* something—about herself, about Orlando, about love, and/or about human nature generally—that Orlando does not, as it is from this position that she effects her teachings. But I argue that such readings distort Rosalind's character and, more specifically, that the opening assumption I alluded to above obstructs a view of Rosalind on which she, in addition to Orlando, undergoes and undertakes her own education.

Critics and scholars—I am thinking here particularly of Bloom—go astray in fixating upon Orlando's unfitness for Rosalind, which would be one way in which to account for her love for him being "unreasonable." But it is a mischaracterization to suggest that she loves Orlando in spite of his unequal soul. As in the instance of Lysander's flower-addled dismissal of Hermia, where he proclaims that "reason says [Helena] is the worthier maid," it is not the case that Rosalind loves where reason says she should not. Her love is better characterized as nonrational; that is, unreasonable in the sense that reason simply has nothing to do with it. This notion comes out clearly both in the wrestling scene in which Rosalind's heart is first "tripped up" and in her later responses to Celia's hesitations about Orlando.

While Rosalind's first impression of Orlando as a physical specimen is apparently underwhelming—leading her to fear for his life in his bout with Charles—his self-deprecating demurral wins some measure of her heart. This self-deprecation must be understood in terms of the "noble device" with which Oliver has credited Orlando, and it is in response to his perfectly conventional and chivalric humility that Rosalind says, "The little strength I have, I would it were with you" (1.2.182–183). Upon his underdog victory, and partly in response to witnessing Duke Frederick's uncharitable comments about Orlando's lineage, Rosalind presents Orlando with a chain from around her neck—another chivalric convention—and bids him farewell. Orlando does not reply to her: in fact, he has two asides in this scene (1.2.238–240; 1.2.247–248) in which he berates himself for his inability to speak, for having "weights upon [his] tongue" and for being a "mere lifeless block." In direct spite of his manifest and (ironically) declared silence, Rosalind says to Celia,

> He calls us back. My pride fell with my fortunes,
> I'll ask him what he would.—Did you call, sir?
> Sir, you have wrestled well, and overthrown
> More than your enemies.
>
> (1.2.241–244)

I cite the above exchanges, first of all, in order to demonstrate that Rosalind understands herself to be fully in love with Orlando, "overthrown," by the time of her exit from this scene; in love, that is, upon having heard Orlando's conventional self-deprecation and having witnessed his feats of strength. Celia will later cement this reading by referring to Orlando as the man "who tripped up the wrestler's heels and your heart both in an instant" (3.2.207–208), acknowledging that she, too, recognizes the speed with which Rosalind has fallen for him.

Second, and in connection with Celia's comment, I wish to emphasize Rosalind's experience of coming to love Orlando, which she presents as the experience of being "overthrown." Orlando, too, it might be added, describes his love in these terms. In chastising himself for his inability to speak, he suggests that in Rosalind's presence, "My better parts / Are all thrown down" (1.2.238–239), and upon Rosalind's exit, he exclaims, "O poor Orlando! Thou art overthrown" (1.2.249). As in Claudio's experience of the "thronging" of soft desires, which "prompt" him to love, and as in Helena's experience of being "drawn" by Demetrius, Orlando and Rosalind alike experience love as something that exerts an external, inverting, and indeed violent force upon them.

Not every character understands the pair's love as irreducible to something like a cause: Celia's reading of the event, for example, ties Rosalind's falling in love with Orlando to Orlando's victory over Charles, to his athletic performance; Orlando's physical capabilities or skills might therefore be cited as a cause for Rosalind's love. But Rosalind is clearly enthralled or intrigued prior to the wrestling itself: it is Orlando's self-deprecating humility that leads her to say, "The little strength I have, I would it were you." And so one might also point to Orlando's ability to embody or perform chivalric conventions as a reason for Rosalind's love. But several elements argue against this interpretation as well.

Orlando's conventionality is, in the first place, something that Rosalind (Ganymede) finds distasteful in Ardenne, which leads her to scoff at his hyperbolic declaration that he will die upon her rejection. In the second place, relatedly, the exchanges reveal that Rosalind finds conventionality itself, and its particular requirements, quite flexible. She both invents an occasion out of thin air on which she can speak with Orlando—"He calls us back"—and conjures from the same place a reasonable ground for answering his call: "My pride fell with my fortunes, / I'll ask him what he would" (1.2.241–242). Her protestations imply that it would be somehow improper to simply approach Orlando a second time—thus, the invention of the call to which she might or might not respond. She then must further invent a reason not to haughtily refuse: she will "ask him what he would" because her "pride [is fallen] with her fortunes." On no reading can this be construed as a *logical* compulsion: her fallen pride does not require her to answer him, nor does it remove the stain of impropriety in any obvious way. It simply casts the consequences of impropriety aside: it provides her an *excuse*. She seems to imply that since her pride is already fallen, playing fast and loose with acceptable conventionality will do no further damage.

I have offered my view of Rosalind's experience of falling in love with Orlando in the interest of making possible a reading on which the unreasonableness of love—its madness—might fully characterize Rosalind's own understanding of her situation. Of crucial importance to the picture that I am urging of what madness and unreasonableness amount to is the fact that such unreasonableness and madness need not, and cannot, be understood as contradicting any specific, ordinarily operative notions of reason or sanity. In other words, I am at pains once more, as I was in Chapter 3, to argue that it is *not* the case that Rosalind falls in love with Orlando *because* he either is or is not a perfect gentleman, but rather that her experience of falling in love is logically *prior* to any "because" whatsoever (cf. Glendinning 102). If it is not rational, or traceable to fully sufficient reasons, then it is not *irrational* either, but simply, as I want to call it, *pre*-rational.

The wrestling in which Charles and Orlando engage, is scored in terms of "falls"; Frederick cautions Orlando that "You shall try but one fall" (1.2.192), for instance. Rosalind's experience of her burgeoning love is explicitly linked to such "falls," as when she confesses to Orlando that he "has overthrown [in his wrestling] more than [his] enemies." Orlando's reaction to being struck by his experience of Rosalind is to say that his "better parts" have been "thrown down." Celia has Rosalind's heart and Charles being "tripped up" "both in an instant." I note the commingling of the concepts of falls and falling, of throwing down and being overthrown, in order to suggest that in turning back to Orlando for the purpose of speaking with him again, concocting excuses and occasions where there are none in fact, Rosalind does indeed *respond* to a kind of compulsion, an externally experienced demand.

While many critics laud Rosalind, and not without reason, for directing the action of this play, I note merely that Rosalind herself locates the impetus for her actions not in something like her will or her whims or her genius, but rather in something external to her, something that "overthrows" her, something that renders her responsiveness obligatory. If this is not reasonable in terms of anything transcendent, say social or conventional or natural logic, then such responsiveness must be, in one sense, *unreasonable*. But not therefore without reason: In loving Orlando, Rosalind makes precisely the movement of acknowledgment, the ungrounded acceptance of a "new order of significance" that restructures or reorients the objects of the world. In short, her responsiveness exemplifies the madness in love; but it also shows forth something of the reason in madness, as Nietzsche describes the matter (Nietzsche 30).

The extent of the unreason or nonlogic in Rosalind's love is further revealed in the scenes in which Celia raises doubts pertaining to Orlando's sincerity. As excited as Celia might be for Rosalind—"O wonderful, wonderful, and most wonderful-wonderful," etc. (3.2.187–188)—she nevertheless vocalizes her belief that Orlando is "not in" love with Rosalind. Celia's evidence for this conclusion, in 3.4, is the same as Rosalind's, namely, that Orlando has promised to meet them and yet "comes not." When I say that these scenes reveal something of Rosalind's "madness," I attend specifically the ways in which Rosalind and Celia respond to the possibility that Orlando is "as concave as a covered goblet" (3.4.23).

Rosalind opens 3.4 by declaring to Celia that she "will weep," asking "have I not cause to weep?" (3.4.1,4); and she specifies this cause, saying that Orlando's "very hair is of a dissembling color" (3.4.6). In the conventional style of comedy, Rosalind gives voice to her sadness and its causes, which Celia echoes, but Rosalind also alternates these disparaging lines with helpless reminders that Orlando's kisses are as "full of sanctity as holy bread" and that "his hair is of a good color," which Celia likewise concedes (3.4.6–16). Celia's opportunity for assertion—"Nay, certainly, there is no truth in him"—enters as a response to an open-ended question from Rosalind: "But why did he swear he would come this morning, and comes not?" (3.4.17–19). Celia here singles out Orlando's duplicitousness, but a few lines later she attributes the breaking of vows to all lovers quite generally, true and false alike: "the oath of a lover is no stronger than the word of a tapster. They are both the confirmer of false reckonings" (3.4.27–29).

About this exchange, I raise two particular points: whether Orlando's breaking of this appointment is attributed to a personal failing (3.4.20) or whether it is taken as a failing of the general category of lovers entirely (3.4.27–29), and even further, whether this is taken up as a reason to doubt the verity of Orlando's love (3.4.25), none of these ways of understanding Orlando's absence has any *practical* effect on Rosalind's love for or attachment to him. At the end of this scene, as Corin bids them to observe the pageant of Phoebe and Silvius, Rosalind says to Celia, "O come, let us remove. / The sight of lovers feedeth those in love" (3.4.52–54). This fact merely indicates that Rosalind's love for Orlando is neither predicated nor reliant upon his reciprocation, or indeed the factual truth of his love, which recalls both the Benedick-Beatrice matter and Helena's eventual acceptance of Demetrius. The questions that Rosalind raises, and Celia's responses to them, result in Rosalind occupying exactly the position with respect to her love that she did at the scene's opening.

The second fact to note, which underscores what I have said above, is that Celia has not said anything to Rosalind in this scene that Rosalind has not already said directly to Orlando in 3.2. In other words, Celia provides Rosalind with no new information, no new reason to doubt. Rosalind has already, for example, faulted Orlando as "no true lover" in virtue of his inability to tell time by the use of sighs (3.2.296). These faults in Orlando, to the extent that they are faults, go uncorrected; this is a point that traditional interpretations of this play miss. If one wishes to read Rosalind's educational scenes in 3.2 and 4.1 as either teaching or testing Orlando, it must be pointed out that Orlando never passes his exams. If Rosalind is understood to be in doubt about the veracity of Orlando's love, and if she undertakes to remove the doubt through personally teaching him how to love, then she has no evidence, by the time she appears with Hymen in Act 5, that Orlando has *become* a true lover and has taken her lessons to heart. Rosalind doubts (and mocks) his poetry and tells him so, and Celia echoes her doubts of his "brave verses"; Rosalind doubts his love on the basis of his punctuality and tells him so (4.1.37–39); and Celia, as we have seen, echoes this doubt, too; and when, in 4.3., Orlando is once more to appear on time, he once more fails. This time, as Oliver enters to explain, he has the excuse of a lion-mauling, and, granted, he sends the bloody handkerchief for proof, but Orlando never manages to refute the specific grounds for doubt that Rosalind and Celia alike raise to him directly and between themselves in private.

For these reasons, it is a mistake to understand 3.2 and 4.1 in terms of Rosalind attempting to impart some information to Orlando about what it is like to be a lover in order that Orlando might make, at length, an equal partner for her. When critics or scholars like Bloom find the wedding perplexing or disappointing in light of Orlando's failure to learn, they take Rosalind to be merely settling for him. If some such teaching (*such* teaching)—and its proof in Orlando's actions—were in fact a necessary condition for the happiness of their match, we are then forced to deny the happy ending. Some scholars, of course, do.

But I wish to suggest instead that Rosalind's imperviousness to doubt simply indicates that doubt is not at issue here. Rosalind's commentary on Orlando's failings, her accusations that he is no true lover, are meant, I wish to say, as earnest criticisms; but such failings or doubts about his love cannot effect any unhinging of her own love for him. Her love is not—and has never been—dependent upon any particular fact about Orlando, including the truth of his love for her. Readings on which Orlando must learn how to be a true lover from Rosalind's tutelage are not straightforwardly false, but in valorizing Rosalind's capacious intelligence and creativity, such readings fail to see *Rosalind* taking on her own education, a process that, as I have argued earlier, is inherent in any genuine act of teaching-as-initiation whatsoever.

5.3 THE REASON IN MADNESS

Rosalind's education is a process of *finding*, undertaken from a position of engagement in the world. Earlier I pointed out that Rosalind disparages Jaques's approach to "cleans[ing] the foul body of th'infected world" (2.7.60) by means of removing himself to an appropriate critical distance from which to vent his wisdom, or to "blow on whom I please" (2.7.49). Against Jaques's purpose, Rosalind argues that his removal from the world, his adoption of the sojourner's position, renders him incapable of achieving any sort of cleansing. The best of which Jaques proves capable is his Seven Ages of Man speech (2.7.139–167), which, while no mean feat, can hardly count as achieving any "cleansing" effect.

As stated earlier, Rosalind's chastisement also reveals her own view of the process of critical cleansing, which I will instead cast as a conversion of the world: it requires first of all that the benefits of one's own country be enabled, that one be "in love with" one's nativity. The way in which Rosalind has adopted or acknowledged the "overthrown" quality of her love for Orlando manifests exactly this type of engagement with her world. Priest's claim that Rosalind has some "clear-eyed" form of "detachment" that allows her a fuller, more complete view of her emotions is thus exactly backward. Instead of a *view* on her love, she finds herself to have something much more like a *grip* on it. Priest's version of things essentially makes Rosalind into Jaques, and he offers this equivalence as though it were a compliment.

Despite Rosalind's assumed role as ministering to the disease of Orlando's love, her interactions with Orlando in 3.2 and 4.1 do not take the form of any external direction of the action, and particularly not of Orlando; instead, they take the form of what Cavell calls "indirection … the direction of reception, of being approached, the attractive, handsome part of our condition" (Cavell, *This New Yet Unapproachable America* 109). Rosalind never suffers the skeptical temptations of Beatrice or Claudio, the urge to approach the object of her love by means of clutching at it. Rather, as she says herself, "[her] way is to conjure you" (epilogue).

I have already indicated one sense in which Rosalind's approach to loving Orlando can be described in terms of "handsomeness," and that is the sense in which her love for Orlando is taken to be more or less immediately and unreasonably given to her, as in a bequest. She never deviates from a view on which she is "overthrown" from without; her acceptance or acknowledgment of Orlando's effect on her is the very acknowledgment of the attractive, gravitational power of the world. But her invention of Ganymede's "religious uncle," a man who "knew courtship" and "read many lectures against" love (3.2.334–337), is equally evidence of a responsiveness to the affordances of her practical situation, a display of the "handsome part of our condition."

Commonly forgotten in scholarly or critical efforts to praise Rosalind for her wit and wisdom is the sheer *improvisational* quality of her inventiveness, a respect or appreciation of the fact that she is making it all up as she goes along. I raise this issue now to deflect or defuse certain ways of interpreting her initial interaction with Orlando in Ardenne as planned or deliberate, as though she dons or maintains "Ganymede" with the particular project of educating Orlando more or less squarely in mind. While Rosalind initially "suit[s her] all points like a man" (1.3.115) with the aim of discouraging potential "assailants" who might otherwise prey upon her "beauty" (1.1.109,113); and while it is easy, given Rosalind's many later interventions in other characters' lives, to argue that Rosalind enjoys the gender prerogatives that attend her masculine appearance, and that she has ample reason to desire to keep her true self hidden; I wish instead to gesture to the seriousness of the inconveniences that come with her disguise, not the least of which emerges upon learning that Orlando is also in the forest.

Rosalind's very first reaction to accepting Celia's word that the poems hung in trees are indeed Orlando's emerges as: "Alas the day, what shall I do with my doublet and hose!," and this exclamation comes even prior to her litany of questions about Orlando ("What did he when thou sawest him? What said he? How looked he?," etc.) (3.2.214–217). Following Celia's laughing reply to these questions, Rosalind returns immediately to this issue: "But doth he know that I am in this forest, and in man's apparel?" (3.2.224–225). Her realization that Orlando is both in the forest of Ardenne and writing poetry proclaiming his love for her makes her "man's apparel" an immediate and pressing problem for her—*that* is the form in which her disguise first appears to her with respect to Orlando: not as a means of developing a fit partner for herself, but as the reason behind her "Alas the day."

Not only, then, does she not set out or plan to conceal herself from Orlando, but her insistent questions demonstrate that the problem of how to *reveal* herself to him is of the utmost importance for her. Her many improvisations therefore ought to be understood as serving *this* end—her self-revelation. Her abrupt declaration to Celia, eavesdropping on Orlando's banter with Jaques, that she "will speak to him like a saucy lackey, and under that habit play the knave with him" (3.2.289–290), is precisely an improvisational response to this very problem of how to reveal herself *despite* her disguise. It is thus not *pure* invention, but rather a matter of taking up the situation as it presents itself—or in more colloquial terms, a (handsome) matter of letting the world come to her. In responding to the affordances entailed in the situation as she finds it, Rosalind undertakes her self-revelation, which also entails her own education.

Before Rosalind and Orlando first encounter one another in Ardenne, we hear clearly the degree of Rosalind's "overthrown" state. As Celia attempts to recount the story of how she came upon Orlando "under a tree, like a dropped acorn" (3.2.230), Rosalind interrupts her several times to sigh and praise Orlando: "It may well be called Jove's tree when it drops forth such fruit" (3.2.231–232), for example. In addition to the constant praise of Orlando, the several interruptions—and her excusing of them—reveal that a kind of helplessness characterizes Rosalind's experience of her love: it is something of a steady and ongoing "overthrow." When Celia bids her be silent, saying "I would sing my song without a burden," Rosalind attributes her own helpless prattling to women generally. As with other claims of this kind, I wish to remain agnostic as to any validity in Rosalind's attempt at generalization and merely want to emphasize that *her own* experience here is one of helplessness: "Do you not know I am a woman? When I think, I must speak" (3.2.244–245).

Although Rosalind claims her verbal incontinence to be a general characteristic of all women, it is not even the case that Rosalind herself evinces this proclivity outside of the context of her love for Orlando. The only other occasion on which she seems unable to master or control her need to speak occurs in the first Act, when she finds her initial conversation with Orlando too unsatisfyingly brief and invents a cause and a justification for speaking with him further. The helplessness, the uncontrollable expressiveness, that she attributes to all women manifests itself for her exclusively in her dealings with Orlando. I associate this helplessness with the handsomeness of her love for Orlando, the sense in which her love and its expressiveness are not under her control, the way in which she finds herself given over to it.

The helplessness of her overthrow is further apparent, as I have suggested earlier, in the unassailability of her love, in its independence of any particular facts about Orlando. Orlando breaks his promises, swears false vows, risks hyperbole, gives off every indication that he holds Rosalind in a kind of chivalrous idolatry—the very monumentalizing temptation to which Othello succumbs—and yet Rosalind, even having wept at his promise-breaking (3.4.1), even having sneered at his naïve attempts at making a goddess or a statue of her (4.1.88–101; 4.1.138–148), can only say to Celia upon Orlando's departure, "O coz, coz, coz, my pretty little coz, that thou didst know how many fathom deep I am in love" (4.1.195–196). Where critics like Bloom, for example, see Orlando's wooden troubadour practice of romance, and the fact that it is unmended over the course of the play, as evidence of what I have called Orlando's doltishness, his unfitness for so great a heroine, I only emphasize here that *she* finds him equal to her love and that her *finding* it so is neither a logical compulsion nor a deliberate choice. The fact of her love, her engagement with the world thus presented, comes first; the facts about Orlando that appear for her stand out against this nonsensical, pre-rational background.

Rosalind's "speak[ing] to him like a saucy lackey" in 3.2 also makes plain her spontaneous responsiveness to her unreasonable overthrow in precisely the way that her invention of an excuse to speak more with Orlando in 1.3 and her continual interruption of Celia's tale are both likewise visible responses to the helplessness of her condition.[8] Her "helplessness," in this sense, describes her own experience of being in "love with [her] nativity." I do not cite it as any metaphysical limitation of her ability to deny or repudiate the world's attraction. As Cavell's investigations of the tragedies show, such power to deny the world and its claims upon us is an ineradicable aspect of the human condition. What I wish to show in considering her educative interactions with Orlando is that her creative agency requires no disengagement from the world in order to achieve its miraculous effects; indeed, contra Priest, her clear-eyed and happy view of her own emotions occurs precisely in virtue of the condition of her absolute *engagement* with the world, an engagement that is directly manifest in her experience of her relations to Orlando and to the world in terms of being "overthrown," as though, as it were, from without.

Appareled like a man, Rosalind simply discovers herself equipped to "play the knave with" Orlando—to banter and cross wits, as she has just overheard him doing with Jaques in this scene and as she herself has done earlier with Touchstone. By speaking saucily and playing the knave, she responds to the affordances of her situation: her doublet and hose prove to be her allies here, for they allow her to engage in something reminiscent of Benedick and Beatrice's "merry war of wits." Thus disguised, put simply, she finds that she has the liberty to flirt with him rather more unconventionally than in Act 1, and I emphasize here that this is a *finding*. This flirting—and the particular game that she invents in the interest of counseling him out of love—allows Rosalind, ironic though this fact may be in light of her man's apparel, to reveal herself to Orlando and also, no less importantly, to accept Orlando's own self-revelation.

Orlando's self-revelation is the simpler matter here and is easier to illustrate. In 3.2, speaking to the "saucy lackey" that Rosalind pretends to be, he finds himself able to engage, first, in a sort of witty repartee (3.2.300–324), which is a marked change from his Act 1 interactions with Rosalind. As Celia and Rosalind attempt to dissuade him from wrestling in the first Act, Orlando speaks in highly formal and self-deprecating language; after the wrestling, he cannot seem to speak at all, and in fact chides himself for this fact, as we have seen. But in the forest, in the company of Ganymede, Orlando allows the full agility[9] of his mind free range: "A man who had a wife with such a wit, he might say, 'Wit, wither wilt?'" (4.1.157–158). While it is neither fair nor accurate to suggest that the Orlando of Act 1 was deliberately concealing himself in formalities and silence—and while it is also true that in this limited sort of concealment Rosalind found him overwhelmingly appealing in the first place—his ability to speak less formally in Ganymede's presence counts as a revelation of himself nonetheless.

In order to see Rosalind's disguised interactions with Orlando as both the taking on of her education and the achievement of own self-revelation, it will be important briefly to reiterate the different senses of revelation and education at work here from the more conventional readings on which Rosalind reveals some facts about abstract notions such as love (or even herself), and on which Rosalind's education amounts to teaching through skeptical trial what love truly entails. For an example of this latter version of a conventional reading, Rosalind's initial inquisition of Orlando in 3.2 appears to be an attempt both to ironically critique the troubadour conventions of the lover and to ascertain whether or not Orlando's love is genuine. These twin attempts are often conflated in the literature (Beckman "The Figure of Rosalind in *As You Like It*"): the "lesson" that Rosalind would impart, on this view, is that the *conventional appearance* of love is adopted more easily than the commitments of love. Therefore, the ascertaining of the quality of Orlando's love requires a test of his commitment—his commitment to loving Rosalind, that is, in the face of Ganymede's attempt to drive "[her] suitor from his mad humour of love to a living humour of madness."

But Rosalind is not trying to ascertain the true quality of Orlando's love; that is, she is not seeking a *proof* thereof. She rather simply, and very ordinarily, wants to *hear* that he loves her. Having listed her "uncle's marks" of a lover—the untied shoe, the neglected beard, and so on—and having complimented in an underhanded fashion Orlando's looks—"you are rather point-device in your accouterments" (3.2.369–370)—she has *positioned* herself as though she were one in doubt. Indeed, it is this position to which Orlando responds in saying, "Fair youth, I would I could make thee believe I love" (3.2.371–372). But no proof is either offered or requested at this point. Rosalind very nakedly and directly asks him, "But are you so much in love as your rhymes speak?", to which Orlando replies, "Neither rhyme nor reason can express how much" (3.2.382–385). *This* exchange prompts Rosalind's talk of love's deserving a dark house and a whip, and so on, as well as her offer of a "cure." She has said earlier that she "will not cast away [her] physic but on those that are sick" (3.2.347–348); her offer of a cure at this point plainly shows that she responds *practically* to Orlando as if to one ill. But Orlando has proven nothing; he has rather, and simply, *confessed* something. She has enticed him to reveal himself to her, and she has accepted his expression of love as just such a revelation.

Rosalind is not trying to ascertain the true quality of Orlando's love; that is, none of her "curing by counsel" is intended to result in any sort of heightened confidence in the truth or maturity of Orlando's love—nor, it must be added, although this is already entailed in the previous clause, is any of Rosalind's counsel supposed to inculcate new beliefs or behaviors in Orlando with respect to loving. She does not want any version of Orlando that she does not already have; she also does not want (for) any further degree of *certainty*. She wants to be wooed; she wants simply for Orlando to woo her. That is the entire point of the game that she conjures from thin air.

Over the course of Rosalind's game, however, and even in its setup, she does speak often—and often disparagingly—about women, love, and marriage. On a conventional reading, the content of these speeches would constitute the lessons on the above topics that Rosalind wishes to impart, the lessons that Orlando is expected to learn. But such a reading overlooks the other instances in the play of speeches on love, duty, and rejection, from Rosalind as well as from other characters. Rosalind, I will argue, is attempting to reveal something to Orlando, but this is *Rosalind herself* that she wishes him to learn rather than any formalized truths about love, marriage, or the rest. I have said that she wants simply for Orlando to woo her; part of this wooing includes her own revelation.

Two factors lead me to this reading of Rosalind's speeches. In the first place, Orlando is not the only recipient of the *content* of this wisdom from Rosalind: it is therefore doubtful that Rosalind offers her thoughts specifically with the aim of preparing or testing *him*. In the second place, though it is related, Rosalind is not the only *dispenser* of the specific contents of her speeches. The wisdom she offers is, in every sense, *common knowledge*, available to Orlando from other sources and directed by Rosalind at other characters.

But the fact remains that Rosalind's educative effort *is* aimed specifically at Orlando, and that Rosalind is the specific one whom Orlando finds capable of initiating him. When I suggest that this teaching and learning, involving self-revelation, is not reducible to the transmission of knowledge, this is clearly not to deny that nothing special or unique occurs in the pair's interaction; it is only to deny that what occurs might be reducible to something like pure information. Taking Phoebe as an object of comparison, both as a provider and a recipient of the substance of Rosalind's philosophy of love, will help to trace out the uniqueness of Rosalind's particular discourse with Orlando, the sense in which it amounts to her self-revelation.

Phoebe rejects, scorns, and flies from Silvius's love, and in her scorning of him, she gives voice to the very same knowledge Rosalind elsewhere bestows upon Orlando. The character of the interactions, though, is altogether different. 3.5 opens with Silvius pleading with Phoebe to mend her tone: "Say that you love me not, but say not so / In bitterness." (3.5.2–3). He proceeds to draw an analogy on this basis between Phoebe and "the common executioner," noting that even one so accustomed to slaughter "Falls not the axe upon the humbled neck / But first begs pardon. Will you sterner be / Than he that dies and lives by bloody drops?" (3.5.5–7). This exchange comes one scene prior to Orlando's similar protestation: upon hearing Rosalind declare to him that "in her person I say I will not have you," Orlando replies, "Then in my own person I die" (4.1.86–87). Both Orlando and Silvius seem to attribute death-dealing power to their mistresses' rejections.

Phoebe's response to Silvius differs, though, from Rosalind's to Orlando in several respects, most particularly in the way it opens: "I would not be thy executioner. / I fly thee for I would not injure thee" (3.5.8–9). Prior to any assertion pertaining to Silvius's exaggeration of Phoebe fatal power is the more directly expressed refusal of any relation to him at all. He accuses her of hatefulness. Her reply is, in essence, "I don't dislike you. I nothing you."[10] Only then does Phoebe address Silvius's hyperbole:

> Lie not, to say mine eyes are murderers.
> Now show me the wound my eye hath made in thee.
> Scatch thee but with a pin, and there remains
> Some scar of it.
> [...]
> But now mine eyes,
> Which I have darted at thee, hurt thee not;
> Nor I am sure there is no force in eyes
> That can do hurt.
>
> (3.5.19–27)

Having first denied that even the barest sort of connection existing between executioner and victim applies to the two of them, Phoebe proceeds to discount the very possibility that "there is murder in mine eye" (3.5.10) and, indeed, that eyes "can do hurt" at all.

The content of Rosalind's retort to Orlando is strikingly similar to the latter portion of Phoebe's: when Orlando claims that he will die if Rosalind will not have him, Rosalind likewise rejects the hyperbole: "Men have died from time to time, and worms have eaten them, but not for love" (4.1.99–101). Orlando doubles down on his claim, protesting that "her frown might kill [him]" (4.1.103). "By this hand," says Rosalind, "it will not kill a fly" (4.1.104). Both Silvius and Orlando swear they will die upon their lover's rejection; both women simply seem to scoff at the dire implications of such a rejection, the ability of an eye or a frown to do such mortal damage.

But when Phoebe herself falls in love with Rosalind's "man's apparel" and claims just the same mortal vulnerability to Rosalind's judgment that she scorned in Silvius, Rosalind responds with the same dismissal of the hyperbole that she leveled at Orlando, but she offers it in a much different way. In Phoebe's letter, she asks Rosalind to affirm her offer of love, "Or else by [Silvius] my love deny, / And then I'll study how to die" (4.3.63–64). When Phoebe later confronts Rosalind personally on this matter, she accuses Rosalind of showing insufficient concern: "Youth, you have done me much ungentleness" (5.2.72). Rosalind's resulting quip expressly severs or repudiates any sense of obligation to Phoebe implied in the latter's complaint: "I care not if I have," she says (5.2.73).

To Phoebe, then, Rosalind offers the same sort of response as that which Phoebe offers to Silvius, one that disowns any responsibility whatever for the other's feelings. That is to say, both Rosalind and Phoebe, in rejecting professions of love from those men (or "men") whom they do not love in kind, are primarily concerned to reject the lover's asserted claim *on them,* rather than simply turning up their noses at the hyperbole of the lover's melodramatic appeals. In other words, when presented with love-pleas declaring that certain death will result from rejection, both Rosalind (to Phoebe) and Phoebe (to Silvius) respond more or less to the effect that "I care not." The implication of any sort of a relationship entailed in the very entering of such pleadings is straightforwardly denied.

Each claim has two aspects: the general hyperbolic assertion that, essentially, looks can kill; but more directly, each lover enters this claim in the *genitive*; Phoebe thus refuses Silvius in the second person; she refuses to be "*thy* executioner," while Orlando claims that "*her* [Rosalind's] frown might kill" him. Each of these claims offers or extends a particular kind of relationship; it asserts or implies a bond between subject and object: Rosalind's frown will not kill just anyone, after all, and Phoebe's eyes are only mortally dangerous to Silvius. Phoebe's refusal to be "*thy* executioner" and Rosalind's haughty "I care not if I have" to Phoebe are both denials of *this* specific claim, the way that the lovers single *them* out.

But when Rosalind professes to Orlando that her frown "will not kill a fly" and that "men have died from time to time ... but not for love," these assertions are entered under the conditions of *accepting* the individuating nature of Orlando's claim, of taking on the relationship in which *her* frown is possessed, if not of a fatal power, then certainly of heightened significance for *him*. Her scoffing at the melodrama in Orlando's claim is notably different, then, from a rejection or repudiation of his claim upon her as a whole. This is one sense in which Rosalind reveals herself to Orlando—that is, as one for whom she is an education. It *matters* to Rosalind that Orlando take her counsel in a way that it does not matter to Rosalind if Phoebe does. Thereby Rosalind acknowledges Orlando's claim on her.

As Bloom has said, "Rosalind criticizes love from within its realm." Contrasting the way in which Rosalind chides Orlando for his melodrama with both the way in which (a) she simply refuses Phoebe's claim upon her and also the way in which (b) Phoebe likewise refuses Silvius's claim clarifies Bloom's intuition. Being "within its realm" is expressed precisely in her acknowledgment of Orlando's claim upon her; her critique of his rhetorical flourishes is therefore only a critique *thereof*. In direct opposition to Jaques, who thinks it necessary to first disengage with the world in order to "cleanse" it, Rosalind's very condition of engagement allows her to criticize the form of Orlando's expression without this slipping into criticism of the expression itself.

5.4 THE EDUCATION(S) OF ROSALIND

I have said before that Rosalind offers her educative efforts with respect to Orlando at least partly in the service of her own self-revelation, and I wish to augment this picture by focusing on how this revelation is implicated in her own education *in* love. Having prepared the ground by demonstrating that Rosalind's disquisitions on love are not well understood in terms of attempting to convey information to Orlando, or sounding the true depth of his commitment to her, it will perhaps be more possible at this point to hear the sense in which her descriptions of women, lovers, and marriage amount to revelations of herself.

Having heard Orlando confess that "Neither rhyme nor reason can express how much" he loves her, Rosalind offers to cure him "by counsel." In response to Orlando's question as to whether she "did ... ever cure any so," Rosalind reels off a narrative from which I have previously quoted, a story that ends with Rosalind driving her "suitor from his mad humour of love to a living humour of madness" (3.2.390; 3.2.403–404). The pedagogical techniques she describes to Orlando hold particular interest for my reading in three different ways. In the first place, the frame of Rosalind's proposed cure is that her suitor "was to imagine [her] his love, his mistress," and under the power of this imagination "come every day to woo [her]." Earlier I suggested that Rosalind, rather than seeking a test or proof of Orlando's love, wants simply for him to woo her. Offering this particular form of curing him certainly achieves that effect.

But, in the second place, the way in which this imaginary wooing might effect a cure for her suitor, the way in which she might, as she proposes to Orlando, "wash your liver as clean as a sound sheep's heart, that there shall not be one spot of love in't" (3.2.406–408) is to imagine *herself* a particular sort of mistress to him. The "cure" that she promises is a(nother) kind of "madness"—"forswear[ing] the full stream of the world" and living instead "merely monastic" (3.2.404–405). In other words, she frames her cure as an attempt to drive Orlando out of love and into insanity. I note two things with respect to this second point of interest: first it is easy to see why Rosalind is often taken to be testing Orlando's love: and if he can persevere in the face of the act she promises to put on, then he must truly love her.

But the second observation undercuts this image of a trial once more: the fact of the matter is that there are precious few similarities between her actual "curing" of Orlando and the sort of "cure" that she advertises to him early on. In 3.2, she clearly describes the type of mistress it would take (or has taken) to cure a lover of his illness. It is difficult at best to see the sense in which she ever, in the later Acts of the play, embodies or performs for Orlando the mistress she describes here. In the earlier instance of curing, she claims that she would,

> Being but a moonish youth, grieve, be effeminate, changeable, longing and liking, proud, fantastical, apish, shallow, inconstant, full of tears, full of smiles; for every passion something, and for no passion truly anything, as boys and women are for the most part cattle of this colour—would now like him, now loathe him; then entertain him, then forswear him; now weep for him, then spit at him.
> (3.2.394–400)

For the time being, I simply point out that the only instances in Acts 4 and 5 bearing even a glancing resemblance to this description of her cure occur in 4.1: she shifts fairly abruptly from scolding him for being an hour late at 4.1.41–46 to a much more inviting pose a few lines later: "Come, woo me, woo me, for now I am in a holiday humour, and like enough to consent" (4.1. 64–67). After a small piece of instruction, her tone shifts again: "Well, in her person, I say I will not have you." At the end of her ensuing lecture against his hyperbole, she once more changes her attitude abruptly. For the jarring effect, I begin quoting from the conclusion of the lecture, there being no lines between the two: "By this hand, it [her frown] will not kill a fly. But come, now I will be your Rosalind in a more coming-on mood; and ask me what you will, and I will grant it" (4.1.104–106). Certainly, putting on a more "coming-on mood" upon minimal—or in the absence of—provocation, and just as suddenly, and without cause or explanation, saying that she "will not have" him manifests the "changeability" that she promises; but these swings hardly rise to the "now weep for him, then spit at him" standard of her curing story.

Meanwhile, where Rosalind does in places demonstrate some of the actual extremes she describes, she undergoes these extremes only before *Celia*. She *is* full of smiles, proud and fantastical, longing and liking; but only when she cannot be bothered to "cry holla" to her tongue as Celia recounts the story of stumbling upon Orlando. She *does*, likewise, here profess that she "will weep" on account of Orlando failing his appointment. But even if these greater extremes feel somewhat unjustified to Rosalind (she asks Celia in 3.4, as though seeking affirmation, "But have I not cause to weep?"), they lack the kind of capriciousness Rosalind describes to Orlando.

The point of detailing the therapy that Rosalind embarks upon is to show that it remains unclear in what sense she can be said to have embodied the cure that she describes to him in Act 3. The "Rosalind" that she imaginatively performs for Orlando in the later Acts is not in any straightforward way a fulfillment of the (misogynistic) pattern that she lays out in her narrative, wherein she will be flighty, apish, and so on.

My third area of interest in Rosalind's pedagogical methods arises directly from this discrepancy between the cure that she promises and the cure she delivers. The narrative that she offers promises a cure, and its frame allows her something that she wants, namely, to be wooed by Orlando. But her promise of a cure absolutely depends upon her requirement that her suitor, both Orlando and the one in her tale, is "to imagine [her] his love, his mistress" (3.2.392–393). When she promises Orlando a cure, the form of the cure requires him to "call [her] Rosalind and come every day to [her] cot to woo [her]" (3.2.410–411). The mutual imagination that Rosalind and Orlando enter into over the course of their courtship is absolutely central to understanding the sense in which the lovers *teach* and *learn* of and from each other, as well as the sense in which Rosalind's "lessons" can be construed as an authentic revelation of herself, both to herself and to Orlando.

I have been at pains throughout this chapter to militate against taking this courtship as a *test*, at least on a skeptical or scientific model, where Rosalind is, as it were, positing and attempting to refute a doubt in the form of a null hypothesis (in this case, that Orlando is *not* a fit suitor for her). I have also militated against understanding this courtship in terms of Rosalind's *educating* Orlando, where this education is modeled on providing him with new information, or in other words, with uncontested and incontestable facts that she possesses (and is certain of), and that he lacks. At the same time, however, what motivates and indeed necessitates the lengthy analyses undercutting both of the above views is the fact that neither of the views is entirely or obviously wrong. Indeed, the fact that a sort of testing and teaching is obviously going on in this courtship seems to demand precisely the views that I militate against. The insufficiencies of these models, therefore, need not and should not lead to the denial of any obvious facts; the insufficiencies simply demand an alternative view of teaching and learning, one that I have located in Cavell's philosophy.

Their charade, as Rosalind orchestrates it, is indeed a test but not one for Orlando alone: Cavell's perfectionism, as he and others have called it "proposes confrontation and conversation as the means of determining whether we can live together, accept one another into the aspirations of our lives" (Cavell, *Cities of Words* 24). Rosalind wants Orlando to woo her; in order to achieve this end, she in her man's apparel invites him to *imagine* her as his Rosalind, which also requires her to imagine *herself* as "Rosalind," that is, to imaginatively project a Rosalind for him to woo. The role played by this imaginative function—one that allows each of the lovers the opportunity to practice or try out, as it were, how to go on with one another—breaks out of the rigidity in the insufficient models of teaching and testing I described earlier. Neither Rosalind nor Orlando need now be assumed to possess or to lack any specific facts, whose importance and relevance must likewise be known a priori. Nor must Orlando or Rosalind now be assumed to hold firm and aprioristic standards for an acceptable lover, say standards that take the form of a rubric. Rather, in engaging imaginatively in a sort of "moral reasoning" (Cavell 32), they might rather be understood as negotiating—and in *that* sense learning, revealing, and testing—the field of a projected romantic future.

Linking Cavell's thoughts on the role of imagination in teaching and learning to Rosalind and Orlando's imaginative projection of themselves and each other over the course of their forest courtship requires that one underscore the way in which Rosalind's performance of herself through Ganymede exemplifies Cavell's sense of achieving the conversion of the world. Throughout his writings, though it eventually comes to bear the name of "perfectionism," Cavell is concerned with the way "the very conception of a divided self and a doubled world, providing a perspective of judgment on the world as it is, measured against the world as it may be, tends to express disappointment with the world as it is" (Cavell, *Cities of Words* 1). This notion of a divided self and a doubled world arises for Cavell not only out of Freud but also out of Emerson; it is Cavell's engagement with Emerson that explicitly occasions his discussions of "perfectionism." The central perfectionist idea that Cavell takes from Emerson is one that Cavell sometimes calls "nextness of the self to the self" (Cavell, *The Senses of Walden* 107); this bifurcated self is at once a completed and an ongoing project: "The self is always attained, as well as *to be* attained" (Cavell, *Conditions Handsome and Unhandsome* 12). Elsewhere Cavell puts the matter like so: "I forerun myself, a sign, an exemplar" (Cavell, *Conditions Handsome and Unhandsome* 54). The doubled self refers to a present (attained) version and a future (unattained) one toward which one aspires.

The divided world shares the same structure: we have the world as it is, which disappoints in various ways, and we have the world as it may be, which might not disappoint. The expression of disappointment with a present state of affairs need not take the form of slandering the world as it is, say the form of Jaques's nihilistic refusals. Undertaking to improve the world from within, as it were, expresses "disappointment with the world as it is" through what one might call being in "love with one's nativity." On Cavell's readings of Emerson's notions of self-reliance, conformity, and aversive thinking, a person's "aversion" to "conformity"—a person's self-reliance—"is not to be understood as a turning away from the society that demands conformity more than as a turning toward it, as in a gesture of confrontation," a confrontation that ultimately "takes the form of making myself intelligible to those concerned" (Cavell, *Cities of Words* 22). Under these conditions, the way in which Cavell brings together the divided self and the doubled world makes sense:

> What I call Emersonian Perfectionism I understand to propose that one's quarrel with the world need not be settled, nor cynically set aside as unsettleable. It is a condition in which you can at once want the world and want it to change—even change it, as the apple changes the Earth, though we say the apple falls.
> (Cavell, *Cities of Words* 18)

Helping to bring about this unattained but attainable world requires as a first step making such a future intelligible to others, which also includes making oneself, or one's future self, intelligible both privately and publicly.

In *The Claim of Reason*, Cavell pursues the same idea, even if it occurs without the "perfectionism" label: "[T]he human individual, to win freedom, must be something that can fight for recognition, which now means, vie with its incorporated interpretations of itself for a voice, for the leading voice, in its history" (Cavell, *The Claim of Reason* 474). When Beckwith points to the "miracle" of the fact that mutual intelligibility is "forged anew and through each conversation" (Beckwith 5), she draws upon Cavell's notion that making oneself (publicly and privately) intelligible occurs through a process of "confrontation and conversation as the means of determining whether we can live together, accept one another into the aspirations of our lives" (Cavell, *Cities of Words* 24). I note and underline the way in which "mutual intelligibility" is fastened to and inseparable from imagining "the aspirations of our lives": self-revelation, on this understanding, is not, or not only, the revealing of *facts* about oneself; it also includes, of necessity, an aspirational, imaginative projection.

Therefore, the parsimony underlying the more traditional and problematic readings of Rosalind's "education" of Orlando lies most basically in a parsimonious notion of what Rosalind's demand that Orlando "imagine me his love" calls for, what the notion of "imagination" at work here amounts to. Specifically, the ordinary assumption is that "to imagine" Rosalind as Orlando's love is more or less directly opposed to *confronting* Rosalind as his love in the flesh, that is, in real life. Confronting Rosalind in real life, then, is supposed to be a confrontation with what one might call the *factual* Rosalind. This is the same assumption behind or beneath the view on which Rosalind *knows* something about herself and about love that Orlando does not, and she must on that basis convey it to him in disguise, as conventional propriety and Orlando's own chivalry would render it impossible to do as herself. "Confronting" another, on this standard view, is a fairly straightforward matter of merely being in their (undisguised) presence.

But Cavell's notes on a "divided self and a doubled world," which requires an individual to "fight for recognition" by "[vying] with its incorporated interpretations with itself" through "confrontation and conversation" with others as a means of testing out or struggling to achieve the "accept[ing of] one another into the aspirations of our lives," and which ultimately amounts to and expresses "a demand or a desire for the reform or transfiguration of the world," highlight the extent to which the sense of *imagining* that Rosalind requires of Orlando is not strictly a function or consequence of her disguise. Confronting another, on this view, is a significant labor precisely because revealing oneself (one's selves) requires much more than standing before another: Beatrice and Benedick, as well as Oliver and Orlando, have already figured the insufficiencies with the standard view on which mutual intelligibility *just happens*.

Meanwhile, on Cavell's view, teaching and learning is the extension and acceptance of mutual intelligibility through aspirational or imaginative processes—and is thus more suggestive, here, of a reading on which Rosalind and Orlando engage together in an attempt to express and negotiate their imaginations of themselves and each other. What they reveal to themselves and each other is not merely factual, then, but also, and perhaps mainly, aspirational. What Rosalind teaches Orlando—what she reveals to him—is therefore, and authentically, herself.

In inviting Orlando to "imagine [her] his love," she invites him into a relation in which his imagination of her—one expressed already in his poetry, wherein Rosalind is a divine amalgam of Helen, Cleopatra, and Lucretia (3.2.142–145)—might be mixed, challenged, or molded by an outside influence, her own influence, through Cavell's "confrontation and conversation." If there is a test here, and it is not unreasonable to say that there is, it is not a test of Orlando's *love* but of Orlando's capacity to imagine in concert *with* someone else, to accommodate an imaginative confluence with another person. Inviting Orlando to imagine her his love allows Rosalind also to play herself imaginatively and thusly to reveal herself. This revelation is not accomplished by the *content* of her dubious self-descriptions (as apish and shallow and so on), but is rather *directly manifest* in the practical relation that she and Orlando take up with respect to one another, the relation that allows her to tease and banter, to remind and counsel, to plead and demand, to elicit and make promises, to *be*—and to *have*—a lover. Her performance of herself, having invited Orlando to woo her, amounts to confronting his imagination of himself and of her with her own imagination of him and of herself; or in other words, and simply, it amounts to a genuine courtship. What is it that Rosalind *is doing* in 3.2 and 4.1? She is, in the fullest possible sense of this phrase, *being herself*.

Bloom says that Rosalind "instructs us in the miracle of being a harmonious consciousness that is also able to accommodate the reality of another self" (Bloom 211), and, far from being at all incorrect, he is, as I take it, more incisive than he knows. When he praises Rosalind in this way, Bloom has her performance of Ganymede in mind, Rosalind's ability to embody two persons at once. But the "other self" that Rosalind accommodates is not Ganymede: *that* "self" is so thoroughly and swiftly cast off in Act 5 that none among the forest's population even thinks to ask after the whereabouts and disappearance of the "fair youth," even in the celebration of so many marriages that Ganymede "himself" precipitated. The "other self" that Rosalind "accommodates" is, rather, Orlando.

Rosalind and Orlando, through the process of their imaginative wooing, find themselves capable of going on together, that is, of tangling their imaginative capacities happily or productively. What Rosalind and Orlando reveal in their imaginative romance, then, is both just what Bloom says and also significantly more: they prove capable of that which neither Lear nor Othello can manage, or bear. They find themselves, in 4.1, in particular, *reveling* in what, on Cavell's reading, is the very source of "Othello's torture": "the premonition of the existence of another, hence of his own, his own as dependent, as partial" (Cavell, *The Claim of Reason* 493). By imaginatively projecting, out of "the way [they] now hold the world," "a future way [they] could help it become," what Rosalind and Orlando reveal to themselves and each other, what they teach and learn of themselves and each other—what, in short, they *find* as the result of their imaginative labor—is accurately described by Bloom as a "miracle." To find oneself capable of accepting "one another into the aspirations of [their] lives" is most completely what it means to accommodate the reality of another self.

5.5 CONCLUSION

As You Like It, on the interpretation I have offered here, may not seem immediately to fit with the particular patterns related to skeptical disavowal that I have traced in the other two comedies considered in this book. Once Orlando and Rosalind have each recognized his or her love for the other—and these recognitions occur more or less simultaneously in 1.3—neither lover finds this commitment open or susceptible to meaningful doubt, and neither experiences or acts upon any temptation to repudiate or deny the claims that such a relation implies. There is no magic flower to create mischief in this play, nor any proud disdain to raise an internal obstacle to the lovers' eventual union. When Bloom suggests that there is no genuine danger in *As You Like It*, I take it that the overwhelming amount of time that the two characters spend bantering and wooing in Ardenne is the primary fact to which he is responding.

But it is inaccurate to claim that no genuine danger appears at all: In fact, I note two different varieties of danger that stalk and direct the action from the opening Acts, and a consideration of these, together with relating them to Rosalind and Orlando's imaginative conversion in courtship, will help draw this analysis to a close.

Jaques and Oliver typify these two varieties of danger: in the former case, Jaques retreats from and refuses the claims of the world under the guise of a kind of idealism; in the latter case, Oliver, along with Frederick, in the initial Acts, refuses and repudiates the world in an opposite movement, say, a movement of *Realpolitik*, an attempt to clutch at the world. Where the perceived corruption of the world impels Jaques to remove himself from its infection and infectiousness, Oliver and Frederick's own corruption impels them to banish or expel that which threatens to expose the shameful rot in themselves.

If Jaques bears a glancing resemblance to Othello in his expressed urge to maintain his own purity through perfecting his independence, the affinity between Lear's motivation (as Cavell understands it) and that of Frederick and Oliver is still clearer: the possibility that their true value will be found out and found lacking—that their unworthiness will be exposed by comparison with another—impels them to cast out the world, and specifically those objects of comparison, through plots of murder and orders of banishment. Jaques evinces some of what Nietzsche calls an ascetic sort of nihilism, a despising of the world figured as the loving embrace of an otherworldly purity. Meanwhile, Oliver and Frederick evince Emerson's "unhandsome" aspect of the human condition: their response to a certain sense of disappointment in their relation to the world and to others manifests itself in a sort of "clutching," which has none of the transfiguring effects they imagine it to entail.[11]

In *As You Like It*, the particular responses that Jaques, on the one hand, and Oliver and Frederick, on the other, enact are rejections or repudiations primarily and directly of *others*, of the claims upon them levied by a community. In this concluding section, I wish to recall Cavell's connection of the type of skepticism to which these characters succumb with the notion of "disappointment," and the ways in which these relate both to Cavell's thinking on conversions or transfigurations inherent to "perfectionism" and to the aforementioned movements of repudiation. Much earlier I drew attention to the ways in which claims such as those that Orlando and Oliver voice (unsuccessfully) to one another in the play's opening scene are fundamentally claims to community; I also said, quoting Cavell, that "the wish and search for community are the wish and search for reason" (Cavell, *The Claim of Reason* 20).

I have already indicated, perhaps obliquely, that Orlando and Rosalind's "confrontation and conversation" enable them to find and to found the reason in the madness of their love, which is to say that they find themselves capable of going on with it—that is, they find and found this capacity in the very act of sharing and embodying their love with one another, much in the way Beatrice and Benedick do. In investigating Oliver's conversion in Act 4, I would like to draw out the way in which this, too, amounts to finding reason in a nonrational relation to others, to a community; and I would also like to demonstrate how this conversion reverses the nature of his appeals to his brother in the play's opening scene.

For Cavell, as we have seen several times, skeptical withdrawal is one sort of response to a certain truth, what he has called "the truth in skepticism." The truth he has in mind is most basically that we *cannot* approach the world, that we cannot get it nearer. Skepticism pictures the above situation as one in which we are by nature, as it were, cut off from the world and thus in need of a *method* or a *means* of approaching it, of bridging this gap, a method that we have heretofore lacked. What this view scants, on Cavell's understanding, is precisely the sense in which, if we cannot approach the world, this is because we are already there, because "there is no nearer … to get." He does not deny, then, the truth that the skeptic sees, that we cannot approach the world; nor does he deny the sort of disquieting sensation to which this fact gives rise, the sense of disappointment it involves. This is what he means in his reading of Emerson, when he says that "that itself is what is disappointing, that this is what there is" (Cavell, *This New Yet Unapproachable America* 108).

Cavell does deny, however, that skeptical *responses* are therefore warranted, that skepticism holds out the possibility of discovering such an approach to the world, say, a method. Instead, on his reading, adopting a skeptical stance with respect to the facts and values of our lives precludes the very possibility of *inhabiting* the world in the way that we ordinarily do, that is, when our lives are, in Dreyfus's words, "permeated by relevance" (Dreyfus, "Overcoming the Myth of the Mental" 49).

But Cavell also takes his own perfectionism—embodied in the attempt to enter into a new way of holding the world, and thereby transfigure or convert it—to respond to or to evince this same disappointment with the world, implying, as it does, a comparison with a better, ideal world. Perfectionism—the attempts at achieving a conversion of the world—therefore seems to risk something of Jaques's particular withdrawal, the danger of worldly rejection in the name of a certain idealism.

The crucial distinction to be drawn between Jaques's withdrawal in the pursuit of an objective vantage and the pictures of perfectionism and acknowledgment figured in Orlando and Rosalind's courtship, as well as in Oliver's conversion, lies in the *character* of one's disappointment, as I wish to call it; or more specifically, a measure of how thoroughly one discovers one's disappointment to color one's experience of the world. I note once more that in the classical skeptical investigations, a Descartes or a Hume takes up skeptical questions in isolation from others, in the study or by the fireplace, and that, for Hume, skepticism loses its grip when he engages the world in the form of public sociability. If the world is disappointing, this disappointment is not necessarily therefore perpetual. Cavell points to this distinction himself when he says that "[t]he sense of disappointment with the world as a place in which to seek the satisfaction of human desire is not the same as a sense of the world as cursed, perhaps at best to be endured, perhaps as a kind of punishment for being human" (Cavell, *Cities of Words* 3).

In Cavell's perfectionism, divided selves and doubled worlds, at the very least, provide something of a de facto public context, but a public context that must be taken up, accepted, or inherited. This public context might be a macrocosmic form of what Richard Eldridge has called in passing a kind of "multi-vocal self." Perfectionism, as opposed to skepticism, requires that one "fight for recognition"—that is, recognition of oneself by others, which Cavell has equated with a struggle for "a leading voice in [one's] history" (Cavell, *The Claim of Reason* 474). Eldridge has pointed out in conversation[12] that "leading voice" is a technical term in music, referring to the member of a four-part harmony that moves out of the current harmonic chord to a dissonant position, compelling the other voices to follow in order to reestablish the harmony. A disappointment with an existing harmony, so to speak, is not a disappointment with harmony as such; and moving away from that harmony by a step or a half-step need not be understood as expressing any drive for dissonance.

The distinction, then, between skeptical and perfectionist responses to the disappointing state of the extant world has directly to do with whether or not one pictures disappointment as something that is in principle possible to overcome in isolation, or whether one takes the inclusion of others to be necessary. It is important to see that, on the latter view, "self-knowledge," a term that emerged in the discussion of Frye early in the chapter, is inherently expressed as or in, as Cavell says, a knowledge "simultaneously turned toward oneself and toward one's contribution to the communal" (Saito and Standish 213). Oliver's pivoting in the play from murderous and "most unnatural" villain to Celia's redeemed husband best figures the way in which the conversion of the world in *As You Like It*, when it is successful, is achieved via a groundless and unreasonable—a pre-rational—commitment to others.

The publicness of Oliver's situation is never far from his mind; in fact, it provides him with the very motivation for his fratricidal plot in the play's first Act. Speaking of Orlando in soliloquy, Oliver says, "Yet he's gentle; never schooled, and yet learned; full of noble device; of all sorts enchantingly beloved; ... and especially of my own people, who best know him, that I am altogether misprized" (1.1.157–161). Oliver takes it upon himself in isolation, as it were, to solve the problem of his misprizing through a kind of clutching at the esteem of "own people." In attempting to erase Orlando from the world, he imagines that his people's love will simply devolve to him by default: no fighting for recognition—indeed, no interaction with his own people at all—is required. Oliver's murderous response to the shame of his own misprizing is an attempt at correcting the misprizing without exposing the shame that attends it.

However, when Oliver reappears in Ardenne in Act 4, delivering his brother's bloody handkerchief to Rosalind, the nature of his response has undergone a complete transformation. To Rosalind's question "What must we understand by this [handkerchief]," Oliver replies, "Some of my shame, if you will know of me / What man I am, and how, and why, and where / This handkerchief was stained" (4.3.95–98). Following Oliver's offstage encounter with Orlando, Oliver bears his confession before him, offering knowledge of "some of [his] shame" by which others might know him. Later, as Celia and Rosalind ask whether he is not Orlando's brother, his reply bespeaks Cavell's multi-vocal self: "'Twas I, but 'tis not I. I do not shame / To tell you what I was, since my conversion / So sweetly tastes, being the thing I am" (4.3.136–138). Oliver's self-exposure, owning the shamefulness of his former actions, directly opposes his earlier attempts to conceal himself. His references to a "doubled self"—the one that is and the one that was—describe or mark out his "conversion." In relating the tale of this conversion, he narrates the sort of engaged brotherly responsiveness that he and Orlando had alike repudiated in Act 1.

In the play's opening scene, Orlando and Oliver face each other across a chasm, each appealing to the "custom of nations" in order to advance or enforce a certain claim upon the other. As we have seen, the "custom of nations" is not self-interpreting, and thus, as each brother voices his claim in virtue of the same custom, each is to that extent justified in refusing the other's demand. In Oliver's tale of the snake and the lion, however, despite the fact that Orlando twice turned as if to abandon his sleeping brother, his "kindness" and his "nature" compelled him to "give battle to the lioness" on his brother's behalf (4.3.129–131). It is only after, and indeed on the basis of, Orlando's intervention that the scene of their fraternal reconciliation takes place, which Oliver describes in terms of the bathing of their "recountments" to one another "from first to last" in "tears" (4.3.140–141). Orlando's responding to the felt obligation of protecting his brother—the sort of obligation that had previously been made to stand on ceremony, as it were—occasions Oliver's own responsiveness; it deflates and circumvents the need for a mediating component, upon whose absence or failure their relation in the play's first scene had foundered.

Though Orlando might provide a reason for battling the lioness, and though Oliver in fact attributes Orlando's action to his "kindness" and his "nature," no such reason proved capable of moving Orlando thusly in the first scene. In this sense, that Orlando's response in 4.3 enacts or picks out or expresses a particular duty in this particular situation—a response that he can justify or explain post hoc—it is a *reasonable* response. In contrasting this with the fact that neither Oliver nor Orlando was able to make such a movement in 1.1—that, in other words, neither brother recognized any reasons in that circumstance as compelling particular, say gracious, responses—Orlando's *finding* himself obliged to rescue his brother is itself unreasonable, or pre-rational. Such a finding, however, *founds* the context in which the brothers can recount their experiences with and for each other, rendering the pair mutually intelligible. Stirm is thus correct to notice the parallels between the brothers' relationship here and Rosalind and Celia's relation from the first Act, but my analysis makes clear that this similarity is not reducible to any facts pertaining to gender in particular.

Rather, recalling Frye's claim that "humorous characters" are humorous in virtue of their lack of "self-knowledge," I wish to say now that the "self-knowledge" Oliver possesses in 4.3 is indeed self-knowledge, but that it is expressed, and is only expressible, in his responsiveness to Orlando's own acknowledgment, in Oliver's taking up the position of a brother with respect to Orlando, and in making the conditions of his own existence to that extent partial, dependent. His self-knowledge is not the discovery of previously undiscovered facts about himself; it is a reorientation of those facts "toward [his] contributions to the communal," toward another.

While Dale Priest identifies Jaques, with "scornful aloofness" and "cynicism," as I have noted earlier, and while these are not entirely inaccurate characterizations, the pejorative sense in these epithets is too strong. Jaques's melancholy, after all, has something like the good of the world in view, as on the occasion, in 2.1.25–45, when he bemoans the fate of a gored and suffering deer. Upon meeting Touchstone and finding a exemplar therein, he purposes to "cleanse the foul body of th'infected world" with the "medicine" of his wit (2.7.60–61). The play does feature an "infected world," and its body is indeed "cleansed" by the play's conclusion, but Jaques has nothing whatever to do with the reanimation or conversion of the world. His view of the self-sufficiency of his own wit—and this despite his many attempts to recruit others to "rail against our mistress the world" (3.2.272)—estranges him from both the world and from others. He adopts, then, even if in the interest of cleansing the world of its infection, a skeptical position: his madness, as I have already said, is to "forswear the full stream of the world" (3.2.404).

The stark consequence of adopting this sort of stance is manifested at the end of the play. Jaques had removed himself from the world and from others with the express purpose of dispensing medicine, of effecting a cure; but, in addition to the fact that his medicine has no obvious effect on the extant state of affairs, he finds himself without a place in the converted or healed world. His repudiation or failure to acknowledge the claims of the world and others upon him is unreconstructed. Even as the Duke Senior says, "Stay, Jaques, stay" (5.4.192), he declines. He is for "other than for dancing measures" (5.4.191). Instead, Jaques seeks "matter to be heard and learned" "out of these convertites" (5.4.182–183). These consequences of his repudiation are not stark in terms of any sort of finality or any particular tragedy; instead, Jaques's continuing self-exile at the end of the play shows forth what one might call the limits of acknowledgment, the fact that the (existence of) the world is to be, and must be, *accepted*; and that this acceptance can be invited but not compelled. Jaques's self-exile at the end of the play demonstrates the reverse of what I earlier attributed to Hume's thinking on skepticism: if the skeptical threat is *perpetually* eradicable, the possibility of failure here, or denial, is nevertheless and ineradicably *standing*.

If Bloom is correct to claim that no "authentic harm" attends the action of the play, then, this is not because the characters or the contexts of this play differ meaningfully from those of more fraught and obvious examples like *Hamlet* or *Macbeth*. That Orlando and Rosalind themselves do not appear to struggle with skeptical temptations with respect to their romantic relationship means neither that the acceptance or acknowledgment that the pair figures is easily accomplished nor that such skeptical threats are entirely absent from the play, even in the lives of the romantic leads. While Oliver speaks of his conversion, of a double self, in explicit terms in 4.3, his narrative of Orlando's action also describes a conversion, after all: Orlando's position in the play's opening scene, no less than Oliver's, amounts to a failure of acknowledgment, an attempt to rely upon a legalistic logic where such logic is powerless to effect the brotherly connection that each sibling seeks; and Orlando's turning away in this opening scene must later be made whole.

It is in fact directly against a background of the possibility of this sort of failure—one also hinted at in Rosalind's attempt to establish abstract conditions for her merriment in 1.2—that Rosalind and Orlando's imaginative engagement with each other can perform its exemplary work or can stand out as exemplary at all. It is precisely because the motivations of Jaques and Oliver are comprehensible, if deplorable, responses to a disappointment with the world "as cursed" that an expression of a similar disappointment— a "sense of disappointment with the world as a place in which to seek the satisfaction of human desire," as Cavell has it—takes the perfectionist or imaginative form of the world's conversion. In this respect, like the other comedies taken up in this study, *As You Like It* reveals the full scope of the joys and consequences attending our various available responses to the "truth in skepticism."

NOTES

1. The way in which Frye's "moral norm" is to be distinguished from what he calls "morality" is mirrored in the way Cavell attacks "moralism" along the lines of an Emersonian conformity. "Morality" or "moralism" in the pejorative sense would merely be the same type of bondage to a social custom that Frye's "self-knowledge" is supposed to move beyond. Frye's "moral norm" and the "self-knowledge" that goes with it doubtless owes a great deal to Kantian ideas about the relation of autonomy to the moral law. Cavell certainly owes a similar debt to Kant, but I will be concerned to show the ways in which Cavell's emphasis on conversion and conversation render autonomy more obviously public than it is in either Kant or in Frye's depiction.
2. This is not unique to Frye as theorist, as far as Cavell is concerned. In fact, as I noted in the early chapters, this is what Cavell seems to take *anyone's* work to reveal—an inability to know in advance what to make of the work.
3. This spelling follows my edition of the complete works (see Chapter 3 references, pg. 86) and comports with Shakespeare's source in Thomas Lodge's *Roslynde*; I am aware that most editions print "Arden."
4. In perhaps an ironic note, or at least an interesting one, among the readings that occasions Stirm's response through its incompleteness is one done by Montrose: "'The Place of a Brother' in *As You Like It*." On Stirm's interpretation, Montrose's

attention to the social construction of gender and power dynamics is too heavily focused on the fraternal pairs and overlooks the importance of Rosalind as Celia.

5. I will stop making explicit note of when Rosalind is and is not operating in disguise. Perhaps this will need to be its own point, offered with its own support, but however far the costuming and suiting like a man are taken to allow Rosalind to speak more freely than her gender and social position would generally afford, I find it difficult and unnecessary to draw a clear distinction between a "Ganymede" that she performs and any more fundamental "Rosalind" that she likewise performs. This difficulty, it seems to me, has also to do with the fact that the distinction is also hard for Rosalind herself to draw, as evidenced by both her capacity to exercise her inventive powers prior to disguising ("He calls us back," she says to Celia in 1.2.241, taking another opportunity to speak with him despite the fact that he has done no such thing) and also the fact that while in disguise Celia must on occasion remind her that she is supposed to be a man. I therefore question—indeed, deny—the value of making this distinction in viewing Rosalind's words and actions as expressing her character.

6. Rosalind's reference here to driving a man out of love and into an ascetic life is an interesting gender inversion. In the plays of Shakespeare and the critical tradition thereof, the spiritual life and the good marriage are commonly understood as the two ways in which to control or contain specifically female sexuality (Dusinberre, *Shakespeare and the Nature of Women*; Levine, *Women's Matters*): we see examples of this in Hamlet's "Get the to a nunnery!" injunctions and in Theseus's offer to Hermia of "single [convent] life" as a third choice beyond death or Demetrius. Historically speaking, asceticism is not merely a female phenomenon, and Rosalind's explicit association of the male monastic life with "a living humour of madness" emphasizes this fact. For Rosalind's invented suitor, the ascetic life does not serve as an appropriate alternative means of policing his sexual desire, as it appears in Hermia's case. This is to say, it is not offered as a means of preventing the practical consummation of a love relationship, but is rather presented as the insane cure for the insanity of love.

7. It is precisely in such a moment of the breakdown of an order of significance that Macbeth, in his own tragedy, says that "There's nothing serious in mortality; / All is but toys" (2.3.115–116).

8. In moving toward a discussion of Rosalind's self-exposure or self-revelation under the condition of her disguise, I must emphasize that despite the potential connotations of my repeated invocations of "helplessness" or "powerlessness" in characterizing Rosalind's relation to Orlando and to the world, these terms, in my analysis, have a demonstratively positive valence. They are not invoked in the interest of denying Rosalind's agency, but they rather map out the sense in which Rosalind finds—and allows—the world to approach her.

9. I do not say that it is any remarkable ability. I merely say that it is *his* full wit.

10. A quick search reveals that the source of this wonderfully apt formulation—I knew I'd heard it somewhere else—is the TV show *Scrubs*, Season 1, episode 6, entitled "My Bad."

11. This is also related to Nietzsche, in fact. In *Ecce Homo*, Nietzsche rails (in a very anti-Deleuzian way) against responding to unpleasing elements of the world through attempts to efface or eradicate them, which he also and elsewhere relates to the "instinct against life." In *Ecce Homo*, he merely points out that

what it means to love the world cannot be accomplished by loving *some* of the world and repudiating the rest: "Nothing in existence may be subtracted, nothing is dispensable."
12. At a symposium, "Kant and Cavell on Perfectionism and Education," held in Stockholm, Sweden, 6–7 September 2013.

REFERENCES

Barber, Cesar Lombardi. *Shakespeare's Festive Comedy: A Study of Dramatic Form and Its Relation to Social Custom.* Princeton, NJ: Princeton University Press, 2011. Print.

Beckman, Margaret Boerner. "The Figure of Rosalind in *As You Like It*." *Shakespeare Quarterly* 29.1 (1978): 44–51. Print.

Beckwith, Sarah. *Shakespeare and the Grammar of Forgiveness.* Ithaca, NY: Cornell University Press, 2011. Print.

Bloom, Harold. *Shakespeare: The Invention of the Human.* New York: Riverhead, 1998. Print.

Calvo, Clara. "Pronouns of Address and Social Negotiation in *As You Like It*." *Language and Literature* 1.1 (1992): 5–27. Print.

Cavell, Stanley. *Cities of Words: Pedagogical Letters on a Register of the Moral Life.* Cambridge, MA: Harvard University Press, 2005. Print.

———. *Conditions Handsome and Unhandsome.* Chicago: University of Chicago Press, 1990. Print.

———. *The Claim of Reason.* New York: Oxford University Press, 1979. Print.

———. "The Normal and the Natural." *The Cavell Reader.* Ed. Stephen Mulhall. New York: Blackwell, 1996. Print.

———. *The Senses of Walden: An Expanded Edition.* Chicago: University of Chicago Press, 2013. Print.

———. *This New Yet Unapproachable America: Lectures After Emerson After Wittgenstein.* Chicago: University of Chicago Press, 2013. Print.

Cavell, Stanley, and Northrop Frye. "Foreword." *A Natural Perspective.* New York: Columbia University Press, 1995. 159. Print.

Dreyfus, Hubert L. "Overcoming the Myth of the Mental: How Philosophers Can Profit from the Phenomenology of Everyday Expertise." *Proceedings and Addresses of the American Philosophical Association* 79.2 (2005): 47–65.

Dusinberre, Juliet. *Shakespeare and the Nature of Women.* London: Macmillan, 1975. Print.

Eldridge, Richard. *Stanley Cavell.* New York: Cambridge University Press, 2003. Print.

Eldridge, Richard Thomas. *Literature, Life, and Modernity.* New York: Columbia University Press, 2013. Print.

Erickson, Peter B. "Sexual Politics and the Social Structure in' As You like It.'" *The Massachusetts Review* 23.1 (1982): 65–83. Print.

Frye, Northrop. *A Natural Perspective: The Development of Shakespearean Comedy and Romance.* New York: Columbia University Press, 1965. Print.

———. "The Argument of Comedy." *Narrative Dynamics: Essays on Time, Plot, Closure, and Frames.* Columbus: Ohio State University Press, 2002. 102–109. Print.

Frye, Northrop, Troni Grande, and Garry Sherbert. *Northrop Frye's Writings on Shakespeare and the Renaissance*. Toronto: University of Toronto Press, 2010. Print.

Glendinning, Simon. *On Being with Others*. New York: Routledge, 1998. Print.

Levine, Nina S. *Women's Matters: Politics, Gender, and Nation in Shakespeare's Early History Plays*. Newark: University of Delaware Press, 1998. Print.

Montrose, Louis Adrian. "'Shaping Fantasies': Figurations of Gender and Power in Elizabethan Culture." *Representations* 2 (1983): 61–94. Print.

Nietzsche, Friedrich. *Thus Spake Zarathustra*. New York: Algora Publishing, 2003. Print.

Priest, Dale G. "Oratio and Negotium: Manipulative Modes in *As You like It*." *Studies in English Literature, 1500–1900* 28.2 (1988): 273–286.

Saito, Naoko, and Paul Standish. *Stanley Cavell and the Education of Grownups*. New York: Fordham University Press, 2012. Print.

Stirm, Jan. "'For Solace a Twinne-like Sister': Teaching Themes of Sisterhood in *As You Like It* and Beyond." *Shakespeare Quarterly* 47.4 (1996): 374–386. Print.

Tvordi, Jessica. "Female Alliance and the Construction of Homoeroticism in *As You Like It* and *Twelfth Night*." *Maids and Mistresses, Cousins and Queens: Women's Alliances in Early Modern England* (1999): 114–130. Print.

6 Coda

The central question engaged by the work on display in this book—both the literary scholarship and the labor of the characters in the plays under investigation—is of an existential nature. Roughly stated: what is to be done with the notion that our fundamental relation to the world is not one of knowing? Understanding the motivations for various human activities and relations along the lines of what I have called an avoidance-acknowledgment continuum rather than or besides a knowledge-ignorance spectrum represents one sort of response to this notion, but certainly nothing like a complete one. In the first place, it is profoundly dubious that anything like a "complete" response, where this completeness would be embodied in an abstract or general formula, exists at all: searching for such completeness would both beg and deflect the question. In the second place, the very assertion of and reliance upon the concepts of acknowledgment and avoidance in studying literature, in particular, risks precisely the reification of a method, of a certain form of *theoretically* approaching the task of reading that such concepts were originally invoked to circumvent. Acknowledgment and avoidance become conceptually necessary in virtue of the very fact of the limitations of such theoretical approaches.

For these and other reasons, acknowledgment and avoidance are not themselves master terms according to which human action or literary meaning become finally or ultimately intelligible. Acknowledgment and avoidance are neither a level more abstract nor a level more concrete than the concepts of knowledge and ignorance. Put another way, if part of the danger of skepticism, as Cavell perceives it, lies in "the attempt to convert the human condition, the condition of humanity, into an intellectual difficulty, a riddle" (Cavell, *The Claim of Reason* 492), then it is still not clear that *nothing* pertaining to human life or the human condition might be fruitfully conceived as an intellectual difficulty or a riddle. Indeed, one might say that the greatest of difficulties in coping with the condition of humanity lies in demarcating issues that can be productively addressed through something like problem solving and those that require something more like an embodied or attitudinal reorientation. To render the issue still more complex, it is further unclear that such reorientations are neatly separable from—or always achievable without—anything like intellectual engagement. It may well be the case that no such demarcation is possible; certainly, following the hints established in the first two chapters of this book, any *project* aimed at generating a method of demarcation is apt to end in failure.

When we are left, as people and as scholars, with the fact that our fundamental relation to the world is not one of knowing, the scholarly and existential difficulties of situating the intellectual endeavors of study, reflection, discussion, and writing within the shuffle and flow of ordinary life come to the fore. In Cavell's explorations of *Lear* and *Othello*, for instance, the problem of a tragic avoidance emerges as the inclination to treat all aspects of love relations, both filial and romantic, in disengaged or logical terms, in terms that understand love to be the effect of certain manipulable causes (*Lear*) or amenable to and indeed reliant upon or produced by ocular or otherwise public proof (*Othello* and *Lear*). What is avoided, on this model, is precisely the possibility that attempts to foreclose upon or to overcome skeptical doubts are self-defeating, that there exists any relation to the world at all that is irreducible to an epistemological problem.

In order to bring out the ways in which the skeptical temptations figured in *Lear* and *Othello* are especially and perhaps uniquely spectacular in their consequences, though by no means extraordinary as temptations in themselves, I have offered readings of three of Shakespeare's more widely read comedies under the working hypothesis that the genre of comedy, no less than tragedy, features these skeptical temptations as well, albeit with (often) entirely different outcomes. Each of the comedies treated in this book has, in addition to supporting or corroborating the aforementioned hypothesis, revealed particular inflections of the skeptical urge.

In *Much Ado*, two different sorts of doubt afflict the primary romantic pairs: Claudio, like Othello, struggles with the urge to transform his love for Hero, originally experienced as something that happens to or comes over or befalls him, into something like an object that he possesses, can be shown to possess, and can have stolen from him. Beatrice and Benedick, meanwhile, grapple with a view of loving as dependent upon verifiable facts, that is, as following from or requiring the truth of another's love as a first condition. The paradox that this pair faces at the altar is that, under such conditions, no sort of mutual affection can get started at all, as each is made to wait upon the confession of the other.

In *Dream*, one finds an *Othello*-like pattern in Egeus's treatment of his daughter's filial duty, which, like Claudio, figures the love and obedience in question as something of an abstract object, something that he may possess and command, something that can be "filched," and something that, in short, requires nothing from him in the way of recognition or acknowledgment, to say nothing of maintenance. One finds also, as in *Much Ado*, a prevailing view of love as requiring or following from an epistemological certainty: Demetrius and Lysander take turns characterizing and mischaracterizing Hermia and Helena as though their loves were logical consequences or causal effects of the distinguishing features of each.

Finally, in *As You Like It*, the skeptical temptation toward withdrawal affects both the romantic aspect of love and a familial articulation, exemplified in the moment when Oliver and Orlando attempt to mediate or negotiate their love and duty for one another in terms of an identical and therefore inadequate appeal to the "custom of nations." In this, one finds yet again a view of loving as logically compelled by certain facts—in this case facts pertaining to patrilineal descent and the customs governing the allotment of property and mutual responsibilities of brothers. But further, in the character of Jaques, we receive another picture of skeptical withdrawal, one not directly related to loving another specific person in any obvious way.

For Jaques, the world's corruption requires a sort of redemption or conversion, and his various and alternating endeavors to eloquently or insouciantly rail against the state of things are offered specifically at "cleans[ing] the foul body of th'infected world" (2.7.60). His raillery, however, takes the form of removing himself explicitly from the course and stream of everyday affairs in order to comment upon them; and one finds, at the play's conclusion, not only that Jaques's well-meaning efforts at world-transformation have been ineffectual, but also that, in the converted or redeemed world on which the play closes, Jaques has forfeited (and continues to forfeit) his place in the new world. If the movement of initial withdrawal from the course of the world, as also in *Dream* and *Much Ado*, is reversible without the satisfaction of skeptical demands, then Jaques, no less than Lear or Othello, serves to show that achieving such a return is neither foregone nor easily effected.

The Cavellian concepts of acknowledgment and avoidance, as ways of marking or characterizing differences among available modes of response to the temptation to draw back from the world in order to know it better or to get it nearer, will be as various and variously applicable as the manifestations of the urge to skeptical withdrawal summarized above. Such temptations may or may not pertain specifically to love. In all cases, while "avoidance" names a basic unresponsiveness to the immanent conditions of one's involvement in the world, the criteria for responsiveness in any particular situation are at least somewhat contextually dependent. What will count as sufficiently evidencing "acknowledgment" in any given set of circumstances is internal, for the most part, to that set of circumstances. Therefore, neither acknowledgment nor avoidance is straightforwardly available in any specifiable or formalizable set of actions or dispositions: there is no one *thing* that it is to acknowledge the existence of, and one's relation to, the world.

In this way, although it is tempting in something resembling a conclusion to draw together and generalize from the examples of successfully overcoming, and of failing to overcome, the urges toward skeptical doubt in Shakespeare's comedies, such a project would be inherently misguided. It may not get any better or more specific than Cavell's comment in *The Claim of Reason* that in some cases skeptical doubts are "countered not by saying that a fact about the world is otherwise than you supposed, but by showing that your world is otherwise than you see" (Cavell, *The Claim of Reason* 180). Acknowledgment is, on this view, simply a willingness or a capacity to see the world as otherwise in the specific absence of any altered facts. While one might show instances or examples of such a capacity, or of acknowledgment itself, these would of necessity fall short of both definitions and prescriptions. While one might show that Helena, for example, at the end of *Dream,* has come to accept as *love itself* the very feature she had earlier characterized as love's childlike immaturity—namely, its ability to "melt" like "hail" (1.1.245–246) or like "snow" (4.1.165)—and while one might rightly say that this conversion of Helena's stance with respect to this characteristic amounts to acknowledging a certain aspect of the human condition, it is both impossible and unnecessary to generalize from such an example. The concept of acknowledgment simply becomes no clearer with generalization; what acknowledgment *is* is directly manifest in Helena's claim to eventually "have found Demetrius like a jewel, / Mine own and not mine own" (4.1.190–191).

The notion that the world is something that can both go dead and become otherwise—that these are standing possibilities inherent in the condition of being human—flies in the face of one of the most basic tenets of modern academic research projects, namely, Weber's famous sense of the world's disenchantment, in light of which any human responsiveness to the world is at best superfluous and at worst obfuscatory of the truth. Instead, as it is imagined, the (truth about the) world stands resolutely and statically over against the vagaries and changeability of (subjective) human concerns. Stripping away, partitioning out, or otherwise accounting for one's subjective standpoint with respect to the facts of the world becomes the very first step in the pursuit of anything that will count as scholarly knowledge.

So it is as well in literary studies: the impasse between the post-structuralists and the evocritics that I discussed in the opening chapters might be understood as a disagreement over the relative possibility of achieving the world's perfect disenchantment. The discussion in the Introduction of the assumption shared by each side of that debate—a "rules-as-rails" picture of things, according to which either the world is objectively the way it is anyway or else we are (subjectively) free to impose and create "truth" where we will—has already revealed the significant difficulties intrinsic to taking the gap between mind and world, or mind and mind, as a starting point, difficulties that Fogelin groups together as the "paradox of interpretation." In returning to these matters in a Coda, in light of the foregoing readings of Shakespeare's comedies, it will perhaps be more possible to recollect the salutary effects of taking a Cavellian position with respect to literary investigations, or to lay them out more coherently.

In terms that emerged in the *As You Like It* discussion, the post-structuralists and the evocritics share an assumption that the world, and literary meanings in particular, require(s) *approaching,* either as the result of our a priori estrangement from objective truth or as a consequence of the need to impose meaning or value upon literary works. But the very notion that literature requires *approaching* at all, the assumption of this a priori estrangement, reifies differing brands, or views, of skeptical withdrawal. On one side, such withdrawal is a first and necessary step in re-taking (knowledge of) the world purged of doubt or superstition. On this view, we are too *close* to the world, too bound up with it, and this nearness confuses or clouds our view; our estrangement is an epistemological one, to be assuaged with and through the clarity of greater distance, say objectivity.

On the other side, such true knowledge of the world is simply precluded (and in this way, post-structuralism is the more virulent form of skepticism): there is no vantage from which the type of clarity the other side imagines necessary would be possible. Instead, any cloudiness or confusion must be (and is) overcome by something like subjective, willful intervention. To the extent that significance exists at all, such significance is entirely up to us.

Each of these positions scants to an extent the ramifications of Cavell's "truth in skepticism," the truth that skepticism records. Since *knowing* does not express or characterize our fundamental relation to the world, neither the discovery of objective facts about the world nor the imposition of subjective truths upon the world will be either necessary or sufficient to dispelling the sense of the world's estrangement that motivates each project. The sense of the world's estrangement is not itself, in other words, the manifestation of "an intellectual lack" (Cavell, "Knowing and Acknowledging" 68).

Skepticism's truth lies in the potential for estrangement from the world; skepticism's diabolical temptation lies in its promise to once and for all foreclose upon this possibility through securing a tight epistemological connection to the world and to others. But taking the skeptic up on this offer has the very opposite effect, as we have seen over and over again. It is merely another iteration of Dreyfus's comment: "if you strip away relevance and start with context-free facts, you can't get relevance back," either by inference from the facts themselves or by anything like free subjective choice (Dreyfus, "Overcoming the Myth of the Mental" 49).

The assumption that Dreyfus and Cavell share—one from which a Cavellian way of reading literature stems—is one that I have quoted before: that we "are always already in a world that is organized in terms of our bodies and interests and thus is permeated by relevance" (Dreyfus 49). Although the truth in skepticism demonstrates that such relevance can be lost or refused, both Dreyfus and Cavell take a fundamental engagement with the world through public practices as the ordinary or default state of affairs. While literary theory—all the various differing methods of achieving an understanding of literature—takes the need to establish a way of approaching literature as a first principle, and thus assumes the abrogation of the ordinary functioning of relevance, a Cavellian practice of (scholarly) reading makes no such assumption.

For precisely this reason—that no "approach" to reading literature is on offer in a Cavellian perspective—the difficulty of undertaking such a practice of reading is hard to overstate. In seeking to do justice to the sense of relevance that permeates our lives and that is embodied particularly in our practical and social dealings with language and literature, both the processes and the products of reading will be, and do, something different—but not less—from what literary scholarship as it is more traditionally conceived has heretofore imagined.

David Rudrum puts the difficulty associated with a Cavellian reading practice succinctly: "In a nutshell, if Cavell's writings on literature show us anything, it is that no serious student of either literature or philosophy can rest on the laurels of a theoretical or methodological approach to his or her subject" (Rudrum 3). One must, instead, enter into the reading of a work, or the thinking with a work, prepared to learn anew and again what sorts of things reading and thinking are. Harking back to Cavell's own foreword to Northrop Frye's work, it is rather the case "that you do not know a priori which terms are to do the theoretical work in his prose, as if nothing short of the powers of each word in the language is sufficient to understand the powers of language" (Cavell and Frye xiv). Here, the process of reading, whether of Frye's criticism or of Shakespeare's plays, is a matter of learning from the work itself "which terms are to do the theoretical work," a process that eschews the possibility, or at least the utility, of bringing an explicit, a priori methodology to bear upon a given work.

Stephen Mulhall has called this a "peculiarly reflexive conception of the task of reading" (Mulhall 193), associating it, on the same page, with a "Wittgensteinian practice of recounting criteria as a mode of thinking whose prosecution constitutes a reanimation of words, self, and world—a way of declaring and so enacting one's own existence and that of others through the full acknowledgment of the life in (that is, our life with) words." Kevin Cahill brings together the sense of individual reflexivity in such a reading practice—the way in which such reading is *personal*—with the sense of such a reading practice's (structural) *publicness*: "A mark of Wittgenstein's later thought, then," he says, "is the idea that 'authentic' clarity in philosophy is inseparable from our acceptance that the meaning of our words is in a certain sense dependent on what shows up as mattering to us" (Cahill 141), which Cahill opposes to a more standard, say abstract, way of "approaching" texts. In such a standard literary practice, one that either seeks or denies objectivity, one that, in short, puts any notion of *responsiveness* out of play,

> we enter into a vicious cycle where it becomes nearly impossible to teach the habits of thought required for responding to features of our lives and world not envisaged from the disengaged stance and where the world increasingly loses any power to evoke those responses in us.
>
> (Cahill 141)

The continuing insufficiencies of structural accounts of determining meaning, coupled with the existential fact that we experience and share in determinate meaning in ordinary conversation, simply shows once more the accuracy of Cavell's "truth in skepticism." There is something connective or stabilizing, something *regular*, that criteria or bare facts just do not do, but that we nonetheless find from moment to ordinary moment done, accomplished.

Responsiveness or acknowledgment—the acceptance and inheritance of public ways of going on in our lives with words and others—is not offered, then, as a systematic explanation of the determination of the meanings of words, but is rather cited as a baseline condition of mutual intelligibility. Agreement in form of life is, on this picture, less a metaphysical given than a matter of ongoing responsiveness—to recall Fogelin once more, an ongoing matter of "join[ing] a consensus in *action*" (Fogelin 28). Acceptance and inheritance of public concepts, being the condition of mutual intelligibility, also entails the possibility and emergence of new applications of concepts, or of new readings of literary works. This fact links a Cavellian practice of scholarly reading with a Cavellian sense of the purpose of scholarly production, which is to say, teaching.

As Richard Eldridge notes, "Mastery and fluency within a life with concepts are hence to be understood ... as matters of a grasp of patterns together with an ability both to imitate and to redirect gaze and interest—to respond anew to life" (Eldridge, *Literature, Life, and Modernity* 15). Characterizing "mastery and fluency" in terms of a capacity both "to imitate" others in applying concepts and "to redirect gaze and interest" links one's own learning—from a work, as from others—with the ability to make such learning *public*, in redirecting *others'* gazes or interests on the extended assumption that one's way of looking at the world, because originating in the imitation of public practice, will be intelligible to others with whom one might hope to find oneself in agreement. The shift may seem subtle, but the distinction between a Cartesian attempt to achieve certainty that there are *others like myself* and a more Heideggerian-Cavellian quest for *those among whom I am one too* is profound.[1]

The nature of making claims pertaining to literary works, then, cannot be simply a matter of establishing proofs, collocating coherence, or asserting (merely) personal truth. Such views of scholarly claims tend to assume the irrelevance of agreement in form of life, or, put another way, they assume that truth is guaranteed or ensured in virtue of an aprioristic logic of determination. Although claims about literary meaning or value or significance are of necessity matters of self-expression, their ability to redirect or reorient the gazes of others renders them effectively claims to community, which is roughly what Cavell means in saying that "the wish and search for community are the wish and search for reason" (Cavell, *The Claim of Reason* 20). Eldridge characterizes the public nature of his own claims to community as follows:

> 'We' as I use it (and as it is typically used by philosophers of certain kinds) is meant to be improvisatory and invitational: to invite others to share in and test a thought for themselves. It is not meant to be a report on the results of research into what countable individuals have in fact said or thought or felt. Claims about how we respond, what we feel, and what we are like are, therefore, in a distinctive way vulnerable, naked, and exposed.
>
> (Eldridge 23)

The sense of vulnerability, nakedness, and exposure that Eldridge cites here acknowledges and takes seriously the possibility of a community's refusal or denial, the possibility of the failure of recognition or intelligibility, the discovery that one is, in virtue of having made an unintelligible or unshareable claim, to that extent isolated from others as from oneself, from reason and community at once.

Rudrum notes similar stakes in his consideration of entering Cavellian claims:

> To stake a claim is metaphorically to stick one's neck on the block: it is to make a statement in the public domain that asserts something one believes to be the case and about which one presumably feels strongly enough to declare it openly and publicly. Whether or not it contains, implicitly or explicitly, an appeal to the grounds that would justify, defend, or otherwise argue for its content *qua* claim, it is nevertheless a provisional kind of utterance, but one whose provisionality awaits ratification in the form of uptake in and from the public domain to which it was addressed. To put it another way, "*claim* designates my pretension to speak in the name of the community."
>
> (Rudrum 15)[2]

Such pretensions, as in Eldridge's thinking above, can always meet with failure or incomprehension, denial, or repudiation. The "ratification" to which Rudrum refers is importantly expressed as "uptake in and from the public domain"—that is, as acceptance and inheritance rather than as something like verbal confirmation or assent. It is not something like a community member saying, "yes, that's right, I agree"; it is, rather, the community member finding him- or herself capable of going on with the content of the claim, of putting it to use in "respond[ing] anew to life," of discovering him- or herself capable of being shown that "the world is otherwise than you see," of seeing both the possibility and value of something like a "future way" in which we might "hold the world."

It is on these grounds that in the Introduction and Chapter 2, especially, I advocated a reorientation of literary scholarship on a certain model of teaching and learning, rather than a strict theoretical epistemology. The *defactoist* view, as I adopted the term from Fogelin in the opening chapters, most basically claims, along the lines suggested by Stephen Mulhall, that the fundamental relation to the world is *practical*, that the world that we *have*, to the extent that we *have* it at all, is grasped or engaged as part of "a consensus in *action*." Cavellian reading practice, as I have sketched it above and throughout this book, adopts a defactoist perspective insofar as it takes the pursuit of answering any questions as to *how* meanings—the various meanings we have and discuss and point to—are both determinable and determined to be idle intellectual extravagances. The confusion of our ability to perceive, negotiate, and publicly discuss the significance of literary works with a cognitive achievement effected according to some comprehensible and general process, as Wittgenstein also conceives of the problem, merely distracts and indeed precludes us from making any *use* of this (miraculous) ability.

When I argued earlier in this book that a defactoist perspective serves a "deflationary" purpose, the deflated target is precisely the notion that we as literary scholars must solve or declare our positions on such metaphysical or intellectual riddles as a prerequisite of engaging in the valid study of literature. Following the considerations of Fogelin, Mulhall, Dreyfus, and Cavell, any view of sharing, justifying, or negotiating the significance of this or that literary piece that requires solving an epistemological problem pertaining to other minds will end up mischaracterizing its object.

"Teaching and learning" refers to a reading and scholarly practice that aims at joining a consensus in action through professing, negotiating, and rebutting views; through staking claims to belonging among (at least some) others in virtue of one's grasp of the world; and through finding oneself to belong in the world as illuminated in the views of another. I do not say that this is what the intellectual endeavor of literary scholarship *ought* to be. Thinking upon the structure of the academy in the Western world of the early 21st century, with its expectation that literary scholars will give lectures and mentor students, publish papers and monographs, conduct discussions and conversations in seminars, attend conferences, edit journals collaboratively, and so on, I simply aver that this is what the intellectual endeavor of literary scholarship *is*.[3]

A recent discussion in another subfield of literary scholarship highlights the distinction to be drawn between achieving a stable answer to a metaphysical or epistemological question of determination and the practices of teaching and studying literature. William A. Johnson, working within the context of Comparative Textual Media (CTM), pushes back against some of his colleagues, objecting to Marshall McLuhan's famous attempt to map the message onto the medium, which is obviously one answer to the sort of metaphysical or epistemological question pertaining to the "message's" determination. Johnson points out that "the textual medium is ... one component in a complex *system* of reading and writing behaviors," a system that he calls "reading cultures" and "reading communities," and that he describes as consisting of "medium, literary text, writer and reader [...] deeply embedded within society, culture, politics, ideology" (Johnson, "Bookrolls as Media" 119). His study of the bookroll in high Roman antiquity implicates the material textual object itself in enabling a certain *"tightness"* of the interactions between, for example, "literariness and economic benefit or textual acuity and social hierarchy" (Johnson, "Bookrolls as Media" 119–120). The ancient medial technology of the bookroll is, as Johnson shows, inseparable from what it means—or meant—to *read*, and the ability to engage literary texts itself is bound up with questions of social standing, patronage, the morality of leisure time itself, and so on. But on his view, the medium's relation to any particular message can only be understood in terms of this deep sociocultural embeddedness. There is something, once more, that studying the artifactual *medium* cannot do or cannot do alone.

While in this most recent work, Johnson problematically advocates adopting an "approach" to literary art that would attempt to take account of something like this system in its entirety, an earlier piece of his is in fact more salutary, since it dodges the dangerous assumption that such a system and all its relations, especially under the condition of constant historical change, *can* and *must* be "known" in its entirety in order to do what it is that literary scholarship does. In that earlier piece, Johnson notes that

> Much of what we do in higher education, both institutionally and individually, is to work toward the construction of particular types of reading groups. In a successful humanities class, we are not so much teaching texts as creating a reading society. ... Individually we as teachers work toward creating the disposition that a particular text (the one we are studying in the class) is meaningful and relevant: it is part of what you need to apprehend the knowledge and to experience that sense of meaningfulness that bonds the group together as a productive, self-validating unit. These group dynamics—the construction of the attitude that Plato is *important*, that Plato *should be interesting*—are fundamental to education, and fundamental to the high intellectual experience.
>
> (Johnson, "Reading Cultures and Education" 20)

Johnson here adopts some troubling language around the "construction" of meaning and the importance of "self-validation," both of which underestimate the objective or external valences of truth and knowledge—the senses in which literary meaning is not *experienced* as up to us alone and in which the aim of literary study is likewise experienced as bearing upon something larger than self-validation. But he nonetheless astutely underscores the fact that meaningfulness and relevance are "fundamental to education, and fundamental to high intellectual experience," which also, along with his concept of the "reading society," emphasizes the inherently *public* nature of "high intellectual experience" and thereby links his view of teaching and learning to a Cavellian sense of going on in agreement with others as "a matter of our sharing routes of interest and feeling, modes of response, senses of humor and of significance and of fulfillment" (Cavell, *Must We Mean What We Say?* 52).

Johnson offers the classroom, directed according to a syllabus or curriculum, as a mode of intellectual exchange within which issues of meaningfulness and relevance are found and founded. But there is no distinction in *kind* to be drawn between this picture of a "reading community" and, for example, the reading public constituted through participating in the engagement with and discussion of published journal articles, or that community on display in giving, receiving, and interrogating conference presentations. These endeavors, too, stake provisional claims to community; they declare and exemplify "routes of interest and feeling, modes of response," and the rest; and for that reason they also require a public uptake, an acknowledgment, in order to *work* as literary scholarship. Johnson's education, like the very practice of "reflexive" reading that Mulhall finds in Cavell, like the practice of scholarly reading and writing in general, is a matter first and foremost of making oneself exemplary, or of revealing oneself and one's views to others in the hope and expectation of ratification or uptake, or of undertaking the provisional joining of a provisional consensus in a certain way of holding the world.

In undertaking the Cavellian readings of Shakespearean comedy that I have offered here, I have urged against the temptation to generalize too hastily with such concepts as "avoidance" or "acknowledgment." Such a temptation to generalize reflects a view on which the particular cases themselves are so to speak impure. Therefore a retreat into the middle distance for the purpose of perceiving the common or transcendent element lying in or above all the cases is imagined to enable an unadulterated view of the essential nature of any given phenomenon. In the Introduction, pointing to the disagreement between the evocritics and the post-structuralists, I noted that the bipolarity of the confrontation hinges upon precisely this notion of essence, and I said that "this is a bipolarity I will wish to question." The defactoism inherent in the picture of a literary scholarship modeled upon the practical endeavor of teaching and learning, rather than upon a quest for epistemological foundations, offers one means of resisting or circumventing the temptation of this notion of essence as generality or transcendence.

In addition to defusing the temptations of this kind of essence, however, a defactoist recitation of examples itself—the public recalling or reminding of our criteria—constitutes another view of essence entirely, one that I discussed in Chapter 2 under the Wittgensteinian epigraph, "Essence is expressed in grammar." These reminders, pertaining, for example, to love (or to acknowledgment, to comedy, to knowledge), trace the logical spaces that these concepts occupy in our practical lives. To paraphrase Wittgenstein, if you say you are in love, and if I say you are not, it nevertheless remains *love* that I say you are not in. As Cavell puts this notion of grammar and grammatical criteria,

> [Wittgensteinian] criteria do not relate a name to an object, but, we might say, various concepts to the concept of that object. Here the test of your possession of a concept (e.g., of a chair, or a bird; of the meaning of a word; of what it is to know something) would be your ability to use the concept in conjunction with other concepts, your knowledge of which concepts are relevant to the one in question and which are not; your knowledge of how various relevant concepts, used in conjunction with the concepts of different kinds of objects, require different kinds of contexts for their competent employment.
>
> (Cavell, *The Claim of Reason* 73)

A common contrast with claiming that one is "in love," a contrasting concept often offered in the case of *Romeo and Juliet*, is to say that one is "in lust." If I say that you are in lust, then we nevertheless express grammatical agreement on what sort of a thing *love* is, including the fact that it is conceptually related to lust. Our argument over whether you are in lust or in love will then proceed to outline the putative boundaries between these two concepts, which will further demonstrate and confirm that we share the form of life in which love and lust are complementary concepts, ways of making sense of particular types of comportment or disposition. Compare this with a set of instances in which I say "you are not in *love*, you're in *red*," or "in *trouble*," or "in the *key of G*." It is no longer clear that we share the form of life necessary to so much as *begin* an argument or a conversation. This would be an occasion on which we would stand facing each other, like Benedick and Beatrice at the altar, palms outward, with nothing to say. We would, in the most important sense, have nothing to discuss.

An expression such as, "You are not in love," and the discussion following it, in every actual case puts on display and makes vulnerable the grammatical criteria of our concepts, including, importantly, the axes of relevance that relate these concepts to one another. This is my way of reading Wittgenstein's sometimes controversial claim about the aim and purpose of philosophy in general, which I also take to be the aim and purpose of literary scholarship: "I want to say here that it can never be our job to reduce anything to anything, or to explain anything. Philosophy really *is* purely descriptive" (Wittgenstein 18). In the *Investigations*, Wittgenstein says that "philosophy must not interfere in any way with the actual use of language, so it can in the end only describe it. For it cannot justify it either. It leaves everything as it is" (Wittgenstein, Anscombe, and Hacker. §124). Taken in light of the work of Cavell, Eldridge, and Rudrum above, the *act* of describing the facts of the world, the space of our concepts—the act, that is, of recalling and offering reminders of our criteria—yields nothing like bare propositions, but rather results in, and proceeds from, the very provisionality discussed earlier, a naked and vulnerable pretension to speak for others. The act of description records our own individual responses to the world, and it offers them publicly and communally for testing, an offering denoted by the use of "we." The scholarly reading of literature and the writing up of our readings are just such descriptive practices.[4]

In my readings of three Shakespeare comedies, I have taken pains to draw out the ways in which the crises faced by various characters in various moments constellate worries around one's relation to oneself, one's family, one's beloved, one's friends, one's home. While it is entirely ordinary to take such moments of crisis in the tragedies as inherently instructive to audiences or readers, even to the point of conveying or communicating a message, it has hardly been so common to understand the emergence of such impasses in the comedies as expressing or demonstrating these same legitimate concerns, or offering similarly educative possibilities. This is a shame: the tragedies are frequently read as dramatizing the loss of one's grip on the world, or its going dead; yet all too rarely do critics and scholars attend to the recollective movements in Shakespeare's comedies—that is, to the ways in which characters facing the same sorts of skeptical impasses find themselves capable of returning to or inheriting the world.

Cavell's readings of *Lear* and *Othello* show that the motivating force underlying the movement and action of each tragedy originates not with any a priori estrangement from the world, but rather in what Cavell elsewhere calls a tendency to "become restive with" one's ordinary "conviction in the world." The tragic threat arises in virtue of the fact that "we have the power to undermine ourselves" in pursuing a better, but nonexistent, sort of conviction (Cavell, *Little Did I Know* 376). In attempting to perfect their independence, both Lear and Othello cut themselves off from the source of their happiness and fulfillment. Lear and Othello respond alike to their restiveness in conviction with what Cahill calls a "reflective detour": they attempt to restore the conviction under threat through the intervention of something like a contract, in Lear's case, and with "ocular proof" in Othello's. Cavell explicitly calls that which is imagined to restore us to the world an "unachievable or rather illusory rationality" it is a particular form of (theoretical) *knowledge*, one superior to the *knowing* embodied in everyday getting around in the world, that beckons Lear and Othello to their tragic, skeptical withdrawals.

Not only do the comedies that I have read herein feature the threat of skeptical withdrawal in roughly equal measure to the tragedies of *Lear* and *Othello*, but the threats arise in response to the same sorts of fears, the same restiveness: over filial and familial obligation, over the tightness or directionality of a romantic attachment—over the intersection, in short, of knowledge and love. As I have argued throughout this book, if tragedy can be read as the drama of skepticism, then comedy can be read as the drama of acknowledgment, the drama of conversion. Taking comedies, no less than tragedies, as exemplary of the possibilities for—or of the grammar of—the human condition, might then supplement the instruction that students and scholars freely accept from the tragedies.

If Othello's unslakable thirst for proof shows us something of the limits of knowing in relation to the conduct of human life, then it also shows us something of the beloved other's peculiar power—the power of love—to occasion or evoke the restiveness that seems to require a superhuman consolation. If Orlando and Rosalind's bantering in the forest shows us something of the playful and imaginative performativity of love, then it also shows us a complementary sort of epistemology, complementary, that is, to the "unachievable or illusory rationality" that Lear and Othello seek. In the comedies, we do not have to *infer* the grammar of acknowledgment from the failures of a tragic hero; the grammar of acknowledgment is, rather, displayed for us, directly, in characters' *finding* themselves (once more) "in love with [their] nativity." Perfectionism, to the extent that Rosalind and Orlando's courtship enacts its conversion of the world, names a nonskeptical axis of response to the disappointing frailty of our connection to the world as it is, and it is conducted by *doing* rather than *knowing*. Put better, the imaginative perfectionism that Rosalind in particular displays deflates the urge to treat doing and knowing, knowing and loving, as inherently separable in the first place.

I am reminded, at the close of all this, of Milan Kundera's *Ignorance*, in which he traces out the origins of the concept of "nostalgia," which he links to a suffering born of absence, of being out and away from one's home, from one's people, from one's beloved. The Czech phrase that he cites—"*styska se mi po tobe*"—he translates as "I yearn for you"; "I'm nostalgic for you"; "I cannot bear the pain of your absence" (Kundera 5). He goes on to note that the Spanish word for nostalgia, "añoranza," comes from the Catalan verb "enyorar," which in turn comes from the Latin "ignorare." Kundera says, "In that etymological light nostalgia seems something like the pain of ignorance, of not knowing. You are far away, and I don't know what has become of you. My country is far away, and I don't know what is happening there" (Kundera 5).

Kundera's thinking on nostalgia twines together the many threads coursing through this Coda, indeed, through this work: that the experience of being out and away, of being separate, is the experience of pain or disappointment; that such nostalgia is articulated equally in terms of absence from home figured as the world and in terms of absence from home figured as another; and that this painful separation from the world and from another is "something like the pain of ignorance." Othello and Lear respond to the painful experience of their uncertain distance from those whom they love as though they were responding not to something *like* ignorance, but to ignorance itself, something that proof or certainty might overcome. Rosalind and Orlando respond to their uncertain distance from the world and the ones they love by, as it were, imaginatively *being there*. The desire for a return signified in nostalgia may be expressed in terms of an intellectual lack, but the return itself is not achievable by something like the supplying of knowledge, say by hearing the news (of home, of one's beloved). This has implications for Shakespearean comedy, for the intersection of loving and knowing, and for the broader field of literary studies as a whole: The return itself and the knowledge it entails are only achieved together, by *returning*. The experience of ignorance that Kundera recognizes in nostalgia is alleviated just as Rosalind and Orlando demonstrate: by imaginatively moving to take up a renewed inhabitation in an animated world to which we find ourselves to belong.

NOTES

1. I owe the discovery of this formulation—which Heidegger himself uses (Heidegger, MacQuarrie, and Robinson, *On Being and Time* 118)—to Simon Glendinning's work. On his reading, "One of the central features of Heidegger's reframing of the problem of other minds lies in its questioning whether being with others is a 'relation' which is, primarily, epistemological in character" (Glendinning, *On Being with Others*. 58). Glendinning's view, obviously, is directly in line with the argument of this text.
2. I feel compelled to say again that, although this formulation bears some striking resemblances to the major tenets of reader-response theory, it is not the case that the truth or correctness of a claim is determined or determinable by community checks, that is, by polling members of a community as to their level of agreement. Truth or correctness is, in an important sense, not at issue. One's membership in and intelligibility to others, one's capacity to speak to, for, and with certain others, is. One's recognition as possessing the ability to redirect gaze and interest is what is at stake.
3. The rise of MOOCs might be seen as a *direct result* of confusing the (grammatical) essence of literary scholarship with the abstract facts or established claims to stable truth that emerge from such collaborative, negotiated, groundless work.
4. Marjorie Perloff also makes this point, with particular reference to Wittgenstein (Perloff, "The Poetics of Description").

REFERENCES

Cahill, Kevin. *The Fate of Wonder: Wittgenstein's Critique of Metaphysics and Modernity*. New York: Columbia University Press, 2011. Print.

Cavell, Stanley. "Knowing and Acknowledging." *The Cavell Reader*. Ed. Stephen Mulhall. Malden, MA: Wiley-Blackwell, 1996. Print.

———. *Little Did I Know: Excerpts from Memory*. Stanford, CA: Stanford University Press, 2010. Print.

———. *Must We Mean What We Say?*. Cambridge, UK: Cambridge University Press, 1969. Print.

———. *The Claim of Reason*. New York: Oxford University Press, 1979. Print.

Cavell, Stanley, and Northrop Frye. "Foreword." *A Natural Perspective*. New York: Columbia University Press, 1995. 159. Print.

Dreyfus, Hubert L. "Overcoming the Myth of the Mental: How Philosophers Can Profit from the Phenomenology of Everyday Expertise." *Proceedings and Addresses of the American Philosophical Association* 79.2 (2005): 47–65.

Eldridge, Richard Thomas. *Literature, Life, and Modernity*. New York: Columbia University Press, 2013. Print.

Fogelin, Robert J. *Taking Wittgenstein at His Word: A Textual Study*. Princeton, NJ: Princeton University Press, 2009. Print.

Glendinning, Simon. *On Being with Others*. New York: Routledge, 1998. Print.

Heidegger, Martin, John MacQuarrie, and Edward Robinson. *Being and Time*. New York: Harper & Row, 1962. Print.

Johnson, William A. "Bookrolls as Media." *Comparative Textual Media*. Ed. N. Katherine Hayles and Jessica Pressman. Minneapolis: University of Minnesota Press, 2013. 101–121. Print.

———. "Reading Cultures and Education." *Reading between the Lines: Perspectives on Foreign Language Literacy*. Ed. Peter C. Patrikis. New Haven, CT: Yale University Press, 2002. 9–23. Print.

Kundera, Milan. *Ignorance*. New York: HarperCollins, 2002. Print.

Mulhall, Stephen. *Stanley Cavell: Philosophy's Recounting of the Ordinary*. New York: Oxford University Press, 1998. Print.

Perloff, Marjorie. "The Poetics of Description: Wittgenstein on the Aesthetic." *Parallax* 4.4 (1998): 79–89. Print.

Rudrum, David. *Stanley Cavell and the Claim of Literature*. Baltimore, MD: Johns Hopkins University Press, 2013. Print.

Wittgenstein, Ludwig. *Preliminary Studies for the "Philosophical Investigations," Generally Known as the Blue and Brown Books*. Oxford, UK: Basil Blackwell, 1958. Print.

Wittgenstein, Ludwig, G. E. M. Anscombe, and P. M. S. Hacker. *Philosophical Investigations*. 4th ed. Malden, MA: Wiley-Blackwell, 2009. Print.

Index

acknowledgment (engagement in the world; recovery): in *As You Like It* 141–46, 152–54, 157, 162, 173–74; Cavell on avoidance and 69, 78, 90–91, 94, 98–99, 121, 180–81; as coming from learning what we're already familiar with 21, 27, 81; failure to learn as isolation from 35, 39–40, 79–80, 107, 120–21, 139, 146, 173; finding-as-founding as form of 13, 75, 122; as linking people to the world and to each other 4, 21, 37–45, 66–68, 73–79, 82, 167–68, 182; in *Midsummer Night's Dream* 88, 94, 98–100, 116–19; as public 21, 77–78; Shakespeare's comedies as drama of 20–21, 45, 66–67, 71, 74–75, 79, 122, 190–91; studying, in literary scholarship 178–84, 188; of what one "cannot fail to know," 21, 71, 76, 80, 82–83; See also avoidance; community; conversion; "finding" as "founding"; love; recognition; responsiveness
agreement (human) 37–42, 134, 184; See also "form of life"; Wittgenstein, Ludwig
Allegories of Reading (de Man) 9
Alpers, Paul 14
Althusser, Louis 127
anti-foundationalism 46–48; See also deconstructionism; groundlessness; post-structuralism
"approaching," 26, 50n1, 170, 181–83
"Argument of Comedy" (Frye) 134
Aristotle 93
Artificial Intelligence 29
As You Like It (Shakespeare) 125–77; avoidance in 134, 139–40, 144–47, 154, 169; Bloom on 131, 144, 149–50, 154, 157, 161, 167–68, 173; conversion in 139–41, 155, 165–66, 169, 174; disquietudes in 127, 147–50; skepticism in 143–47, 162, 168, 180
attraction. See "handsome and unhandsome" concept; responsiveness
Augustine (saint) 28
avoidance (of the requirements of love; withdrawal): *vs.* acknowledgment in Shakespeare's tragedies 2–3, 13–21, 45, 53, 64, 190–91; in *As You Like It* 134, 139–40, 144–47, 154, 169; Cavell on acknowledgment and 69, 78, 90–91, 94, 98–99, 121, 180–81; in life 41; in literary criticism 128, 130; as a method in literary scholarship 178–82, 188; in *Midsummer Night's Dream* 88–91, 94, 103, 106–7, 109–12, 114–17, 120–21; in *Much Ado about Nothing* 53, 68, 70–73, 75–79; in *Othello* 103, 110, 112, 114, 168, 179; in teaching and learning 39; See also acknowledgment; conversion; disappointment; isolation; reason; skepticism
"The Avoidance of Love" (Cavell) 13–16

banishment: in *As You Like It* 125, 131, 134, 139–41, 169, 173; in *Midsummer Night's Dream* 88
Barber, C. L. 125
Beauvoir, Simone de 49
Beckman, Margaret Boerner 144, 158
Beckwith, Sarah 41; on literature's therapeutic powers 3, 36, 42, 48, 166; on Shakespeare studies 36–37, 84n7; on skepticism 76, 107

belonging. See acknowledgment; world
Benston, Alice N. 87
bequest. See inheritance
Best, Stephen 22n3
bipolarity: in *Midsummer Night's Dream* 88–89, 100; between structuralists and post-structuralists 10–11, 25, 27, 188
Bloom, Harold: on *As You Like It* 131, 144, 149–50, 154, 157, 161, 167–68, 173; on post-structuralism 9–10
The Blue Book (Wittgenstein) 28
bookrolls 187
Booth, Wayne 5
Boyd, Brian 8–9
Bradley, A. C. 82–83
Bromell, Nick 22n5
Butler, Judith 22n6

Cahill, Kevin 64, 183
Calvo, Clara 149
Carroll, Joseph 8
causal explanations: in *As You Like It* 151–52; Henze on, in *Much Ado about Nothing* 57–58, 61; Oatley on, for characters' emotions 93–95, 98–99, 105, 113, 119; search for 12, 33, 43, 47, 71–72, 81; See also certainty; knowledge; reason
Cavell, Stanley: on avoidance and acknowledgment 69, 78, 90–91, 94, 98–99, 121, 180–81; on "conversion," 72, 165–67; on "finding" as "founding," 13, 48, 75, 102–3, 122, 191; on Frye 128–29; on the importance of making sense of literary works 27, 45, 47, 187–89; as influence on author's methodology 82; on isolation 3, 20, 81; on "perfectionism," 168–74; reading practice of 3–4, 45, 47–48, 119, 128–31, 182–88; on self-knowledge 74–75, 79, 171; on setting aside skepticism through defactoism 45, 49; Shakespearean readings by 2–5, 13–21, 34, 45–48, 63, 71, 80, 107, 112, 118–19, 134, 157, 168–69, 179, 190–91; on "taking on our education," 42; on training and initiation 34, 37, 39, 44, 144; on "truth of skepticism," 13, 19, 25–26, 28, 36, 43–44, 47, 170, 178, 182, 184; on Wittgensteinian grammar 188–89; on Wittgenstein's "form of life," 12, 40–42, 102–3; on Wittgenstein's scenes of teaching and learning 40–42; on world "going dead for us," 35, 68
certainty: attempts at overcoming skepticism through 2, 19–20, 64, 69–70, 184–85; literary scholarship's pursuit of 4, 7–13, 31, 62, 82–83, 181–82, 188; See also causal explanations; foundationalism; knowledge; reason; skepticism
character(s): intentionality ascribed to literary 26, 47, 93–94; literary scholarship's interest in 5, 8–10, 13, 23n7, 45–47, 61, 93; "right-thinking" vs. "humorous," 126–27, 129, 131, 134, 136, 173
Cities of Words (Cavell) 80
Cixous, Hélène 9
The Claim of Reason (Cavell) 39, 71, 166, 180–81
cognitive psychology 7–8, 45–47, 81, 96–99; See also emotion; "evocriticism"
Coleridge, Samuel Taylor 46
comedies (Shakespeare's): as drama of acknowledgment 20–21, 45, 66–67, 71, 74–75, 79, 122, 190–91; happy endings of 1–2, 13, 20–21, 48, 53–58, 62–64, 81, 108, 121–22, 125–28, 139, 141, 169, 180; "screwball," 3, 80, 112, 123n5; skepticism as driving 1–3, 48, 73, 179; skepticism in *As You Like It* 143–47, 162, 168, 180; skepticism in *Midsummer Night's Dream* 88–89, 106–11, 116–18, 179–80; skepticism in *Much Ado about Nothing* 1–2, 20–21, 53–54, 63–66, 68–70, 79–81, 89, 139, 155, 179; tragedy as lurking within 63, 108, 110, 116, 119, 134, 179, 190; See also acknowledgment; disquietudes; love; *titles of specific Shakespeare comedies*
"commonsense understanding," 31–32, 34, 37; See also practical know-how
communication. See conversations; language
community: "claims to," 138, 169, 184–85; comedic resolution as return to 125–27, 139; public nature of 44–45, 76–77, 118–19, 138, 171, 182; of readers 186–87; See also acknowledgment; conversations;

isolation; language; love; public nature; teaching and learning
Comparative Textual Media 186
Conant, Jim 64
"consensus in action," 38–40, 184, 186
conversations: in *As You Like It* 156–59, 162–65, 172; in community 44, 184; as miraculous 48–50, 166–69, 186; as needed in literary scholarship 32, 44–45, 47–50, 82–83, 184, 186; See also language
conversion: in *As You Like It* 139–41, 155, 165–66, 169, 174; comedy as drama of 190–92; defined 21, 72; love as 119; in *Midsummer Night's Dream* 107–10, 116–21; in *Much Ado about Nothing* 66, 72–74, 77–78; See also acknowledgment; recognition; redemption; responsiveness
Cook, Amy 8
Cook, Carol 55
Cosmides, Leda 8
"creative discovery," 23n6, 74–78, 105
criteria: Cavell's philosophy and 4, 180, 183–84, 188–89; Much Ado and 54, 59, 70–76, 78–80; skepticism and 43–44, 70, 75–76
cross-dressing (in *As You Like It*) 155–58, 161, 165, 167–68, 175n5
culture 11–12; See also political activism

Dahl, Espen 13
Dawson, Anthony 64–65
death *vs.* marriage: in *Much Ado about Nothing* 54–56, 63
deception: claims of, in *As You Like It* 147–49, 155–56; in *Much Ado about Nothing* 54–64, 68–69, 71, 75–77, 87, 149
deconstructionism 5–7, 10, 12, 25, 27–28
defactoist view: author's use of 21n1, 43, 185–86, 188; exemplarity in 44, 48, 88; Fogelin on 4, 43, 49, 185–86; as means of dissolving skepticism 30–31, 43–50, 135–37; practices of 25–52, 185–86; value of, in literary scholarship 27; See also Cavell, Stanley: reading practice of; literary scholarship; practical know-how
de Man, Paul 6, 9–10
denial. See avoidance

Dennis, Carl 54
dependency (and love) 18–20, 114, 116, 168, 173
Derrida, Jacques 5–6, 8–9
Descartes, René 3, 27, 30, 40n2; skepticism of 43, 170
Dewey, John 21n1
Diamond, Cora 91
disappointment (disenchantment) 118, 120, 165, 169–71, 174, 181, 191
disquietudes: in *As You Like It* 127, 147–50; defined 56; examining, in literary scholarship 83; in *Midsummer Night's Dream* 87, 90, 93, 97, 99–100, 103, 105; in *Much Ado about Nothing* 56, 62–63, 81
divided (or doubled) self 165–68, 171–72, 174
divine power (gods): in *Midsummer Night's Dream* 89–91, 101, 105–6, 112, 114–16
doubled worlds 165–67, 171
double self. See divided self
doubt. See skepticism
Dreyfus, Hubert: on "a new order of significance," 22n6, 74, 101, 105; on "commonsense understanding," 31–32, 34, 37; on "creative discovery," 23n6, 74–78, 105; on everyday know-how 28–29; and "form of life," 37, 39; on Homer 102; on infinite regress 28–30, 34; on literary practice 186; on the rationalist picture of the mind 50n2; on relevance 98–99, 170, 182; on "the detached attitude," 65
Dreyfus, Stuart 29
Dumm, Thomas 90–91
Dutton, Denis 8

Eagleton, Terry 112
Ecco Homo (Nietzsche) 175n11
education: in *As You Like It* 139–41, 150, 154, 156, 158, 162–68; as a bequest 130; "taking on one's own," 42, 44, 48, 73–74, 79, 106, 121, 130, 150, 154, 156, 158; as training and initiation 34, 37, 39, 44, 144; transmission model of 44, 144, 147–48, 150, 153–54, 160; See also conversations; "creative discovery"; "finding" as "founding"; ignorance; knowledge; reading; self: knowledge of; teaching and learning

198 Index

Eldridge, Richard 138, 145, 171–72, 184–85, 189
Emerson, Ralph Waldo 45, 72, 102, 122, 125, 128, 165–66, 169–70
emotion: Harré on 8, 26; Oatley on 8–9, 45–46, 93–101, 103, 105, 113, 119, 121; See also dependency; isolation; love; shame
engagement (with the world). See acknowledgment
epistemology: new facts as inadequate to solve problems of 13–17, 21, 25–32, 42, 46, 68, 73–74, 89, 98, 100, 179–82, 188, 191–92; skepticism in modern 3–4, 13, 25–26; Wittgenstein on questions of 26–32, 36
Erickson, Peter B. 125, 144
essentialism. See "evocriticism"; foundationalism
"everyday know-how." See practical know-how
"evocriticism," 98, 127; overcoming the bipolarity of post-structuralism and 45–47, 188; on the universal nature of the human (in literary scholarship) 8–11, 26–27, 31, 34, 38, 41–42, 49, 82, 181–82
evolutionary theory 7–9; See also "evocriticism"
exemplarity: in *As You Like It* 174; defactoism as dealing with examples of 44, 48, 88; in *Midsummer Night's Dream* 112; as a task of literary scholarship 82–83, 130, 188
exile. See banishment
existential issues 36, 125, 178–82, 184
"Experience" (Emerson) 102

facts (new). See knowledge
"finding" as "founding": in *As You Like It* 125, 128–29, 131, 139–40, 143, 154–58, 167–69, 172, 191; Cavell on 13, 48, 75, 102–3, 122, 191; in *Much Ado about Nothing* 83; See also self: knowledge of
Findlay, Alison 66
Fischer, Michael 3
flower (in *Midsummer Night's Dream*) 93–100, 102–8, 119, 121
Fogelin, Robert: on consensus in action 38–40, 184, 186; on defactoist stance 4, 43, 49, 185–86; and "form of life," 37–39; on the "paradox of interpretation," 28–30, 32, 34, 36,
100, 135, 141, 181; on publicness of teaching and learning 33
formalism. See New Criticism
"form of life," 12, 37–42, 102, 134, 144, 184, 186
foundationalism (in literary scholarship) 10–12, 25–26, 28, 36, 45–47; in *As You Like It* 135–43; flaws in 53–63, 83; Wittgenstein as defying usual explanations of 38; See also epistemology; "evocriticism"; "finding" as "founding"; knowledge; reason; transcendent
Freud, Sigmund 165
Friedman, Michael D. 55
Frye, Northrop 171, 183; on Shakespearean comedy 125–32, 134–37, 173

gender issues: and *As You Like It* 141–44, 155–59, 163–64, 172, 175n6; and Frye's criticism 125–27, 134–35, 137; in *Much Ado about Nothing* 55; See also cross-dressing
"Genealogy of Morals" (Nietzsche) 85n9
Giraldi, William 6–7, 10
Glendinning, Simon 83, 123n3, 192n1
gods. See divine power
Gottschall, Jonathan 8–9, 11
Grady, Hugh 10, 87
grammar (Wittgenstein on) 37, 40–41, 64, 188–91
gravitation. See responsiveness
Greenblatt, Stephen 50
groundlessness (in *As You Like It*) 131–35, 152, 171
Guilhamet, Leon 88
Guyer, Paul 94

Hamlet (Shakespeare) 85n11, 144, 174–75
"handsome and unhandsome" concept 102–3, 128, 155–57, 169
happiness 121–22, 125–28, 135; See also acknowledgment; love
Harré, Rom 8–9, 26
Hartog, Hendrik 17
Hawkes, Terrance 10
Hazlitt, William 87
Heidegger, Martin 42, 50n6, 51n8, 99, 102, 122, 125; on disquietude 56; on "reception," 72; on self-knowledge 79
Henry IV, Part I (Shakespeare) 129–30, 144

Henze, Richard 49, 54–63, 67–68, 70–71, 75–76, 81–83, 87, 144, 149
Hume, David 3, 173; skepticism of 43–44, 170
Hunt, Maurice 54, 98

ignorance: avoidance distinguished from 16–17, 69; and nostalgia 191–92; See also knowledge; teaching and learning
Ignorance (Kundera) 191–92
illness: demands for epistemological explanations as an 42; skepticism as an incurable but perpetually cured 44, 48, 118, 173
imagery 14, 57, 61; of stones and statues 18–19, 90–92, 108, 114, 157
independence. See dependency; isolation
information. See knowledge
inheritance (bequest): in *As You Like It* 133, 135–36; education as 130; language as 40, 44, 50, 51n6, 184; love as 155
intentional fallacy. See messages
intentionality (of literary characters) 26, 47, 93–94
isolation (independence; privacy; separateness): failure to teach or learn as dooming one to 35, 39–40, 79–80, 107, 120–21, 139, 146, 173; Kundera on 191–92; in life 15; overcoming, in comedy 3, 81, 88, 108; in Shakespeare's tragedies 2–3, 19–20; shame and 16–17, 134, 171; "truth of skepticism" linked to 25, 36, 40–41, 102, 173; See also avoidance; disappointment; skepticism

James, William 22n1
Johnson, William A. 186–88
Julius Caesar (Shakespeare) 129–30
justice. See law
justification. See reason

Kant, Immanuel 40, 85n10, 97, 101
Kastan, David 82
Kelly, Sean Dorrance 102
King Lear (Shakespeare) 134; *As You Like It* compared to 169; avoidance in 179; Cavell's reading of 190–91; *Midsummer Night's Dream* compared to 89, 112; skepticism in 1–2, 4, 13–18, 20, 29, 71, 168

"*King Lear* and the Theory of the Sight Pattern" (Alpers) 14
knowledge (new facts) attempts at overcoming skepticism through 3, 13, 64–65, 69–71, 92, 181–82; as being in plain view 3, 42, 53, 71, 73, 78, 118, 159; of each other, as failing 132–34; of how to go on 32, 118–19, 130, 145, 168–69; as inadequate to solve epistemological problems 13–17, 21, 25–32, 42, 46, 68, 73–74, 89, 98, 100, 179–82, 188, 191–92; literary scholarship's attempts to establish 4, 7–12, 31, 62, 82–83, 181–82, 184; as mischaracterizing "our fundamental relation to the world," 27–29, 40–41, 65–66, 83, 178–79, 186, 191; as not lacking in various Shakespearean crises 14–15, 19, 21, 53, 69–71, 73–74, 118, 136–40, 153, 159, 164–67, 173, 182; teaching and learning a an alternative means of, in literary scholarship 27, 32–37, 43–50, 114, 183–92; and transmission model of education 44, 144, 147–48, 150, 153–54, 160; See also acknowledgment; avoidance; education; epistemology; "finding" as "founding"; practical know-how; reason; self: knowledge of; skepticism; teaching and learning
Kundera, Milan 191–92

Lamb, Charles 87
language ("linguistic turn"): as an expression of character 47; as a bequest 40, 44, 50, 51n6, 184; contemporary literary scholarship's attention to 4–13, 26–28, 36; Heidegger on 50n6; imagining, as "form of life," 37–38, 144; "impurity" of 13; learning to use 32; as miraculous 48–49, 166–69, 186; Wittgenstein on 183; See also conversations; grammar
law: in *As You Like It* 133–34, 174; in *Merchant of Venice* 87; in *Midsummer Night's Dream* 87–93, 97, 99–101, 103, 108–9, 112–16, 120–21, 134
Leavis, F. R. 5
"Lecture on Ethics" (Wittgenstein) 48–49

Lee, Randy 87
Leibniz, Gottfried 50n2
Lewalski, B. K. 66
Liebler, Naomi 87
lies. See deception
"the linguistic turn." See language
literary scholarship: attention to language in contemporary 4–13, 26–28, 36; Cavellian approach to 181–86; Cavell on the importance of 27, 45, 47, 187–89; character study emphasis in 5, 8–10, 13, 23n7, 45–47, 61, 93; as conducting serious conversations about meanings of literary works 32, 44–45, 47–50, 82–83, 184, 186; defactoist practices of 25–52, 185–86; exemplarity as a task of 82–83, 130, 188; as form of political activism 6–7, 9–11; foundational epistemological assumptions of many approaches to 25–26, 28–29, 31, 40; public nature of 45, 47–50, 82–83, 184–88; purpose of 189–90; as searching for objective knowledge 4, 7–12, 31, 62, 82–83, 181–82, 184; skepticism as reified in some contemporary 13, 31; studying acknowledgment *vs.* avoidance as method in 178–82, 188; teaching and learning as an alternative means of knowing in 27, 32–37, 43–50, 114, 183–92; as teaching us about ourselves 3–4, 48–49, 82; and therapeutic effects of literature 3, 36, 42, 48, 166; use of other academic disciplines in 7–9, 49, 62; See also conversations; defactoist view; "evocriticism"; language; messages; New Criticism; post-structuralism; Shakespeare studies; structuralism
logic. See reason
love: as an inheritance 155; as a causal agent 93–97, 179–80; criticizing, from with its realm 144, 149–52, 162; and dependency 18–20, 114, 116, 168, 173; *vs.* "labor of care," 17–18; madness in 144–54; as a matter of reason and free will 99, 101–2, 104–5, 119, 121, 179–80; as not based on reason 150–54; Oatley's view of, in *Midsummer Night's Dream* 93–97, 99; in *Othello* 191; skeptical temptations regarding, in *Much Ado about Nothing* 1–2, 20–21, 53–54, 63–70, 79–81, 83, 89, 139, 155, 179; See also acknowledgment; avoidance; happiness; marriage and remarriage; recognition; responsiveness

Macbeth (Shakespeare) 114, 174, 175n7
MacKay, Maxine 87
McLuhan, Marshall 186
madness: in love 144–54; reason in 154–62
Marcus, Sharon 22n3
marriage and remarriage: in 1930s and 1940s American films 3, 80, 112, 123n5; in *As You Like It* 135; in *Midsummer Night's Dream* 123n5, 126–27; in *Much Ado about Nothing* 54–56, 58, 63, 69, 72, 76
Marshall, David 87
Marx, Karl 127
The Merchant of Venice (Shakespeare) 87
Merleau-Ponty, Maurice 99
messages (in Shakespeare's works): Frye on 129–30; other scholars' search for 49, 54–63, 82, 190
methodology: author's 82–83, 164; Cavell's 3–4, 182–83
A Midsummer Night's Dream (Shakespeare) 87–124; Cavell on 80; compared to *As You Like It* 133, 142–43; compared to *Much Ado about Nothing* 88–89, 108, 118; disquietudes in 87, 90, 93, 97, 99–100, 103, 105; Montrose on 126–27; resolution of primary lovers' plot in 87–88, 107, 127–28, 181; skepticism in 88–89, 106–11, 116–18, 179–80
Miller, J. Hillis 5
miracles: of comedies' happy endings 1–2, 20–21; intelligibility of communication as 48–50, 166, 168–69; literary scholarship as practice of 83
Moffatt, Laurel 87
Moi, Toril 49
Montrose, Louis Adrian 126–29, 134–37, 174n4
Much Ado About Nothing (Shakespeare) 53–87, 144, 147, 151, 153, 167, 175n6; disquietudes in 56, 62–63, 81; happy ending of

53–58, 62–64, 66, 68, 81, 108, 169, 180; isolation in 35, 41, 75, 81; *Midsummer Night's Dream* compared to 88–89, 108, 118; skepticism in 1–2, 20–21, 53–54, 63–66, 68–70, 79–81, 83, 89, 139, 155, 179
Mulhall, Stephen 15; on Cavell's mode of reading 3–4, 183, 188; on dangers of skepticism 70, 85n10; on exemplarity 82–83; on foundational epistemological assumptions 25–26, 28–29, 31, 40; on our fundamental relation to the world 186; on "world going dead for us," 35, 37, 41, 68
"multi-vocal self," 171–72
murder. See violence

nativity 146, 155, 157, 165, 191–92
A Natural Perspective (Frye) 128
"Neo-Darwinism." See "evocriticism"
New Criticism (formalism) 5, 7, 14, 23n7, 47–49; and author's methodology 82; and *Midsummer Night's Dream* 87; and *Much Ado about Nothing* 54, 57
New Historicism 8, 10
"new order of significance," 75, 107–8, 113, 119, 138, 146–47, 152, 175n7; Dreyfus on 22n6, 74, 101, 105
Nietzsche, Friedrich 22n1, 50n5, 85n9, 10, 152, 169, 175n11
"nostalgia," 191–92

Oatley, Keith 8–9, 45–47, 56, 127; on *Midsummer Night's Dream* 87, 93–100, 103–5, 113, 119, 121
"order of significance." See "new order of significance"
Othello (Shakespeare): *As You Like It* compared to 157, 169; avoidance in 103, 110, 112, 114, 168, 179; Cavell on 63, 91, 116, 190–91; *Much Ado about Nothing* compared to 63, 66; Oatley on 95; skepticism in 1–4, 14–15, 18–21, 29, 36, 45–46, 54, 56, 64

pain 15
paradoxes: of interpretation 28–30, 32, 34, 36, 100, 135, 141, 181; of rule-following 30, 38
perfectionism 164–65, 168–74, 191; See also acknowledgment; conversion; Emerson, Ralph Waldo

Perloff, Marjorie 192n4
Philosophical Investigations (Wittgenstein) 21, 28, 30–32, 37, 189
Philosophy of Psychology—A Fragment (PPF) (Wittgenstein) 30, 39
Pierce, Charles Sanders 21n1
political activism (in literary scholarship) 6–7, 9–11
postmodern theory 8, 31; See also *specific schools of*
post-structuralism 127, 145; and literary scholarship 5–13, 26–27, 31, 34–35, 41–42, 49, 181–82, 188; and *Much Ado about Nothing* 57; overcoming the bipolarity of evocriticism and 45–47, 188; See also deconstructionism
PPF (Philosophy of Psychology—A Fragment) [Wittgenstein], 30, 39
practical know-how 30–32; and "agreement in form of life," 37–42, 184, 186; as common and public 37, 40; as nonformalizable 29, 34–36; as untouched by literary scholarship 31; See also "commonsense understanding"; defactoist view; reminders
"Presentism," 10
Pressman, Jessica 47
Priest, Dale G. 144, 147–49, 155, 157, 173
privacy. See isolation
proof. See knowledge; reason
Proust, Marcel 8
public nature: of community 44–45, 76–77, 118–19, 138, 171, 182; of everyday avocations 43–44; of literary scholarship 45, 47–50, 82–83, 184–88; of practical know-how 37–40; of teaching and learning 33–35, 40–41, 44, 48, 82–83, 186; See also acknowledgment; community; conversations; language; teaching and learning
Pursuits of Happiness (Cavell) 80

rationality. See reason
Ratner-Rosenhagen, Jennifer 9–10
reader response theory 38, 192n2
reading: Cavell's mode of 3–4, 45, 47–48, 119, 128–31, 182–88; close 23n7, 47–48; "distance," 7; nature of scholarly 44–45; "redemptive," 83; scholarly 45; "surface," 7;

"symptomatic," 22n3; See also conversations; literary scholarship
reason (justification; logic; proof; rationality): in *As You Like It* 138–39, 150–62; defactoist critical approach as not reliant on 48; demands for epistemological 1–2, 42–43, 107, 179, 190–91; love seen as a matter of free will and 99, 101–2, 104–5, 119, 121, 179–80; in *Midsummer Night's Dream* 96–98, 102, 104–7, 113; in *Much Ado about Nothing* 53–55, 59–60, 64–69, 72, 76, 81; neurocognitive views of love and 96–98, 119; See also avoidance; causal explanations; certainty; knowledge
receptivity. See responsiveness
recognition 14–16, 45, 71, 114, 166, 171; appeals to, in *As You Like It* 133; See also acknowledgment; responsiveness
recovery. See acknowledgment; conversion; illness
redemption 66–67, 83, 84n7, 180
refusal. See avoidance
regress: horizontal 79–80; infinite 28–30, 34, 46, 62
relativism (solipsism) 6, 8, 10–11, 38
relevance: Dreyfus on 98–99, 170, 182; of forms of life 41, 44, 187–88; frames of 138, 144, 183, 189
Remarks on the Foundations of Mathematics (Wittgenstein) 32
remarriage. See marriage and remarriage
reminders (of the ordinary and everyday; "criteria") 43–44, 48, 53, 71–77, 80–83, 109–10, 182, 188–89; in *As You Like It* 134, 138–40, 143
repudiation. See avoidance
responsiveness (attraction; gravitation; receptivity): in *As You Like It* 152, 155–57, 172; of Cavell's approach to reading 183–84, 190; in *Midsummer Night's Dream* 89–91, 101–6, 108–9, 114; in *Much Ado about Nothing* 72–74, 78; See also acknowledgment; love; recognition
resurrection (in *Much Ado about Nothing*) 54–56, 63–64, 66, 68
reversion 76
Richards, I. A. 5, 7
Romanticism 5, 9, 82
Romeo and Juliet (Shakespeare) 189

Rorty, Richard 22n1
Rudrum, David 50n1, 183, 185, 189
rule-following paradox 30, 38

Saito, Naoko 145, 171
Savigny, Friedrich Karl von 122n1
Scheff, Thomas J. 55
Schell, Jennifer 22n6
Schwab, Joseph 48
the self: deception of 88–89, 108, 118; as divided or doubled 165–68, 171–72, 174; knowledge of 79, 171; in *As You Like It* 132–37, 173; literature's enhancement of 3, 44–45, 47–48, 82–83, 130; in Shakespeare criticism 74–75, 107, 125–30, 134; "multi-vocal," 171–72; revelation of 156–62, 164, 166–68
separateness. See isolation
Shakespeare and the Grammar of Forgiveness (Beckwith) 36–37
Shakespeare's Humanism (Wells) 8
Shakespeare studies 8–10, 36–37, 84n7; See also *specific approaches, critics, and plays*
shame 16–18, 134, 169, 171
Sharafi, Mitra 122n1
"significance" (new order of). See "new order of significance"
skepticism: in *As You Like It* 143–47, 162, 168, 180; attempts at overcoming, through certainty 2–3, 13, 19–20, 64–65, 69–71, 92, 181–82, 184–85; Beckwith on 76, 107; Cavell on "truth of," 13, 19, 25–26, 28, 36, 43–44, 47, 170, 178, 182, 184; contemporary literary scholarship as reifying 3–4, 13, 25–26, 31; crises of, as infrequent in everyday life 43; defactoist view as means of dissolving 30–31, 43–50, 135–37; of Descartes and Hume 43–44, 170; as driving Shakespeare's comedies and tragedies 1–3, 13–15, 19, 21, 48, 54, 63, 73, 107, 120, 157, 179, 190; as incurable but perpetually cured 44, 48, 118, 173; in *King Lear* 1–2, 4, 13–18, 20, 29, 71, 168; as making the "world go dead for us," 35, 37, 41, 68, 181–82; in *Midsummer Night's Dream* 88–89, 106–11, 116–18, 179–80; in *Much Ado about Nothing* 1–2, 20–21, 53–54, 63–66, 68–70, 79–81, 83, 89, 139, 155, 179; in *Othello* 1–4,

14–15, 18–21, 29, 36, 45–46, 54, 56, 64; "other-minds" *vs.* "external-world," 3–4, 15, 17, 29–30; setting aside of 45, 49, 64–68, 117–18, 143; "truth of," as linked to isolation 25, 36, 40–41, 102, 173–74; See also acknowledgment; avoidance; conversion; disappointment; disquietudes; isolation; shame
social integration. See community
solipsism. See isolation; relativism
Spolsky, Ellen 8
Standish, Paul 145, 171
Stanley Cavell and Literary Skepticism (Fischer) 3
statue imagery 18–19, 90–92, 108, 114, 157
Stern, David 28, 34
Stirm, Jan 125, 141–44, 172
stone imagery. See statue imagery
structuralism 5, 7–8, 10, 12–13, 25, 28, 35, 62, 130, 134

teaching and learning: acknowledgment as coming from 21, 35; in *As You Like It* 131, 134, 144, 162–68; as extending towards one another 35, 38–39, 72–73, 145; failure of 19, 34–35, 38–39, 79; literature's role in, about ourselves 3, 44–45, 47–48, 82–83, 130; by means of examples and exercises (see also exemplarity) 32; in *Midsummer Night's Dream* 106; in *Much Ado about Nothing* 53–54, 72–73, 79; as not necessarily rule-following 31–33; as ongoing 44–45, 47–48; publicness of 33–35, 40–41, 44, 48, 82–83, 186; reading communities as form of 186–87; as training or initiation 32–35, 38, 144, 154, 159–62; See also "creative discovery"; education; exemplarity; knowledge; messages; practical know-how; reminders
themes 14, 57, 61
therapeutic powers: of defactoist view 43; of Shakespeare works 3, 36, 42, 48, 166
Todes, Samuel 22n6, 74
Tooby, John 8
The Tractatus (Wittgenstein) 31
tragedies (Shakepeare's): avoidance in 1–3, 103, 110, 112, 114, 120, 168, 179; Cavell's study of 48, 107, 157; as lurking behind his comedies 63, 108, 110, 116, 119, 134, 179, 190; skepticism as driving 1–3, 14–15, 19, 21, 54, 73, 107, 120, 157, 190; See also *specific Shakespeare tragedies*
the transcendent 41, 62, 83, 88, 128–29, 188
"Truth and Lying in an Extra-Moral Sense" (Nietzsche) 50n2
"truth of skepticism." See skepticism: Cavell on "truth of"
truths. See knowledge; messages; reason
Tvordi, Jessica 126, 144, 149

violence (in *As You Like It*) 132–34, 139, 141
Virginia Quarterly Review 6

Waddington, Raymond B. 87
Weber, Max 181
Wells, Robin Headlam 8, 10
Wells, Stanley 84n1
Western flower. See flower (in *Midsummer Night's Dream*)
Williams, Jeffrey 7
Williamson, Marilyn L. 55
Wilson, Michael Jay 87
The Winter's Tale (Shakespeare) 3, 18, 63
withdrawal. See avoidance
Wittgenstein, Ludwig 90, 130; on assembling what we're familiar with 21, 82; on conjuring tricks 149; defactoism as originating in 49; on disquietude 56, 64, 81; on epistemological questions 26–32, 36; on feeling pain 15; on grammar 37, 40–41, 189–91; on human "form of life," 12, 37–42, 102; on infinite regress 46; on knowing how to go on 119, 122, 125; on language 183; on logical inference's rigidity 75; on the miraculous 48–49, 186; on teaching and learning 32–35, 37–43, 47
the world: acknowledgment as linking people to each other and to 4, 21, 37–45, 66–68, 73–79, 82, 167–68, 182; knowledge as mischaracterizing our fundamental relation to the 27–29, 40–41, 65–66, 83, 178–79, 191; skepticism as making, "go dead," 35, 37–38, 41, 68, 181–82; See also acknowledgment; avoidance; disappointment; skepticism

Zizek, Slavoj 127
Zunshine, Lisa 8

For Product Safety Concerns and Information please contact our EU representative GPSR@taylorandfrancis.com
Taylor & Francis Verlag GmbH, Kaufingerstraße 24, 80331 München, Germany

www.ingramcontent.com/pod-product-compliance
Lightning Source LLC
Chambersburg PA
CBHW052340230426
43664CB00041B/2573